Behaviour Managen
An Essential Guide
and Newly Qualified Teachers

Behaviour Management: An Essential Guide for Student and Newly Qualified Teachers explores the current issues and theories in behaviour management. It encourages readers to think and reflect on their own experiences and offers practical advice for developing confidence in the classroom and quickly adapting to the changing needs of different students and settings.

Each chapter of the book focuses on a different aspect of behaviour management, addressing issues such as building routines, health and safety, mental health and using technology to support behaviour management. It includes:

- Tasks designed to encourage analytical, reflective and original thinking.

- Resources and guidance to develop practice and collate evidence to add to portfolios or other files required by tutors, mentors and assessors.

- Case studies from personal experience that provide tips and tools for effectively managing behaviour.

This book is an essential resource for student teachers, newly or recently qualified teachers and anyone with an interest in developing an understanding of behaviour within schools.

Eleanor Overland is Senior Lecturer in Education at Manchester Metropolitan University, UK.

Joe Barber is Senior Lecturer in Education at Manchester Metropolitan University, UK.

Mark Sackville-Ford is Assistant Trust Director of SEND at The Laurus Trust and formerly a Senior Lecturer in Education at Manchester Metropolitan University, UK.

Behaviour Management

An Essential Guide for Student and Newly Qualified Teachers

Edited by
Eleanor Overland, Joe Barber
and Mark Sackville-Ford

Routledge
Taylor & Francis Group

LONDON AND NEW YORK

First published 2020
by Routledge
2 Park Square, Milton Park, Abingdon, Oxon OX14 4RN

and by Routledge
52 Vanderbilt Avenue, New York, NY 10017

Routledge is an imprint of the Taylor & Francis Group, an informa business

British Library Cataloguing-in-Publication Data
A catalogue record for this book is available from the British Library

Library of Congress Cataloging-in-Publication Data
Names: Overland, Eleanor, editor. | Barber, Joe, editor. | Sackville-Ford, Mark, editor.
Title: Behaviour management : an essential guide for student and newly qualified teachers / edited by Eleanor Overland, Joe Barber and Mark Sackville-Ford.
Other titles: Behavior management
Description: Abingdon, Oxon ; New York, NY : Routledge, 2020. | Includes bibliographical references and index.
Identifiers: LCCN 2019047489 (print) | LCCN 2019047490 (ebook) | ISBN 9781138392632 (hardback) | ISBN 9781138392649 (paperback) | ISBN 9780429402104 (ebook)
Subjects: LCSH: Behavior modification. | Classroom management. | Classroom environment. | Teacher-student relationships. | First-year teachers.
Classification: LCC LB1060.2 .B44145 2020 (print) | LCC LB1060.2 (ebook) | DDC 370.15/28--dc23
LC record available at https://lccn.loc.gov/2019047489
LC ebook record available at https://lccn.loc.gov/2019047490

ISBN: 978-1-138-39263-2 (hbk)
ISBN: 978-1-138-39264-9 (pbk)
ISBN: 978-0-429-40210-4 (ebk)

Typeset in Melior

by SPi Technologies India Private Limited

Contents

Figures

Tables

Editor biographies

Eleanor Overland is a Senior Lecturer in Education at Manchester Metropolitan University, where she works on teacher education programmes, online learning for pre-service teachers and Continuous Professional Development (CPD) for practicing teachers. Her passions lie around computing and the use of technology in education. Previously, Eleanor has worked in a range of schools across Greater Manchester as a classroom teacher and on leadership teams. She has also worked as a teaching and learning advisor for a local authority and been involved in a range of policy and strategic developments in secondary education. She is currently completing her doctoral studies on the implementation of the new computing curriculum in England.

Joe Barber is a Senior Lecturer in Education at Manchester Metropolitan University. He leads the Secondary PGCE English course and taught English in secondary schools and sixth form colleges for 14 years. Alongside this, Joe held several senior positions overseeing behaviour for learning, pastoral care, safeguarding and child protection.

Mark Sackville-Ford is the Assistant Trust Director of SEND at The Laurus Trust working across a range of schools to promote inclusion. He was previously a Senior Lecturer in Education at Manchester Metropolitan University, working within a range of programmes from Teacher Education to doctoral level. His varied career spans a commitment to education and ensuring all children can thrive. His expertise around behaviour was honed when working as a Behaviour Support Teacher for Stockport LA. He has written extensively around behaviour in schools and is the author of 'Critical Issues in Forest Schools'. Mark has a broad research interest rooted in new materialist and post-human methodologies to think more deeply around socio-material assemblages in education and schools. His doctoral thesis explored the ways that affective atmospheres may exist in schools.

Contributor biographies

Sarah Baggaley is a teacher with over 25 years' experience working in primary and secondary schools and has also been an advisory teacher for behaviour within a Local Authority for over 14 years. She has previously led a project developed to provide a more focused, child-centred package of support for children and young people whose school placement has become vulnerable to permanent exclusion. Currently, Sarah is a lead practitioner for restorative approaches within a Greater Manchester local authority, working in schools and within a multi-agency children's service. Her recent MA in Education allowed her to explore the role of values and taking a restorative approach within the contemporary world of education.

Joanna Baynham is a Senior Lecturer in Education in Manchester Metropolitan University. She leads the geography PGCE course as well as being programme leader for the Post Graduate Certificate in Education (School Centred Initial Teacher Education). Jo has worked at Manchester Metropolitan University for 6 years and has taught on a range of courses in both primary and secondary teacher education. Prior to this Jo taught geography in a secondary school in Hertfordshire for 15 years, having a range of roles, including Head of Geography, Head of Humanities, Director of Independent Learning and leading the Humanities Specialist School. Her current research interests are in the different types of knowledge trainee geography teachers need.

Chris Chambers has a career of two halves. The first 18 years was as a history teacher in two secondary comprehensive schools in Greater Manchester. Whilst in school, he had a range of management responsibilities, including Assistant Headteacher, where one of his roles was the creation, implementation and management of a new school behavioural policy. The second half marked a move into higher education; since 2000, he has worked at Manchester Metropolitan University where he is currently a Principal Lecturer. In that time, as a tutor for History Education, he has taught on undergraduate and postgraduate programmes for primary and secondary student teachers. His academic interests focus around the, often artificial, dichotomy between educational theory and classroom practice. This has led to a wide range of research around history pedagogy, assessment and progression, behaviour management, Global Citizenship and classroom technology.

Jedde de Vries is a Senior Lecturer in Physical Education (PE) in the Manchester Metropolitan University (MMU). Throughout his teaching career, he has taught in a wide range of educational settings: primary, secondary, Further Education and in SEN. He has held positions as subject leader and head of department in the Netherlands and Scotland. He is currently course leader of the PE postgraduate teaching programme in MMU and leads the primary PE specialism units. In 2018, he started his doctorate studies within one of his main topics of interest 'physical play.'

Richard A. Dunk is a Senior Lecturer in Education at Manchester Metropolitan University, where he works on teacher education programmes alongside supervising master's study for in-service teachers. Richard previously taught science (particularly physics), mathematics and computing for 9 years in England, Scotland and the Philippines, spending time in both state and independent schools as well as FE colleges. His current research interests revolve around post-qualitative methodologies and a use of modern computational tools in socio-material analysis, particularly the professional development of student teachers, and the way space and technology combine in classrooms.

William Evans has a background in teaching music to secondary school pupils as well as to undergraduate students in a variety of pedagogical roles. William is passionate about teaching music musically and developing more musical lessons in schools. He is a strong believer that musical talent is a myth. In his current role as a senior lecturer at the Faculty of Education at Manchester Metropolitan University (MMU), he is able to pursue both these interests. William teaches on BA, PGCE, SCITT and MA courses, whilst also undertaking research in the field of musically 'gifted' pupils and how they learn. As a keen cycling coach, he is very interested how the elements of HIIT training, so popular in physical training, could be applied to methods of musical practice and development. His main research interests are around this area and is planning write a practice book exploring these ideas.

Anne Guilford was a Senior Lecturer within the Faculty of Education at Manchester Metropolitan University (MMU) for 9 years until summer 2018. She now works as an Associate Lecturer at MMU. Prior to this, Anne taught Design & Technology for 30 years in secondary schools, including a year as an advisor, she was Head of Sixth Form in her final post in school. She has delivered sessions at MMU on Pupil's Mental Health and attended training on supporting the mental health of students and teachers.

Chris Hanley is a Senior Lecturer in Education at Manchester Metropolitan University. He taught English in schools and colleges for 11 years and has worked in teacher education for 10 years. He has had a number of roles at MMU, including teaching on and leading the English PGCE. Currently he is programme lead for the doctor of education course at MMU.

Louise Hayes is a Senior Lecturer in Education at Manchester Metropolitan University and is the computing course lead for the PGCE. Before this, Louise was a Head of Computing for over 12 years at an Independent School. In 2003 she re-trained as a Secondary School teacher, moving from a career in the telecommunications industry, where she worked in a variety of roles for BT plc for 16 years. An advocate of lifelong learning, she has a BA (Hons) in Business Studies, and an MSc in Education Leadership and Management. Louise is nearing the completion of her Education Doctorate with research interests in gender imbalance in computing education. She is an academic advisor on an independent school governing body, an external examiner for the PGCE in Secondary Computing course at University College London, a Barefoot Computing Ambassador, and a course facilitator for the National Centre for Computing Education.

Anna Olsson Rost has a background in teaching history to secondary school pupils as well as to undergraduate students in a variety of teaching roles. Anna is passionate about both history and teaching, and in her current role as a lecturer at the Faculty of Education at Manchester Metropolitan University, she is able to pursue both these interests. Anna teaches on BA, PGCE, SCITT and MA courses, whilst also undertaking research in the field of the history of education. Her main research interests are comprehensive education, discourses of state schooling and education policy. Anna's PhD thesis explored the development of early pioneering comprehensive schools. However, her academic interests are broad, ranging from history textbook analyses to resilience and retention among NQT teachers. Her published works include studies on Cold War discourses, and on the significant impact of forgotten pioneers of comprehensive schooling on nationwide developments during the 1950s and 1960s.

Michelle Noble is part-time Partnership Tutor at Manchester Metropolitan University and a freelance CPD trainer. She taught secondary English for 20 years in a wide range of settings. Her senior leadership posts include whole-school management of Teaching and Learning, Year Team Leader, Raising Attainment at GCSE, NQT Tutor and ITT Line Manager.

Behaviour management for student teachers and NQTs: An introduction

Eleanor Overland

Chapter aims

- To consider how theory can be linked to your practice in the development of behaviour management.

- To determine how the tasks within the book can contribute to your portfolio or assessment evidence.

- To consider different approaches to using the book and how it can support you throughout your student teacher and Newly Qualified Teacher (NQT) journey.

Keywords: Behaviour management; reflection; theory; classroom practice; portfolio of evidence; ethics and data protection

Introduction

Welcome to all student teachers, newly or recently qualified teachers and anyone else with an interest in developing an understanding of behaviour within schools. This book is quite different to others that you may have read about behaviour management. It is not simply a pragmatist's guide with lists of hints and tips, nor is it solely a theoretical book. This text aims to combine a wider understanding of behaviour management, from both historical and theoretical perspectives, alongside providing practical advice and guidance to support you in both your understanding and classroom practice relating to behaviour management.

Our team of authors are all highly experienced educators and have spent many years supporting student teachers and NQTs as they develop their understanding of behaviour management and classroom practice. The team have also supported and marked many student assignments linked to behaviour management in the classroom. To achieve the highest grades, it is essential to be both analytical and reflective in your writing and this book encourages exactly that. In this introduction we will outline exactly how you can use this book effectively to develop your practice and collate appropriate evidence to contribute to your portfolio, files or other evidence required by your tutors, mentors or assessors. We will also highlight ways in which you can use the book to support your academic assignments, the most successful student teachers will be able to combine both.

Most importantly, this book is designed to make you think and reflect on your own experiences and practice. We are all shaped by our own experiences as pupils when we were at school, by what we perceive from the media and talking to others, by what we observe in schools and also by how we are influenced by what mentors and colleagues tell us. This book encourages you to challenge the norms, explore a range of practice and reflect on how your own practice may develop to best fit your own beliefs, values and the pupils you are working with.

Theory into practice

We often find our students can become quite nervous or switch off when they hear the word 'theory'. As student teachers and NQTs, there is often a view that theory is complex and only relevant when tackling the academic aspects of teacher training. This is, of course, not the case and many of the practical guides and policies you will find in schools are underpinned by theory. For example, you may find yourself in a school with a 'zero tolerance' policy on behaviour. This originates from the field of psychology based on 'deterrence theory', which is widely researched in criminology. A simplified version of deterrence theory is that poor behaviour is prevented through fear of punishment or retribution. Knowing this can help you reflect on how this is working in the school and for you in your classroom. It may also help you find research or case studies in other fields that can be transferred to your own experience (Gregory & Cornell, 2009). Having an understanding of the origins of such policies may also provide a suitable starting point for developing your own views and theoretical approaches to behaviour management.

In addition to theories written by academics and researchers, it is also important to remember individuals are a huge part of the process within behaviour management. Your own experiences shape your understanding and development and it is possible to frame yourself within a theoretical framework. Some teacher educators make use of the work of Bourdieu to do this and it provides a useful starting point to help understand your own position within your role as a student teacher or NQT (Kirkby et al., 2017). Think back to your motivation for wanting to train to be a teacher. You may come from a family of teachers and it felt like a natural career choice for you. Perhaps you are a 'career changer' and already have financial security but would now like to work in a school environment and make a contribution to the lives of young people. You may even have been inspired by your own teachers at school and be the first person you know to join the teaching profession. Some journeys to this point will have been much more straightforward than others, some of you will have already had to show true determination and overcome challenges to get here. All of this will impact how you feel in the classroom, how you yourself relate to children in the classroom and how you approach behaviour management.

Your 'primary habitus', as outlined by Bourdieu, occurs within the family. What were the expectations within your home when you were a child? In what way do you think this influences your expectations of behaviour in children now? 'Secondary habitus' develops as you continue through social situations. Institutions and organisations such as schools, clubs and places of worship are 'homologous habitus'. This is key in the development of your personal understanding of your relationship with behaviour management. Not just your own experience in education but the homologous habitus of the school you are in now. It is also worth considering that of your mentor and tutors. Sometimes conflicting views can make for challenging relationships and a level of understanding and empathy can be beneficial. Using a theoretical framework can depersonalise such complexities whilst still allowing for personal differences in experience and views.

Whilst theorising themselves as part of their reflection and development in behaviour management the most successful student teachers and NQTs have a sense of agency, some level of ownership of development in their classroom practice (Huber & Yeom, 2017). Rather than just being told what to do and getting on with it, this book encourages you to think about behaviour differently and so you may want to explore alternative approaches to behaviour management in the classroom. Having 'permission' to do this can sometimes be difficult, particularly where school policies are specific and consistently followed. Assignments and reflective tasks can provide a useful catalyst to allow you to deviate from usual practice. It can allow you to carry out small-scale research in your practice to explore different approaches. You will need your mentors and tutors to support you with this so the more informed you are prior to explaining your ideas, and demonstrating links to other theories and research, the more likely you are to gain their approval. Where school-based mentors are willing to contribute and even participate in the research with you, the impact can be great.

The overall messages we would like you to take from this section are: first, don't be afraid of theory. Think of it as a treasure hunt, trying to identify theoretical underpinning for policies and approaches to practice. Second, remember you yourself are part of the process. Having an awareness of your own 'theoretical framework' will allow you to explore your thinking in a more informed and analytic way. Finally, use your teacher training and NQT year as an opportunity to explore different approaches and have agency over your development in the classroom. As you develop these aspects of your practice you may well discover you would like to go on to carry out further classroom research and perhaps even engage in study for a Master's or beyond!

Developing a portfolio

As a trainee teacher or an NQT you will usually be expected to collect and collate evidence to demonstrate your development and achievements in practice. Often the organisation of these files is linked to the Teachers' Standards but they can also be organised in other structures such as by class or year group you are teaching. Regardless of the structure of the portfolio, student teachers and NQTs are asked to demonstrate how they have developed and met the standards. Demonstrating this for behaviour management can be quite a challenge; sometimes a short interaction in the classroom with pupils can demonstrate huge leaps in your classroom practice but how to capture this and generate evidence is more problematic. The issue with 'evidencing' your progress in behaviour management is that it often does not generate hard evidence or data that can be easily filed and catalogued. You'll also find that your progress with behaviour management does not follow a smooth upward trajectory. Chapters in this book challenge different aspects of your practice; as you make progress in one area or with one particular group of pupils, you may find it takes longer with others.

The key to your development with behaviour management is realising how developing relationships, personalising approaches and being reflective in your approach will evoke subtle changes in your practice that have an impact with your pupils. It is clearly most important to develop your practice in the classroom with the pupils but there will also be a requirement to provide some kind of record to demonstrate your progress. Written lesson evaluations, personal journals and reflective pieces can capture subtleties in developments within your classroom practice. Lesson observation records completed by tutors or mentors can also generate evidence. The problem with this is that we often see student teachers or NQTs generating pages of 'evidence' for the sake of it. Reflective writing should be a purposeful process to give you time and space to organise your thoughts and analysis aspects of your practice. This is appropriate when exploring key incidents and constructively reflecting on your practice but may be an unnecessary process at other times when it is purely for the sake of generating evidence.

Alternative ways to collect evidence, such as video and sound recordings of lessons, have also been suggested. It can be a highly constructive process to record your lessons, particularly to watch them back and reflect on your own practice. Consider carefully how these will be stored and whether it is appropriate to include these as part of your portfolio. Children will be identifiable in the recordings so having these online or in your own personal folders could be problematic and may go against school policies for General Data Protection Regulation (GDPR) or safeguarding. Before you record in any classrooms check the policies for the school: are you permitted to use your own devices? How will you save information securely? When will you ensure the recordings are deleted appropriately? (DfE, 2018).

Collating documentation that may also support the development of your behaviour management could also contain sensitive information and must be treated with care. 'Data-rich seating plans' and other such tools can contain a lot of personal information about pupils. In addition, class lists, particularly those including photos or assessment information, must also be treated with care. Should this information be taken outside the school and do you actually need to have copies within your portfolio? If you are not sure, discuss this with your mentors, tutors and colleagues to ensure you protect the personal data of your pupils. Whilst you are making use of such documentation, just having them as a presence in your portfolio does not actually provide 'evidence' of your progress.

You may be using some of your evidence as part of an assignment. This places a different onus on ethics and permissions for using data and evidence. Data linked to behaviour management can be particularly sensitive and seeking ethical approval must be considered. How will you select the class or pupils to focus on in your assignments? It would be very difficult to gain permission from pupils and parents to use them within your assignments if you are asking them to participate as you've identified they present challenging behaviour. The British Educational Research Association (BERA) produces guidelines for researching in education and they are a useful reference if you need to seek ethical approval for any of your assignments (BERA, 2018).

All authors of this book recommend you are discerning in your collection and collation of evidence for your portfolio. Documents, such as classroom rules or lists of reasons for sanctions, can show an engagement with school policy but are fairly superficial in demonstrating how you personally have developed your practice. Short, focussed reflections and selective evidence from your practice will be far more constructive in developing your practice and will not provide unnecessary additional workload. Throughout the book there are 'tasks' for you to complete. Many of these require research in your placement, a level of reflection or both. Completing and collating these will make really valuable contributions to evidencing your thinking and progress in your development of behaviour management (Zwozdiak-Myers, 2012).

Using this book

Each chapter of this book focuses on a different aspect of behaviour management, but you will soon see there is considerable connection and overlap. It is not necessary to read from cover to cover but to visit chapters when they seem most relevant. You will also find many chapters are useful at any stage of your development, or even before you start teaching practice, as they encourage the development of your thinking and ideas not just classroom practice. The chapters have been ordered in such a way as to support your journey so you could read from start to finish or dip in whenever required. For example, some of our student teachers often find they need to develop their voice when they first begin teaching practice so jumping straight in to Chapter 7 would be an ideal starting point.

Throughout the book there are a number of tasks. These are by no means exhaustive nor may every one be relevant to you and your school. They are designed to encourage the level of analysis and reflexivity required to develop your views of behaviour management. As mentioned earlier, some of the tasks may make a useful contribution to your portfolio or folder of evidence. Where you are using the tasks in such a way it may be worth discussing these with your tutors or mentors as they can also support with these.

Overall, this book is not supposed to be an easy read. We are not apologetic for that. As the new generation of teachers, we fully believe you are capable of being analytical, reflective and original in your thinking. Ultimately, you will be the school leaders and policymakers of the future. So we want you to be challenged and be thoughtful in your development of behaviour management.

References

British Educational Research Associations (BERA) (2018) Ethical Guidelines for Educational Research. Online. https://www.bera.ac.uk/publication/ethical-guidelines-for-educational-research-2018 (accessed 12/6/19).

Department for Education (DfE) (2018) Online. https://www.gov.uk/government/publications/data-protection-toolkit-for-schools (accessed 12/6/19).

Gregory, A. & Cornell, D. (2009) 'Tolerating' adolescent needs: Moving beyond zero tolerance policies in high school. *Theory into Practice*, *48*, 106–113.

Huber, J. & Yeom, J. (2017) Narrative theories and methods in learning, developing, and sustaining teacher agency. In D.J. Clandinin & J. Husu (Eds.) *The SAGE Handbook of Research on Teacher Education* (Vol. 2, pp. 301–316). London: SAGE.

Kirkby, J., Moss, J. & Godinho, S. (2017) The devil is in the detail: Bourdieu and teachers' early career learning. *International Journal of Mentoring and Coaching in Education*, *6*(1), 19–33.

Zwozdiak-Myers, P. (2012) *The Teacher's Reflective Practice Handbook: Becoming an Extended Professional Through Capturing Evidence-Informed Practice*. Abingdon: Routledge.

2

The history of behaviour management: Key theorists and current context

Chris Chambers and Anna Olsson Rost

Chapter aims

▪ To provide a wider historical and political context to the study of behaviour management.

▪ To consider how different theoretical approaches to the teacher–pupil relationship can inform the development of your teacher persona.

▪ To reflect on the extent to which your response to low-level disruption can frame it as a behavioural, or educational, issue.

Keywords: History of behaviour management; philosophy of education; teacher education; theory & practice; Education Act (1944); Newsom Report (1963); Elton Report (1989); Steer Report (2005); comprehensive education; Interventionists; Interactionists; Non-Interventionists; assertive discipline; pedagogy; performativity; inclusion; control theory; critical pedagogy; accountability

Managing behaviour before the invention of classroom management

Given the seemingly central role of classroom management in the eyes of student teachers and their mentors, it is difficult to envisage a time when this was not at the heart of learning the craft of teaching. Yet, 'the systematic study of effective classroom management is a relatively recent phenomenon' (Egeberg et al., 2016, p. 2), probably dating back to the 1970s.

If this were the case, how were teachers trained to manage the classroom prior to the 1970s? Partly, this depended on the locus of the education, which has shifted throughout the last 150 years. As Robinson (2006, p. 20) highlights, the metaphor of a swinging pendulum is an apt one for teacher education; in the 19th century, the apprenticeship model dominated, and this was entirely school-based with no involvement from universities. Teaching was a craft with a student learning the skills of the trade through observation of someone more experienced. Thus, a student would merely copy, unquestioningly, the approach of the teacher. This model was criticised by the Cross Commission (1888) and this led, in turn, to a professional system, with institutions of higher education in control of teacher education. The academic focus of the university courses was often a hybrid of other disciplines; Partington (1999) outlines a curriculum based around the philosophy, history, sociology and psychology of education, where very little attention was given to classroom management. This approach was justified right up to the early 1960s; for example, the Newsom Report (1963) considered it necessary for students to have an introduction to sociological study 'in order that they may put their own job into social perspective and be better prepared to understand the difficulties of pupils in certain types of area' (para. 292).

Yet, even if behaviour was not explicitly addressed, all university courses required practice in the classroom. So, how was a prospective teacher's abilities in this area assessed? Robinson (2004) identified a term prevalent in reports, from the first half of the 20th century, judging a person's effectiveness in regards of their 'power to teach'. For her, this 'touched upon the contentious idea that some teaching qualities are innate and natural, not learned or acquired through training'. Often these reports focused on a student's character and personality. Thus, their classroom presence emanated from their natural authority. In the eyes of some educators, this could correlate to a person's social class and 'intelligence'. This prerequisite of teaching could not be taught or learnt and so any practical elements of university courses centred on 'technical teaching strategies such as exposition, questioning and narration' (Robinson, 2006, p. 32).

However, by the late 1960s this model was censured as 'being ineffective and overly theoretical' (Haydn and Hake, 1995). It took time for teacher education to be reformed and a catalyst for change was the perceived failure of universities to prepare students for classroom management. The Elton Report (1989) stated:

> 'In 1987 Her Majesty's Inspectors of Schools (HMI) carried out a survey of about 300 new teachers in their first year in schools. Among other things HMI asked them how well they felt their training had prepared them for classroom management. We did not find their answers reassuring. HMI say that "most comments on education studies complained of an overemphasis on theory … A substantial number of new teachers felt that discipline and control had not been adequately dealt with on their courses"'. (para. 17)

Kenneth Baker, the then education secretary, announced there was to be 'a revolution in teacher training, switching the emphasis from college-based lectures in the history and sociology of education to classroom experience in selected schools' (Aldrich, 1990, pp. 47–8). Since then, universities have supported the education of student teachers with a greater focus on meeting the required professional standards. As a result, recent generations of student teachers may not have been exposed to the diversity of pedagogical theories related to classroom management. In the current, diverse landscape of initial teacher education, there is probably a need to make clear distinctions between university courses and those that are school-led. The role of the former is in providing student teachers with a theoretical lens through which to view teaching and learning, but also in showing how these ideas can help to shape personal classroom practice.

Classroom management

Changing school structures

A brief overview of the changing structures of the English school system provides further context to enhance your understanding of how education policies have sometimes had unintentional consequences for classroom management. The introduction of the 1944 Education Act meant that, for the first time, secondary education became free and compulsory for all children. Additionally, the school-leaving age was raised to fifteen (from fourteen), although this change was not enforced until 1947. Most Local Education Authorities (LEAs) implemented a divided system of secondary education because it was generally believed that there were different 'types' of children who should be educated in different schools. Grammar schools already existed, and would continue to provide academic schooling for a minority of children: those who had been able to pass the 11-plus entrance examination and who were therefore deemed suitable for an academic education. The majority of pupils, however, would attend secondary modern schools where more vocational education was provided. A small number of LEAs also opened technical schools for pupils to learn scientific, mechanical and engineering skills. Although the vast majority of LEAs only provided two different types of schools, the system that developed during the late 1940s and into the 1950s became known as the tripartite system. The fact that all children up to the age of fifteen were now in attendance at secondary school meant that the intake of children not only grew in regards to numbers, but also differed in terms of pupils' motivation, interest in academic study and aspirations (both pupils' own aspirations as well as parents' and teachers' aspirations for these pupils).

There was even further change to the structures of schooling during the latter half of the 1960s when LEAs started to implement comprehensive schools that would cater for all pupils within particular catchment areas. The Labour government of 1964 requested that LEAs start to re-organise secondary education along comprehensive lines, but local authorities were not required by law to implement comprehensive schools. Nonetheless, throughout the latter half of the 1960s and into the 1970s, a majority of LEAs started to implement comprehensive schools, and by 1977 70 per cent of LEAs had introduced some form of comprehensive education system (Benn & Chitty, 1997).

Considering the change of the make-up of the secondary school population during the 1950s and 1960s, it is perhaps unsurprising that more attention was paid to specific guidance on 'discipline' in governmental reports and recommendations from this period onwards. For example, the Newsom Report in 1963 included a section titled 'Spiritual and Moral Development', where approaches towards discipline in schools were discussed. As you will see throughout this chapter, guidance on behaviour management in schools has often been in response to public debates and issues raised in the press and the media. Despite recurrent OFSTED reports emphasising the fact that a majority of pupils do not display disruptive behaviours, the public debate has often focused on issues related to behaviour management in schools. It is interesting to note that the Newsom Report (1963) recounted some views of teachers and head teachers, with one head teacher quoted as saying: '[F]or all the ballyhoo in the newspapers, I am sure that children are kinder, more tolerant, and have a far wider understanding than they used to have' (Ministry of Education (MoE), 1963, p. 60). The report also commented on the way in which '[S]ome heads are bitterly angry about the harm done to secondary modern schools by grossly exaggerated accounts of indiscipline – which often make it very difficult to recruit staff…' (MoE, 1963, p. 61). Similar contextual aspects also influenced more recent governmental reports and guidance on behaviour in schools. For example, both the Elton Report (1989) and the Steer Report (2005) were, at least partially, responses to concerns in the media that youths were displaying worse behaviours than they had done in the past (Ellis and Tod, 2009, pp. 29, 42). Such were the contexts within which both the above reports were produced, and the consequent recommendations framed, and the Elton Report (1989) made a conscious effort to respond to the accusation that behaviour was somehow a new and threatening problem (DES, 1989).

The study of classroom management

As state schooling grew, and secondary education expanded in Britain and elsewhere, it is perhaps unsurprising that classroom management emerged as an area of academic study. Jacob Kounin (1970) is often credited with being the first theorist to systematically study classroom management. Prior to his work in this field, 'little empirical research had been done on effective classroom management' (Egeberg et al., 2016, p. 2). From his studies, Kounin (1970) believed there should be a connection between classroom teaching and management, and he identified a number of skills a teacher required, beyond the instructional qualities taught previously. The terms – 'withitness', overlapping, momentum, smoothness, and group focus – he used to achieve what he called lesson movement – may no longer be in common parlance, but what they describe are still integral to effective teaching. For example, as a teacher you need the ability to know what is happening in the classroom – withitness – and thus you need to be able to multi-task – overlapping. As a teacher you also need to be adaptable to deal with possible distractions and disruptions to ensure lessons flow – momentum – and this is achieved by maintaining a clear purpose to a lesson and keeping it 'on track' – smoothness. Finally, you need to engage the whole class – group focus. One term, coined by Kounin, is still cited in lesson observations today, and that is the ripple effect. This refers to how a teacher response to the particular behaviour of one pupil might influence the others in the class. Similarly, if a teacher fails to address unproductive behaviours conveyed by one pupil, other members of the class might be disposed to emulate these.

Continuums and classifications

Since Kounin, there have been a wide range of theorists purporting to have the best approach to classroom management. The principles and values, underpinning these theories, are often linked to an author's own understanding of the role of a teacher and their beliefs about the nature of children and these can be conflicting.

One helpful approach to analysing theories is to cluster them across a continuum, and a number of such continua have emerged. An early one, given that a teacher is seen as *in loco parentis*, was to adapt Baumrind's (1970) parenting styles: authoritarian, authoritative and permissive. One critique of Baumrind is that she classified two extremes as being too hard (authoritarian) and too soft (permissive), meaning that the middle way (authoritative) was 'just right'. Within education, these terms have evolved with the rise of 'assertive discipline' (Canter and Canter, 1976) and the attendant disapproval of aggressive or passive approaches to classroom management.

A more sophisticated continuum comes from Louise Porter (2014), who charted the distribution of power between teacher and pupil along with a compound focus on behaviour, cognition, emotion and relationships. Her classifications range from autocratic to laissez-faire, covering a wide range of theories, though in this chapter the focus will be on just three (Figure 2.1).

The danger for a beginning teacher is to assume that one approach is correct and to dismiss the others. It is far better to see them as helpful in creating a framework for the sort of teacher you wish to be. Approaches to discipline will vary depending on how the teacher–pupil relationship is viewed.

Approach of 'Interventionists'

Depending on any given context, it may be that different teacher roles are required and thus it is worth exploring the approaches of three: Interventionists,

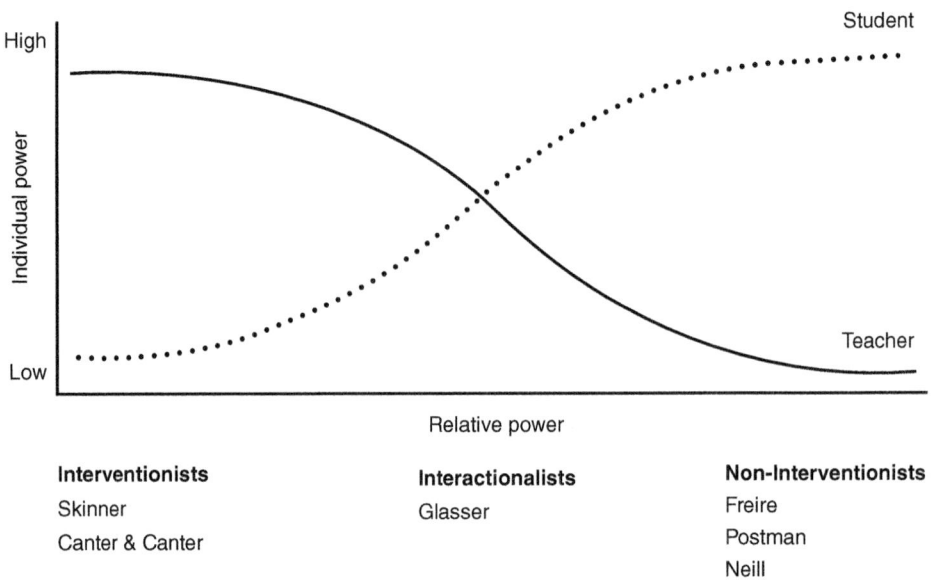

Figure 2.1 Theories of behaviour as a continuum (adapted from Porter, 2007).

Interactionalists and Non-Interventionists. The most common approach taken in many schools is based on behaviourism and the work of the American psychologist, Burrhus Frederic Skinner. This is explored in greater depth in a later chapter. Skinner (1938) dismissed the notion of free will, arguing that human action was dependent on the consequences of our previous actions. He developed the principle of reinforcement: an action is less likely to be repeated if the consequences are bad, whereas, if they were good, the probability of the action being repeated would be stronger. Thus, it is possible to learn good behaviours through rewards and punishments. Skinner called this 'operant conditioning' and there are clear links to a classroom. A pupil will behave positively, in order to be rewarded, but is less likely to break classroom rules for fear of the associated consequence or punishment.

This idea is central to the model of Assertive Discipline articulated by Lee and Marlene Canter (1976), which exemplifies the view of the teacher as an enforcer. The teacher is required to enforce the classroom rules and this should be done in an assertive manner. The ways to develop assertiveness can provide you with some useful tools as a beginning teacher. For example, the focus on the teacher's use of language, popularised by the work of Rogers (1997), can be helpful.

A key critique of the behaviourist view is the way that it frames children. Pupils are portrayed as naturally unruly; they lack any innate morality and need the management of the teacher in order to behave. It is said to limit pupils' autonomy and fails to help them develop any self-discipline. Also, in turn it defines the role of a teacher; the classroom becomes teacher-centred and dominant, with pupils submitting to the will of the teacher.

The approach of 'Interactionalists'

Interventionists are criticised for believing that the root causes of misbehaviour are naughty pupils, disciplined by non-assertive teachers. Another group of thinkers, who are referred to as Interactionists, believe disruption in the classroom is caused by a lack of a positive relationships between pupil and teacher. They advocate what is known as 'control theory' and one of the leading Interactionalist thinkers is William Glasser (1992); the subtitle of his seminal book *Managing students without coercion* focuses on the need to manage pupils without 'operant conditioning'.

Glasser (1992) argued that if the four basic psychological needs of pupils are met, they will be motivated to behave positively; he defines these needs as love, power, freedom and fun. These must be exercised by the pupils without interfering with the needs of their peers. For Glasser, disruptive behaviour is caused by the way a dominant teacher disturbs a pupil's need for power and freedom.

The importance of Glasser's work for a beginning teacher is the emphasis he places on positive relationships between teacher and pupil. He argues this is developed through mutual respect, pupil participation in classroom decisions and crucially by the teacher promoting a pupil's self-discipline. If these values are promoted, a positive rapport is created. Pupils will take responsibility for their own role in the relationship without the need for intrinsic or extrinsic motivation. Thus, the status a teacher has in the classroom is not based on their power to reward or punish, but on their subject and curriculum expertise.

One of the main criticisms of the interactionalist school is the assumption that a teacher can meet the needs of all the pupils in any given class; it is possible that some have additional needs which go beyond the four basic ones Glasser identified. In addition, there can be tensions when giving pupils power and freedom and that can be more difficult to manage for student teachers.

The approach of 'Non-Interventionists'

The Non-Interventionists are critical of the power dynamics of the classroom and owe much to the school of critical pedagogy, espoused by thinkers such as Paulo Freire (2007). Although Freire's ideas in *Pedagogy of the Oppressed* were shaped in his native Brazil, a former Portuguese colony, it is possible to see a reflection in a classroom of pupils, oppressed by the powerful forces of the teacher and school establishment. Freire was also critical of traditional pedagogy which he termed a 'banking model of education'; pupils are simply a *tabula rasa* to receive knowledge from their teachers. This approach discourages any critical reflection and thus reinforces oppression. In contrast, teacher and pupil should be equals. Even Interactionalists promote the status of the teacher as a 'more knowledgeable other' (Vygotskiĭ, 1978) whereas, for Non-Interventionists, teaching should be a 'subversive activity' (Postman and Weingartner, 1969). Postman advocated that pupils should control the curriculum, lesson activities and the assessment. So how can this be of use to a beginning teacher?

It would be a caricature of Non-Interventionists to believe their approach is simply to let the pupils get on with it; there is one key message which is useful and that is the crucial importance of interest. This is not a new idea as it dates back to the early 20th-century educationalist, John Dewey. For Dewey, the term interest indicates the 'engrossment of the self in an object' (Dewey 2008). Thus, a crucial aim of a teacher is to engage pupils in their learning, without resorting to 'extraneous and artificial inducements': rewards, sanctions or the threat of the examination system. Once a pupil is engrossed in learning, they are unlikely to misbehave, but they will require 'discipline', although this is very different to the managerial way in which discipline is framed in schools. MacAllister (2014) summarises Dewey's definition of discipline as 'a disposition of persistence and endurance in the face of challenge and difficulty.' Pupils need to consciously take responsibility for their own learning and development. Self-, rather than teacher-enforced, discipline is the key.

However, the main critique of the Non-Interventionists is that, although theoretically interesting, it can only be truly applied if the school context embraces these philosophies. For example, A.S. Neill (1960) believed that children were innately good and should be allowed to grow without adult imposition of morality and therefore teachers must not enforce rules on pupils. The school he founded in 1921, Summerhill, proudly espouses his thesis, but, as its website states, it is 'still ahead of its time' (2018, online).

Whole-school approaches

Since the late 1970s, research, which influenced government reports and guidelines, appeared to suggest that certain schools were effective in fostering positive working atmospheres and good discipline, whilst others were not (Rutter et al., 1979; Mortimore et al., 1988). Furthermore, these findings proposed that whether or not a school was able to foster a positive working environment was in fact unrelated to the school's catchment area and pupil intake – any school, in any catchment area, had the potential to establish a purposeful learning environment. This seemed to indicate that successful classroom management was something that could be found and created within the schools themselves, and that such successes could be achieved through whole-school approaches. The role of whole-school approaches has become more significant since the late 1980s. The Elton Report (1989) was published at this time, and the report largely accepted the tenet that actual school settings were notable factors for indiscipline among pupils (Ellis and Tod, 2005). This has become a recurring and encompassing belief which can be widely observed in governmental guidance as well as in school behaviour policies. There are very few schools today that lack rigorous whole-school behaviour policies with strict processes to be followed. You might have noticed that the

Teaching Standards (S7) also wholly accepts the effectiveness of whole-school approaches and the necessity to be able to utilise these in order to become a successful teacher (DfE, 2011).

The fact that the Interventionist school is the most popular approach to classroom management is arguably due to the influence of the Canter approach. Schools have devised elaborate systems of rewards to reinforce positive behaviours, and these have progressed from the popular house points, beloved of Harry Potter fans, to app-based schemes like Vivos (2018 online). To deter miscreants, a hierarchical set of sanctions will be in place. If you find yourself in such a context, it is recommended you follow the system. However, that does not mean you do so uncritically and there may be times when this role of enforcer feels unnatural or uncomfortable.

Task I

Conduct focused observations in academic, pastoral and extra-curricular settings (where possible and/or relevant). Compare and contrast the relationships between teachers and pupils in the different settings.

Is it possible to see any links to the three approaches: Interventionist, Interactionalist and Non-Interventionist?

What have you learned from these observations and the reading to inform your own teacher persona?

Why might classroom management be a problematic issue?

Separating behaviour management from teaching and learning?

From an Interactionalist standpoint, treating 'behaviour management' as something separate from teaching and learning is problematic. The Elton Report provided detailed and specific advice on how to manage a classroom, and even though 'classroom management' was considered more than simply 'behaviour management', the report has consequently been criticised for (largely unintentionally) separating behaviour management from teaching and learning (Ellis and Tod, 2005, p. 32). Because of their interest in the potential negative impact of treating behaviour management as a distinctly separate set of skills to teaching and learning, Ellis and Tod (2005) have also pointed out this pattern in relation to other governmental guidelines. For example, they have highlighted this issue in relation to the governmental circular *Pupil Behaviour and Discipline* from 1994 (DfE, 1994). Such criticisms generally emphasise the dangers of treating behaviour management in isolation from the actual teaching and learning that take place in the classroom. Ellis and Tod promote what they have termed 'behaviour for learning' strategies instead, where teachers should consider pupils' relationships with the curriculum, others and the self in order to promote behaviours that enhance learning rather than treating behaviour management as a separate issue (Ellis and Tod, 2005, 2015). By tracking developments over time, Ellis and Tod (2005) have identified this as a growing tendency in government policy and guidance, and they propose that it has now become customary to think of behaviour management as a set of tools that are independent of pedagogy. Porter (2007) provides a helpful example to illustrate that the way in which you as a teacher view particular behaviours in the classroom can influence consequent responses to these particular behaviours. Porter's example is that of disengagement, or what teachers might call 'off-task behaviours' in the classroom. Porter stresses that a teacher's response to pupils being 'off task' can vary considerably depending on whether the teacher views this as a behavioural issue or an educational issue (Porter, 2007, p. 16).

Performativity

As referred to above, teachers have to work within the parameter of their school contexts. However, this does not mean that you should not ask yourself how the type of teaching and learning you adopt in the classroom can also affect the way in which you manage the learning environment i.e. your classroom management. This is particularly pertinent in relation to special educational needs and disability (SEND) pupils, or those children who are less results-driven in their motivation. Issues related to classroom management and accountability have often been viewed as consequences of what has been termed performativity. Ellis and Tod have emphasised that increased accountability affects the way in which schools and teachers view and treat pupils who are seen as having a negative impact on accountability measures (Ellis and Tod, 2009, p. 35). From this point of view, a less flexible curriculum and increasingly stringent accountability measures might change the way in which pupils who struggle to conform to classroom rules and school policies are both viewed and dealt with by teachers and schools. In fact, in a study by Rustique-Forrester it was found that performativity led to 'the marginalization of low-performing students, and a climate perceived by teachers to be less tolerant of students with academic and behavioral [sic] difficulties' (Rustique-Forrester, 2005, p. 1). The 400 per cent increase in exclusions in English schools between 1990 and 1997 has also sometimes been ascribed to the proliferation of accountability measures introduced by the Conservative government (Rustique-Forrester, 2005, p. 5). This system of accountability was also enthusiastically embraced by New Labour in the wake of their election victory in 1997, as illustrated in the document *Excellence in Schools*, where an 'unrelenting pressure on schools and teachers for improvement' was envisaged (Department for Education and Employment (DfEE), 1997b, p. 3).

Inclusion

The New Labour government (1997–2010) was also vociferous in its support for inclusive practices in schools, rather than special education being provided outside of mainstream schools. This commitment was outlined in the document *Excellence for All Children* (DfEE, 1997a). However, as has already been explored, performativity has the potential to influence teachers' and schools' approaches towards managing pupils who are seen as a threat to accountability measures when it comes to GCSE results for example. Therefore, it is unsurprising that these two different agendas, accountability and inclusion, do not always sit comfortably alongside each other (Ellis and Tod, 2009, p. 21). As Ellis and Tod (2009) have pointed out, it might be presumed that school improvement should not only be measured in relation to the raising of academic standards, but should also include improvements and the effectiveness of inclusion. However, today, standards-raising has become the predominant accountability measure (possibly because it is easily measurable compared to inclusion practices). At the time of writing, OFSTED's new draft framework for 2019 (DfE, 2019) has just been published. The new framework seems to suggest that less emphasis will be put on outcomes (i.e. test and exam results) in order for curricula not to become too narrow, and also for a new criterion of 'behaviour and attitudes' to be introduced. The form this will take in practice, and the impact this might have on schools and classroom management, is yet unknown.

So, how are performativity, inclusion and classroom management connected? You might have read about this in the national press, where particular academies have been reported to have refused SEND pupils to attend their schools, stimulating further discussions around issues of inclusion in an education system where standards-raising is at the top of the government's and schools' agendas (*The Guardian*, 24 May 2012; *The Independent*, 3 January 2016). According to DfE figures released in 2018, 4,152 children with disabilities or special educational needs were left without a school place in 2017, compared to 776 pupils in 2010 (*The Times*, 8 April 2018). DfE figures for 2016–17 also showed how pupils with SEND were six times more likely to be permanently excluded from schools in England than other pupils, making up almost half of all permanent exclusions (Department for Education (DfE), 2018).

These types of figures raise questions as to how we view our roles as teachers in regards to classroom management. For example, some might consider what has been termed 'zero-tolerance' behaviour policies a barrier in relation to establishing an inclusive learning environment. It could be argued that if we are to take into account the learning as well as emotional needs of all pupils, then perhaps classroom management strategies need to be scrutinised carefully. Sir Ken Robinson's (RSA: Animate, 2010) sometimes controversial views on Attention Deficit Hyperactive Disorder is an example of how looking at the institution of schooling through a different lens might problematise the issue of classroom management.

Task 2

Reflect on a recent lesson you have observed/taught where low-level disruption – pupils being 'off task' – became an issue.

On reflection, how did you respond to these challenges in the classroom at the time? How are you hoping to adapt your practice to pre-empt similar issues arising with this particular class in future?

Did you view and respond to the situation as (1) a behavioural issue? or (2) an educational issue?

Would you have acted and reflected another way on the same situation if you had viewed it differently? Might there be benefits/drawbacks to viewing such situations in a different way?

The classroom: application and implication

The effective application of theories

Hopefully you will appreciate that this chapter is not advocating one approach over another, as all have their value. Interactionalist and Non-Interventionist ideas are helpful with their focus on being proactive and their respective emphasis on positive relationships and engaging pupil interest. Clearly preventing misbehaviour in the first place is preferable, but the reality is that there will be many times, despite meticulous preparation, when you will have to react to disruption and the ideas of the Interventionists will provide approaches to deal with this. However, it is a false assumption that any theory will work in every school and every class and every pupil. As Daniel Muijs (2010) stated wisely, there are no 'magic bullets' in the classroom. The critical factor is therefore the 'fitness for purpose of particular

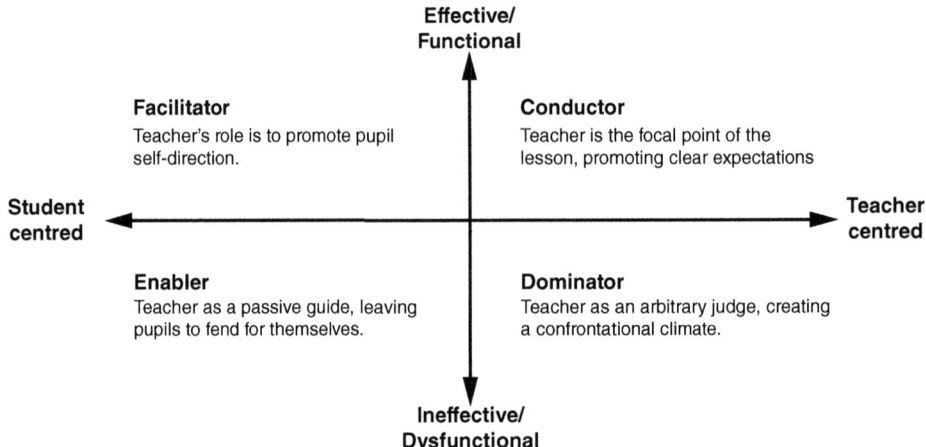

Figure 2.2 Positive strategies to engage all learners (adapted from Shindler, 2010).

pedagogies' (Husbands and Pearce, 2012). A beginning teacher with a range of ideas is better placed to deal with the unpredictable nature of the classroom than one whose repertoire comes from just one school or one mentor.

Nevertheless, there is a big difference between an awareness of different approaches and implementing them effectively so that they work for you in your classroom. Shindler (2010) provides a helpful quadrant (see Figure 2.2) for considering the efficacy of behaviour management strategies. Rather than a false dichotomy between teacher-centred interventionists or pupil-focused Non-Interventionists, Shindler's work highlights that each approach can be both effective or dysfunctional, depending on how the teacher sees their role and implements a lesson. To conclude, using Shindler's terminology, you would be advised to develop your ability to move seamlessly between being a conductor and facilitator, depending upon the lesson topic, learning activities and the pupils you are teaching.

Further reading

Egeberg, H.M., McConney, A. and Price, A. (2016) Classroom management and national professional standards for teachers: A review of the literature on theory and practice. *Australian Journal of Teacher Education*, *41*(7). This article gives a fuller review of theory and practice.

Ellis, S. and Tod, J. (2009) *Behaviour for Learning: Proactive Approaches to Behaviour Management*. Oxon: Routledge. This book gives a more detailed exploration of the historical and political contexts.

Porter, L. (2014) *Behaviour in Schools: Theory and Practice for Teachers* (3rd ed.). Maidenhead: Open University Press. This excellent book gives a good overview of theories and how these relate to behaviour.

References

Aldrich, R. (1990) History of Education in initial teacher education in England and Wales. *History of Education Bulletin*, *45*(Spring), 47–53.

Baumrind, D. (1970) Socialization and instrumental competence in young children. *Young Children*, *26*, 104–119.

Benn, C. and Chitty, C. (1997) *Thirty Years On: Is Comprehensive Education Alive and Well or Struggling to Survive?* Harmondsworth: Penguin Books.

Canter, L. and Canter, M. (1976) *Assertive Discipline: A Take-Charge Approach for Today's Educator*. Seal Beach, CA: Lee Canter & Associates.

Cross Commission (1888) *Final Report of the Royal Commission on the Working of the Elementary Education Acts, England and Wales*. London: HM Stationery Office.

Dewey, J. (2008) *Democracy and Education*. Saint Louis Park, MN: Filiquarian.

DES (1989) Discipline in Schools (The Elton Report). London: HMSO.

DfE (1994) Pupil Behaviour and Discipline (Circular 8/94). London: DfE.

DfE (2011) Teachers' standards. Online: https://www.gov.uk/government/publications/teachers-standards (accessed 29 December 2019).

DfE (2018) Permanent and fixed-period exclusions in England: 2016 to 2017. Online: https://www.gov.uk/government/statistics/permanent-and-fixed-period-exclusions-in-england-2016-to-2017 (accessed 29 December 2019).

DfE (2019) Draft for Consultation: The Education Inspection Framework. Unknown place of publication: Department for Education. (Online) (Accessed on 2 February 2019).

DfEE (1997a) Excellence for All Children. London: DfEE.

DfEE (1997b) Excellence in Schools. London: DfEE.

DfES (2005) Learning Behaviour: The Report of the Practitioners' Group on School Behaviour and Discipline (The Steer Report). Nottingham: DfES.

Egeberg, H.M., McConney, A. and Price, A. (2016) Classroom management and national professional standards for teachers: A review of the literature on theory and practice. *Australian Journal of Teacher Education*, *41*(7), 1–18.

Ellis, S. and Tod, J. (2005) Including SENCOs in behaviour improvement: An exploration of the behaviour and attendance strands of the national strategies. *Support for Learning, 20*, 83–89.

Ellis, S. and Tod, J. (2009) *Behaviour for Learning: Proactive Approaches to Behaviour Management*. Oxon: Routledge.

Ellis, S. and Tod, J. (2015) *Promoting Behaviour for Learning in the Classroom*. London: Routledge.

Freire, P. (2007) *Pedagogy of the Oppressed*. New York: Continuum.

Glasser, W. (1992) *The Quality School: Managing Students without Coercion*. New York: Harper Collins.

The Guardian (24 May 2012) Academies' refusal to admit pupils with special needs prompts legal battles.

Haydn, T. (2004) Evidence versus ideology in education policy; the recent history of initial teacher education in England and Wales and the implications for educational researchers as agents of change. *Educar, 34*, 53–70.

Haydn, T. and Hake, C. (April 1995) A bridge too far? Teacher Training in England and Wales. *International Journal of Educational Reform, 4*(2), 172–177.

Husbands, C. and Pearce, J. (2012) *What Makes Great Pedagogy? Nine Claims from Research*. Nottingham: National College for School Leadership.

The Independent (3 January 2016) Academies turn away children with special needs to 'cherry-pick' pupils, charity warns.

Kounin, J.S. (1970) *Discipline and Group Management in Classrooms*. New York: Holt, Rinehart & Winston Inc.

MacAllister, J. (2014) Why discipline needs to be reclaimed as an educational concept. *Educational Studies, 40*(4), 438–451.

MoE, The Newsom Report (1963) Half Our Future a report of the Central Advisory Council for Education (England). London: Her Majesty's Stationery Office.

Mortimore, P., Sammons, P., Stoll, L., Lewis, D. and Ecob, R. (1988) *School Matters: The Junior Years*. Shepton Mallet: Open Books.

Muijs, R.D. (2010) Changing classroom practice. In D. Hargreaves, A. Lieberman, M. Fullan and D. Hopkins (eds.), *Second International Handbook of Educational Change*. London: Springer, pp. 857–868.

Neill, A.S. (1960) *Summerhill: A Radical Approach to Child Rearing*. New York: Hart Publishing Company.

Partington, G. (1999) *Teacher Education in England and Wales*. London: The Institute of Economic Affairs.

Porter, L. (2007) *Student Behaviour: Theory and Practice for Teachers* (3rd ed.) Sydney, Australia: Allen & Unwin.

Porter, L. (2014) *Behaviour in Schools: Theory and Practice for Teachers* (3rd ed.). Maidenhead: Open University Press.

Postman, N. and Weingartner, C. (1969) *Teaching as a Subversive Activity* New York: Dell.

RSA: Animate. (2010) Sir Ken Robinson – Changing Education Paradigms. (Online video) (Accessed on 2 February 2019) https://www.youtube.com/watch?v=zDZFcDGpL4U

Robinson, W. (2004) *Power To Teach: Learning through Practice*. London: RoutledgeFalmer.

Robinson, W. (2006) Teacher training in England and Wales: Past, present and future perspectives. *Educational Research and Perspectives*, *33*(2), 19–36.

Rogers, B. (1997) *The Language of Discipline: A Practical Approach to Effective Classroom Management*. Plymouth: Northcote House.

Rustique-Forrester, E. (2005) Accountability and the pressures to exclude: A cautionary tale from England. *Education Policy Analysis Archives*, *13*(26), 1–39.

Rutter, M., Maughan, B., Mortimore, P. and Ouston, J. (1979) *Fifteen Thousand Hours: Secondary Schools and their Effects on Children*. London: Open Books.

Shindler, J. (2010). *Transformative Classroom Management: Positive Strategies to Engage All Students and Promote a Psychology of Success*. San Francisco, CA: Jossey-Bass.

Skinner, B.F. (1938) *The Behaviour of Organisms*. New York: Appleton-Century.

Summerhill School (2018) Online http://www.summerhillschool.co.uk (Accessed on 17 September 2018).

The Times (8 April 2018) 'Shameful' cuts hit children with special needs.

Vivoclass (2018) Online https://www.vivoclass.com (Accessed on 24 September 2018).

Vygotskiĭ, L.S. (1978) *Mind in Society: The Development of Higher Psychological Processes*. London: Harvard University Press.

3 Developing routines and minimising disruption

Louise Hayes

Chapter aims

■ To understand how classroom routines enable teachers to communicate shared values and behaviours to drive a positive classroom culture and minimise disruption during a lesson.

■ To know that when a teacher takes a class for the first time how to draw up suitable classroom rules to set expectations.

■ To develop strategies for the beginning of a year, and know the importance of setting a set routine at the start and end of lessons, including how this can be achieved in a number of classroom situations.

■ To be able to plan for a variety of in-class transitions and look at ways of stopping a class and getting pupils' attention to give instruction, move from one task to another and/or to refocus on the teacher or work.

Keywords: Classroom routines; classroom rules; consistency; classroom management; first lessons; lesson planning; phase transitions; timing; pace

Introduction

Routines are often defined as a series of actions that are done in a regular and systematic order. This can be applied to many aspects of our daily lives – for example, the tasks that are performed on a daily basis from when you get up in the morning. As with other areas of life, the same is true in schools and classrooms and research suggests that teachers are particularly prone to this type of behaviour because classrooms are very stable environments and some aspects of the job are quite repetitive in nature (Wood and Neal, 2007; Schwabe and Wolf, 2010).

As a new entrant in the teaching profession, this chapter will help you to consider the routines that you want to establish in your classroom. As part of your school-based training and development, you are going to observe, and practise, a variety of different routines. What you find is that as you progress in your practice, setting routines will become a natural part of what you do as a teacher. However, initially, they are something that you need to carefully consider in your lesson planning; as you gain experience as a professional, you will continue to develop a range of skills that will enable you to respond and adapt to your classes. At first, some things are going to work for you and some things most certainly will not, which is all part of the learning process.

Whilst there is a huge body of work around the theory of routines, particularly within educational psychology, this is intended to be a pragmatic guide to help you develop your routines as you start out as a teacher. In this chapter, we look at the importance of setting and establishing routines for pupils learning and behaviour.

Classroom routines

Teachers in secondary schools, as with their primary colleagues, understand the importance of establishing classroom routines for pupils' learning and behaviour. As a student teacher or NQT teacher, the aim of you doing so is to help you minimise disruption to your lessons, and enable learning and teaching to take place. In practice, getting it right will take time; however, with careful planning you will learn to establish routines in your classroom.

This chapter will look at examples and suggest a series of tasks to help you be able to do this. You will be taking your classes for the first time, and you will need to draw up suitable classroom rules and expectations, such as what to do at the beginning of a year, taking your classes for the first time, and the transitions that take place within lessons. Whilst you may consider setting routines to be far down your priority list, it is worth remembering that setting the right routines at the start will pay dividends in your lessons in the long run. Furthermore, routines are not established immediately but take time to bed in. Once they are, many potential disruptions will be eradicated – in short, working hard to establish routines really does pay off in the long term.

Behaviour management policy

The school will have a policy that sets the standards for pupil and staff behaviour. This document will be supplemented in subjects where there are health and safety considerations, such as in science laboratories and in technology classrooms. As part of your lesson planning, you will need to ensure that you know, and incorporate, the school behaviour management policy into your teaching. This is an important point for you to note because if you do not know the policy well enough, the pupils certainly do know it and will happily tell you if you get something wrong. So, do make this a priority document to read. Teaching Standard S7 asks that you 'manage behaviour effectively to ensure a good and safe learning environment'. Specifically, point A (see Appendix A) focusses on having clear rules and routines in accordance with the school's behaviour policy (The Teachers' Standards, 2013). (Task 1 asks you to consider how you might do this.) What is important for you to consider is that experienced teachers at the school have built up a reputation, may hold a senior position, and have years of experience that is hard to replicate.

Task I Key Subject Knowledge Concepts

Before you start teaching, consider the practical preparations that can be used to manage your lessons. Decide upon the routines that you would like to set in your own classroom; use this chapter to help you, but also reflect on the practice that you have seen in the classroom. Write down what you need to do and include the detail in your lesson plan. You can produce a digital document/film to do this. This may include a number of questions, for example – How will you know the names of the pupils? Do you know (and can you use) the school behaviour policy? What praise will you give to the pupils and how will you issue rewards? Doing this will help you to avoid making meaningless threats and making issues personal. You might want to write down some ready prepared phrases that you will use, for example using the word 'Thank you' rather than 'Please' when you make a request for them to do something.

Remember to be kind to yourself too – you are learning. Be consistent in your practice, if you say you are going to do something, then make sure that you do it and ensure that your follow the school behaviour policy. The pupils will soon get to know if you are the kind of teacher who says one thing and then does something else. What you also need to consider is that this is for both rewards and sanctions; it is easy to focus on the negative, but in giving praise and being positive in your approach, you are likely to get a better response from the pupils. A final point to note here is that if you forget to do something during the lesson, then make sure that you do it later on in the day. Pupils are not going to remind you if you have forgotten to give them a sanction.

The new class

Taking your classes for the first time will be simultaneously both exciting and frightening. At the start of any new term you will experience this feeling. Even experienced teachers will feel some level of nervous energy when returning to school after a break, meeting new classes, and this is particularly the case at the beginning of a new school year.

As a new teacher and face in the school, it is important for you to consider a number of factors that may impact upon you when you start. You are going to be replacing the class teacher for a period of time, and you will need to think about the routines that are already in place, and how you might go about adapting them. There may be some aspects of the routine that you are expected to keep the same, and if you try to change too much, a well-planned lesson or activity can end up falling into disarray very quickly if the routine is not implemented correctly. Even if you think that you have the best-thought-out plan you may need to be prepared for this to happen. Rogers (2015) asks us to consider the benefits of co-constructing classrooms and getting the pupils to create a collaborative classroom agreement (Rogers, 2015). This shared understanding of rights and responsibilities shifts our thinking away from it being solely the teacher's responsibility to manage behaviour (Rogers, 2015). In my role as a student teacher educator, as part of our first sessions on lesson planning, the student teachers are asked to consider the benefits of the following activities when establishing routines, in accordance with a school behaviour management policy:

- line them up outside of the room (where you are able to do so)

- meet them at the door (you may like to check uniform at this point)

- welcome them into the room – remember to smile!

- have the learning outcomes, keywords, homework ready (all written on the board/presentation slide)

- have a starting activity ready for them to do (if you are able to be in the room before the lesson starts, it is good practice to have something prepared on the desks)

- get the pupils to work straight away – it enables you to take control of the lesson.

Establishing your routines

When you start in your placement schools, you will be taking over a timetable from perhaps one, or possibly more, teachers. In your first observations of lessons it is important that you include notes of the routines that you are seeing in all subject area observations. Make sure that you take a notebook and pen with you (you may be able to use a device, but check on your school policy here particularly regarding use of a mobile phone). It is also professional practice, and good manners, to speak to the teacher who you are observing to ask them where they would like you to sit in the classroom. It is important that you are not judgemental of the teacher's lesson that you are observing, and you are not in the lesson to give them feedback. What you are there to do is make notes. Take a note of the time of day the lesson is taking place; the age group of the pupils; the gender balance in the room; how the teacher has seated the boys and girls; what the previous lesson/break/lunch activity was, as all of this will potentially have an impact on the lesson. I have taught many lessons when the pupils were having an injection during the class, this brought about its own level of disruption to the lesson as they came and went to their appointments. A box of tissues was a worthwhile purchase for my classroom and consideration of a task which absorbed the excitement was vital.

First lessons

When establishing your routines in your first lessons it is important that you set out your expectations and it is a worthwhile task to go through your classroom and/or subject rules with the pupils. This will then enable the pupils to be clear about the expectations that you have of them (Task 2 gives an activity for you to consider). You are then able to remind them of this activity if it is necessary to do so at a later stage. Be careful not to make an assumption that something is too simplistic or that the pupils already know it.

Porter (2006) claims that through involving students in self-reflection they can record aspects of their own behaviour, which is 'intrinsically more rewarding than externally imposed controls'. Thus, in allowing students to reflect on behaviour choices this develops their thinking skills so that they understand the value of behaving in an appropriate way.

Task 2 Classroom Contract Lesson Activity

It is important that you ensure that you are working within school behaviour management policies and practices, but there are a number of activities that you may wish to consider that also allow pupils to take some responsibility for their learning and behaviour:

- A pre-prepared document for your subject area with a number of examples of expectations. Have a blank space for a signature and date;
- A group/paired task with a number of behaviour scenarios for the pupils to work through and agree upon;
- A poster task, where the pupils devise a 'top 10' behaviour rules list listing how they may obtain rewards and sanctions (this will create a wall display that is useful to refer to during lesson time);
- Discuss with the class how rewards may be gained in your subject, there may be specific tasks that you consider to be above the normal expectations of work.

The age of the pupils will also play a part. It is worth thinking about what you might do differently with the various year groups. A new class of Year 7 pupils will have a different set of needs to a class of Year 11's, who will likely bring about another set of challenges for you. The differing needs of age groups needs to be considered in your lesson planning. Finding out what works for you, as well as observing experienced teachers, will enable you to prepare for these different needs. In my teaching practice, I remember being advised that a good strategy was to wait until the class was silent until I started talking. I found that this did not work for me until I became more established in the school, and a better strategy was to get the pupils working on a task as soon as they had entered the classroom.

Year 7 pupils are likely to be more receptive to changes than the older year groups. But you may need to spend more time introducing what you may think of as smaller matters, such as where to write the date and title on a page, when and where to note homework, when to turn the page over or move onto the next question/task (Task 3 asks you to reflect on this). You may be surprised at how specific the instructions need to be about what it is you want them to do and when to do it. For instance stating, 'I would now like you to copy the date and title from the board, and include capital letters in your title' ... Again, the subject that you teach will bring its own specific challenges to your routines; as a computing teacher, a regular cry I heard was 'The computer is not working' (it was often not turned on) and 'how do I save/open/find a file?' I found that for first lessons my routine included giving the pupils a demonstration of what I wanted them to do, and in later lessons a reminder of what they needed to do.

The older year groups will have a differing set of needs and are likely to be used to a set of routines that a previous teacher has created. Developing positive relationships with the pupils provides for 'psychological input' (Roffey, 2011), which means that if in your interactions with them you show interest in them, greet them by name, you will increase their motivation and achievement. A further point for you to consider is ensuring that you are consistent in your practice; changing a routine from lesson to lesson is not good practice, unless, of course, an established class routine is not working. Here you can work with a school mentor to plan how to implement a change and gain feedback through a lesson observation.

Task 3 Key Subject Knowledge Concepts

What would be the routines that you would expect the pupils to follow in your classroom? Limit your list to no more than 5. Ensure that the list is specific to your subject as this may differ from a generic school behaviour policy. Present your rules as positive statements.

You may wish to create a digital document that you can use in your lesson planning. For example, teaching in a computer lab brings a differing set of challenges, and a routine would be to 'log onto a computer when instructed to do so by the teacher'. Another may be, stand behind your chairs, take out your reading book/journal/planner/pencil case and put coats on the back of the chair, bags on the floor.

Lesson observations

You are expected to observe teachers in your own, and in other subject areas, as part of your training and development. This is not only an excellent way to gain ideas for routines that you may wish to use in your classroom; it is also good practice for you to have a focus of the observation rather than just sitting passively watching what is going on in the lesson (Task 4 asks you to reflect on this).

You will find that you may get well-meaning advice from experienced teachers on what you should, or should not do, and what works (for them) in a classroom. Denrell and March (2001) warn against the 'hot stove effect' – essentially writing off an effective technique because it is hard to use (Denrell and March, 2001). For example, you may hear 'Oh yeah, that has never worked for this class so don't bother giving it a try'. This may be the case, but in looking to try or adapt a technique in some way, a supportive mentor would challenge this viewpoint, and enable you to give something a try first. It might just work for you!

Task 4 Linked to Standard S7 (Manage behaviour effectively to ensure a good and safe learning environment)

In your observations of lessons, write a reflection in your weekly reflective journal for observations, instead focussing specifically on Teaching Standard S7. In your observations, you may note down the routines that the teachers in the lessons you observed. This will be dependent upon the lessons that you observe – it may be something that you witness inside or outside of your own subject area that catches your attention. For example, note down how the teacher stops a class, how they get the pupils' attention to give instructions, how they move from one task to another and/or how they refocus the class on themselves (the teacher) or their (the pupils') work. This can be very useful to see how this is done in practical subjects, such as PE or drama, or during lab work in science.

A final point here for your own observations is that whilst it is tempting to show all of your teaching skills when you are being observed, the pupils will know you have made changes and will likely respond to you in a different way. If the lesson is being observed, as part of your weekly observations, it may be something that you can ask your mentor to focus on and give you feedback on how it went. If you are being observed as part of your professional review, or by your visiting university tutor, then it is probably best to not attempt a major routine change for this lesson. Even if a new seating plan is attempted, it is likely that your lesson will get off to a very bad start.

In-class transitions/timing and pace

To ensure that the pupils are making progress throughout the lesson, getting the routines that will drive in-class transitions right is just as important as the start and the end of the lesson. Stopping a class and getting pupils' attention to give instruction and to move from one task to another or to refocus on the teacher or work requires consideration and planning. During the lesson, transitions of activities also require a routine to be set up to ensure that valuable time is not lost. Having your resources ready and organised will help you with the pace; you can spend too much time looking for pens, paper and books if they are not ready to use. Think about where you stand in the classroom for different types of instruction. In lesson observations, look at how teachers do this. For example, at the start of the lesson, you may wish to stand at the front of the classroom to give whole-class instructions. For demonstrations, you may have another part of the classroom that you use; the pupils will then know what is going to happen when you move to that space in the room.

Below is a suggested list of activities that you may to consider using in your routine that will drive in-class transitions:

- The use of a timer that is set to count down or up to the end of the task with a sound that attracts attention at the end of the time.

- Count-down strategies, for example from 5 to 1, to stop the class to enable you to give out an instruction.

- Stand at the back/middle of the classroom (in a different space from your start/ end of lesson instruction) to give an instruction.

- Raise your hand in the air and give the pupils a 'thumbs up' when they follow your lead (do this without speaking).

- Place your finger over your lips again with or without a hand in the air, to attract the attention of the class.

What you will soon notice is that it is very easy to lose track of time when you are teaching. I have often observed teachers, and am guilty of doing this myself, who talk for a longer period than necessary, before any learning takes place in a lesson. Whilst it is important that the pupils know what they are expected to do in the lesson, through setting the right pace of the lesson you can optimise focus and behaviour in the classroom. Ayers et al. (1995) state that by controlling task durations, ensuring clear differentiation and establishing a comfortable working environment, teachers can positively affect behaviour by maintaining lesson pace to sustain attention (Task 5 asks you to consider this further).

It is easy to be confused between the difference between timing and pace. This is not an easy balance to achieve; if you move things on too fast, you may lose pupils, but go too slowly and some may lose interest in the lesson and go off task. To keep the lesson to time, it is worth thinking about using a timer – one on the desk or an electronic one that can be used on the computer or in a slide. This will help you to keep your teacher talk to a set time and ensure that pace is better managed during the lesson. In my teaching I found that calling time, such as warnings for how long the task had to go, countdowns to the end of task, pushed the pace, whilst enabling me to give instructions of where the pupils were expected to be at that particular point in the activity. The time of day will also impact upon the flow and energy in the lesson. This is a further point for you to consider – the lesson after lunch may need to have more energy, with activities that are considerate of this; you may even wish to consider using a pupil to keep time if the activity is appropriate for you to do so.

Task 5 Routines

Discuss with another student teacher how classroom transitions routines impact upon pupils and teacher behaviour. Write 500 words that consider how you can build a lesson that considers the methods you will use to manage pace. How do you give pupils time to consider the topic you are teaching and keep pace? How do the activities in your lesson plan set the pace? Will you have quiet points to give the pupils time to note down questions, theory, or give them thinking time? How will you transition through the activities in the lesson?

Organisation of the classroom

The purpose of having an organised classroom is to help you to lay it out for minimum disruption to your lesson. This includes planning lessons so that your resources are planned, available and easy to access. You are also able to control and organise the physical layout of the classroom, including how seating plans and seating configuration can be used to affect pupils' behaviour. If you are lucky enough to teach in the same classroom, you are in the privileged position of being able to organise your layout and resources to suit your teaching. If this is not the case, having easily readily available resources is the next best thing and a box will enable you to have access to a number of the items that you may need. Here, it will depend upon the lesson activities, but you can prepare to have some essential items that will help you in both cases. In organising them into plastic wallets, or small boxes, you will be ready prepared for the lesson. It is worth you including items that you will need, for example a glue stick, pen, pencil, scissors, sticky notes, marker pens, etc. … If you are in the same room it is easier to put them out ready for the lesson; if you are having to move you may wish to think about who will help you to (ask or choose a volunteer) to pass them around at the start of the lesson. Having pupils do this at the start of the lesson can also mean that you are free to observe that all routines and instructions are being followed.

A further point to consider is the physical layout of the classroom. In some classrooms, you are able to move the desks around if you wish to carry out individual, paired or group work. Moving the desks around is easier to do at the start of the lesson, rather than mid-way through. If it is possible to get into the room before the pupils do, then you will be able to move the desks to suit your planning. If it is not, again, volunteers at the start will help you move them. Your classroom layout will, of course, be subject- and school-dependent, but with a carefully organised room the behaviour of pupils can be considered.

Seating plans

Seating plans, as well as the seating configuration, can affect pupil behaviour and having one in place allows you to control the learning environment. When you are creating seating plans for your classes you will need to think about a variety of aspects, including the desk arrangement, the layout of the classroom and pupil profiles. Your timetable and the rooms you are teaching in will give you a clear idea of the room layout. Obviously, certain subjects, such as PE, Drama and Science, will have their own specific needs to consider, as would be the case if you are in a computer room. As you get to know the pupils, it is highly likely that you will change the plan after a lesson or so anyway. In your early planning you need to consider medical needs, for example who needs to be sat near the front of the classroom, or to be able to see the board. If an alphabetical seating plan is created, this is not always the best option, as some pupils may need to be seated next to a positive role model, and pupils may find they are working next to the same pupil all day if this is not taken into account. The school may also have a policy on seating plans, so you will be expected to take this into account.

A further benefit of a seating plan is that it will help you to know the names of the pupils, especially in the early days of meeting a class. Among the key things for you to consider including in your plans are;

- Medical and SEN needs of the pupils.

- Pupil profiles and behaviour data.

- Academic achievement record.

I was sometimes asked by the pupils if they could sit with their friends; I learned at an early stage in my teaching career that this was not a good move and that it would often lead to off-task behaviour. In setting consistent standards of behaviour and a firm but polite 'no', the pupils soon stopped asking. Or you may wish to use this can be a bargaining tool for positive reward and this can work well for some pupils.

Another benefit of having a seating plan when you place your pupils according to where you want them to sit when doing group work, including thinking about how you move them to work in pairs or groups. For instance, when you move from working in a pair to a group of four, and from groups of four to eight. Plan ahead so that when the two in front turn around to work with the two behind, the pupils are already sat in the correct groups. The benefits to this are not only for classroom management, as pupils do not need to move around the room to get into their groups, but equally for considering distractions or unwanted behaviour as well as potential health and safety risks such as tripping hazards. In undertaking group work the following points may be considered, although this is not a comprehensive list:

- The lesson activity that you are undertaking – is it a carousel of tasks with the need for movement around the groups?

- Will the groups be working on individual, paired and group tasks at the tables?

- How will you stop the class for discussion or get them to move onto the next task?

The focus of this chapter is on classroom routines; however, it is also important for you to think about the group dynamics, and how you might support a classroom that supports diversity, gender and ability needs. Not only is this good differentiation, which will very much depend upon the school in which you are based, but the gender balance in groups, and the abilities of pupils, will be important for you to take into account when you are setting up group work.

Conclusions

The objectives of this chapter were to understand how classroom routines enable teachers to communicate shared values, and behaviours, to drive a positive classroom culture and minimise disruption during a lesson. What can hopefully be seen from this is that it is something which is not separate from classroom management, organisation and planning as well as relationship building.

What is also important is that you are not frightened to try things out. Even the most experienced teachers have lessons where routines are disrupted impacting upon behaviour and pupil progress. The chapter has covered some strategies that will give you ideas to help and guide you to minimise disruption, from taking a class for the first time, what to do at the beginning of the year, and pace and transitions in lessons. Furthermore, do ask for feedback from mentors in your lesson observations on specific areas; it will not only give you evidence towards your teaching standards, but will give you a clear understanding to the benefits of the routines you are using.

The importance of observing other teachers has been stated earlier, and using the time wisely whilst in the lesson. Observe outside of your subject area too, and think about what would and would not work in your lessons. I found some great techniques in doing so that worked for me in my computing lessons after watching a drama and languages teacher. Finally, when you plan your lessons, think of the simplest things that are going to impact upon the routines. For example, how much movement you want in your classroom? Where are the bag racks? What do pupils do with their coats/blazers? These things are a common source of controversy – and having a routine removes this as a recurring issue in lessons, even on hot or cold days! How are you going to store books and who will hand them out to the class? If equipment is needed, think about how you want the pupils to collect it (you might want to choose a class helper to do this for you).

In summary, spending time on your routines will pay dividends to your lessons and relationship with your pupils, as will knowing the school behaviour management policy and having a box of tissues to hand at all times for those unexpected classroom interruptions! I wish you the best of luck!

References

Ayers, H. et al. (1995) *Perspectives on Behaviour, a Practical Guide to Interventions for Teachers* (2nd edn.) London: David Fulton Publishers.

Denrell, J. and March, J.G. (2001) Adaptation as information restriction: The hot stove effect. *Organization Science 12*(5): 523–538. (Accessed online: 24 April 2019). https://impact. chartered.college/article/sims-teacher-journal-clubs-evidence-based-practice/

Department of Education (2013) The teachers' standards. https://assets.publishing.service. gov.uk/government/uploads/system/uploads/attachment_data/file/665522/Teachers_ standard_information.pdf.

Porter, L. (2006) *Behaviour in Schools: Theory and Practice for Teachers* (2nd edn.). Maidenhead: Open University Press.

Rogers, B. (2015) *Classroom Behaviour: A Practical Guide to Effective Teaching, Behaviour Management and Colleague Support* (4th edn.). London: SAGE.

Roffey, S. (2011) *Changing Behaviour in Schools: Promoting Positive Relationships and Wellbeing*. London: SAGE.

Schwabe, L. and Wolf, O.T. (2010) Socially evaluated cold pressor stress after instrumental learning favors habits over goal-directed action. *Psychoneuroendocrinology, 35*(7), 977–986.

Wood, W. and Neal, D.T. (2007) A new look at habits and the habit-goal interface. *Psychological Review, 114*(4), 843.

Appendix A: Teacher Standard for Behaviour

S7: Manage behaviour effectively to ensure a good and safe learning environment

Standards	Unsatisfactory Progress	Requires Improvement	Good	Outstanding
a) Have clear rules and routines for behaviour in the classroom, and take responsibility for promoting good and courteous behaviour in the classroom and around the school, in accordance with the school's behaviour policy	Rules and routines not established or consistent in accordance with the school's behaviour policy. Limited awareness of and engagement with the responsibility for promoting good and courteous behaviour in the classroom and around the school.	Clear rules and routines for behaviour in the classroom applied in accordance with the school's behaviour policy. Takes responsibility for promoting good and courteous behaviour in the classroom and is beginning to do so around the school.	Clear rules and routines for behaviour are well established and implemented consistently in accordance with the school's behaviour policy. Consistently reinforces good and courteous behaviour in the classroom and around the school.	Pupils demonstrate a shared understanding of rules and routines for behaviour which are embedded and implemented consistently in accordance with the school's behaviour policy. Actively encourages pupils to behave well in the classroom and around the school and display high levels of courtesy and cooperation.

(Continued)

Standards	Unsatisfactory Progress	Requires Improvement	Good	Outstanding
b) Have high expectations of behaviour and establish a framework for discipline, consistently and fairly, with a range of strategies, using praise, sanctions and rewards consistently and fairly	High expectations of behaviour rarely or not yet evident. Use of praise, sanctions and rewards neither consistent nor fair.	High expectations of behaviour are evident. Establishes a framework for discipline, deploying strategies, including the use of praise, sanctions and rewards applied consistently and fairly.	Maintains high expectations of pupils' behaviour. Establishes and maintains an effective framework for discipline, consistently and fairly incorporating the use of praise, sanctions and rewards.	Sustains high expectations of behaviour, which are integral to learning. Establishes and maintains a very effective framework for discipline, consistently and fairly, using a wide range of strategies.
c) Manage classes effectively, using approaches which are appropriate to pupils' needs in order to involve and motivate them	Pupil involvement and motivation is limited by ineffective class management.	Manages, involves and motivates classes effectively using approaches, which are appropriate to most pupils' needs.	Demonstrates a wide range of approaches in managing, involving and motivating classes in ways appropriate to pupils' needs.	Manages a high level of pupil motivation, involvement and engagement throughout the lesson using a wide range of approaches appropriate to pupils' needs.
d) Maintain good relationships with pupils, exercising appropriate authority, and acts decisively when necessary	Has difficulties establishing or fails to establish effective relationships with pupils. Authority lacks confidence and interventions are ineffective.	Maintains appropriate relationships with most pupils creating a supportive learning environment. Is able to exercise appropriate authority and act decisively when necessary.	Makes timely and appropriate interventions to maintain good discipline.	Strong relationship with pupils ensures a productive and inspiring learning environment. Ensures that any matters relating to pupil behaviour are addressed immediate thus maximising their learning.

The motivated classroom

Joanna Baynham

Chapter aims

- To explore theories behind developing levels of motivation in the classroom.
- To reflect on mindset theory and whether this can have an impact on pupil motivation.
- To consider strategies to develop levels of motivation in your classroom practice.

Keywords: Motivation; intrinsic; extrinsic; intrapersonal; interpersonal; mindset

Introduction

Understanding what motivates pupils in your classroom is an important part of learning to be a teacher. Being able to see beyond the immediate behaviour the pupil is showing helps you to create a positive classroom environment in which all children can flourish. In order to create this positive classroom environment, you need to understand the theories of motivation, the psychology that underlies this and how this leads to the creation of a motivated classroom. This chapter will explore these theories of motivation and how your understanding of this can link to Bennett's 3 Rs of routines, responses and relationships (Bennett, 2016) with the aim of creating the motivated classroom. As beginning teachers the use of positive language can be challenging, so understanding theories and the psychology of motivation can support you in developing your relationships with pupils. Managing behaviour in the classroom is not just about what we as teachers do to the children in front of us. It is also about understanding how children learn and whether their needs are being met.

Germaine Greer has been quoted as saying 'The world's a wonderful place: how can geography teachers make it so boring?' (Germaine Greer cited in Molyneaux and Tolley, 1987, p. 10). As a geography teacher I was rather offended by this statement but it made me think: did pupils think my lessons were boring? Did they think geography was boring? You may not be a geographer, but you can apply the same sentence to your own subject. What is the pupil's experience in your lessons? How motivated are pupils in your lessons?

Task 1

Write a paragraph about how you think pupils perceive your lessons. You could choose a specific lesson to focus on or think more generally about a series of lessons with a specific class. What was the lesson like from a pupil's perspective?

There is a lot of research around pupil perceptions of school, teachers and different subjects. Try looking at research in your subject or phase to see what you are up against!

Theories of motivation

Motivation is a highly complex area. We are all affected by different things in different ways. Motivation is intrinsically linked to the way we learn, our learning styles and preferences, our engagement with what we are learning and our participation in learning. It is about critical engagement and metacognition but underlying this it is making us more aware of what exactly motivates us to learn. Understanding what motivates pupils in your subject area, and in your lessons, will help you to consider how the behaviours you see in your classroom can be addressed by looking at how and what you are teaching. 'Motivation is the cornerstone of the entire learning process. People learn when they want to learn, when they are desperate to learn' (Hughes and Potter, 2002, p. 63).

Motivation is a difficult word to define. It can mean many things. In an educational context motivation is often taken to mean '(The) desire to learn and the capacity to cope with challenges, setbacks and obstacles' (McLean, 2004, p. 7). It has also been described as 'the drive' to do something (Tileston, 2010). Motivation is the state of being motivated; in reality, however, in psychological and educational terms it is not that simple. It also incorporates our biological needs that motivate us to keep clean, eat and drink as well as feel loved.

By the 1980s much of the research being conducted around motivation was based on values, suggesting that motivation was what you get out of something rather than knowing what and how you are learning. Higgins and Sorrentino (2016) concluded that motivation and cognition are actually inseparable. Before this many people had studied the two processes separately yet, without the ability to think and do, we are unable to motivate ourselves to do anything. We need to understand what is going on inside our heads before we can understand why we are motivated about some things and not others. With many pupils this can be seen as they move through their school career. As they get older some disaffected students decide what they want to learn and what they don't, and they begin to value some subjects more than others. It is worthwhile considering how pupils might value the subject you are teaching them.

Task 2

In Task I you were asked to reflect on how pupils might perceive the subject you are teaching them. Now consider the value that pupils may put on the subject you are teaching them.

For primary teachers you may want to consider how pupils put values on different subjects, and for secondary teachers consider the value pupils put on your subject compared to others.

How does this affect pupils in your subject/classroom?

We still, however, need to appreciate that there are different types of motivation. As adults, we tend to understand what motivates us as we are able to reflect on our past experiences. As a teacher I believe we become increasingly reflective on our own motivation and this helps us to better understand what is happening in the classroom, but how can we help children to become motivated and understand what it is that motivates them?

Task 3

What was your favourite subject at school?
Why did you enjoy this subject?
What motivated you to become a teacher?

Intrinsic and extrinsic motivation

Usually, motivation is described as either intrinsic or extrinsic. Either the motivating factor is coming from within yourself, or it is coming from something or someone else.

When we want to do something for the enjoyment of doing it, and we have a feeling of pleasure from doing it we are intrinsically motivated to do it (Deci, 1975). The act of doing that thing is what motivates us and the feeling we get from doing it rather than the end goal. As teachers we attempt to nurture this intrinsic motivation by allowing children to be curious and delight in what they are doing. This is particularly apparent in younger children, who ask lots of questions. As they go through school, what happens to the number of questions they ask? Does this intrinsic motivation wane? In my experience as pupils go through secondary education their motivation becomes more focused on the extrinsic goals of examinations and the intrinsic elements become harder to find. This is not always the case, but the intrinsic nature of why a pupil does something may not always be apparent. However, as pupils get closer to their exams, we need them to have a mixture of both intrinsic and extrinsic motivation in order to achieve their potential.

We need them to go from a sense of being controlled, in which the teacher is telling them everything they need to know and do, to a sense of autonomy, self-determination and intrinsic motivation so they can perform to the best of their ability (McLean, 2012). As the pupils move from one extreme to the other, they follow what McLean calls a 'regulation continuum'.

Interpersonal and intrapersonal

Weiner (2000) describes motivation as being either intrapersonal or interpersonal. He says that although the boundaries between intrapersonal and interpersonal motivation are ill-defined, there are distinct characteristics between the two areas. Intrapersonal is when you have set yourself a goal and it is down to you to reach it. It is self-imposed and related to self-esteem, guilt, shame and other thoughts that are self-directed. Interpersonal motivation, on the other hand, is the feelings or pressures that others can put on you. This may be from teachers or parents. It is the idea that someone is evaluating you.

In the last three decades or so there has been a shift in thinking surrounding motivation and the focus on what is happening internally rather than external factors. The notion of 'self' appears to play an important role in motivation, even from a very young age (McLean, 2012). 'Our current understanding of the self, however, is fast evolving and it is a great challenge to grasp its complexities. Individuals are no longer seen as responding to, and being manipulated by, external stimuli. They are seen as being motivated by personal goals, competency beliefs and personal evaluations of their worth' (McLean, 2012, p. 8). According to Deci and Ryan (1985), it is a basic aspect of human nature that we need to feel proficient, self-sufficient and loved by others. This feeling of being able to succeed therefore becomes very important. When success is not achieved that feeling of failure is also important and can sometimes be the stumbling block for children in school.

> **Task 4**
>
> Reflect on the ideas of McLean and Deci. To what extent do you think external and internal factors affect a pupil's motivation?

These attempts at defining motivation begin to give a clearer understanding of motivation and the reasons behind it. However, it does not even start to comprehend why some pupils are highly motivated and others struggle to get motivated about anything. I agree that there are things that we do for ourselves and that we also like to do things to please other people, whether it be our peers, teachers, parents or employers, but the complexities of so many factors mean it is very personal. There are both intrinsic and extrinsic reasons for our motivation.

Task 5

Go back to what you wrote for Task 3. This was getting you to think about what motivated you at school. What motivates you now? What are the intrinsic and extrinsic factors, and what are the interpersonal and intrapersonal ones? Write a paragraph discussing this.

Therefore, teachers need to create an environment in which children feel motivated. The best teachers will create a classroom environment where the 'teacher's task is not to motivate students to achieve but to provide the opportunities for achievement that will be motivating. Teachers can best influence how students motivate themselves by setting up the optimal conditions that helps shape their beliefs about their ability, how they approach learning, how they make sense of their progress and how competent they feel' (McLean, 2012, p. 8).

Mindsets

Believing that you can do something means you are more likely to achieve. I can think of many children I have taught who came into my lessons already feeling like they had failed, and I can think of others who relished any challenge I gave them. Carol Dweck sees this distinction in terms of two different mindsets: a fixed mindset and a growth mindset (Dweck, 2017). The fixed mindset assumes that your intelligence is fixed and cannot change. This gives a sense of having to work with what you've got. Dweck suggests the opposite of this is the growth mindset, where we believe we can improve and use failure to better ourselves; by putting in more effort we can improve our outcomes. Many schools have used her work to encourage children to move from the fixed to a growth mindset. How can we get pupils to believe in themselves? Sometimes they naturally have that growth mindset but others need more support. How you see yourself affects everything you do and there are many factors that can affect that sense of self. This can range from how you are spoken to at home to how a teacher lets you know you didn't do very well on a test. These things can stay with us for a very long time. As teachers we need to be really mindful of this.

Dweck has also criticised the way in which some schools have embraced her theory. She has stated that a growth mindset is not just about effort. The intention of developing a growth mindset is to reduce the learning gap but by praising effort the teacher is not addressing learning and therefore hiding the learning gap. She goes on to say that teachers should be encouraging pupils to consider different strategies they can use to improve their learning rather than just telling them how to do it. This then gives them a range of strategies to help improve their learning (Dweck, 2015). I believe that this idea of a growth mindset cannot be regarded as the only strategy. There needs to be a range of strategies that allow pupils to thrive.

The motivated classroom

McLean (2004) describes what he calls the motivated classroom. He describes motivation as having drivers and dimensions. He says that there are four features of learning contexts that teachers employ to drive student self-motivation. The first driver he describes is engagement. Teachers must show students that they are interested in their pupils. Secondly, he says that teachers need to make it clear to pupils how they can achieve the desired outcomes and goals. This is known as the structure driver.

Once teachers have set up this climate in the classroom, they can then reach optimal motivation by reaching the stimulation driver. This relates to the quality of teaching and learning within the classroom. He states that 'Students are intrinsically motivated when they want to do something for its own sake, interest and enjoyment. Relevance, challenge, control, curiosity and fantasy are some of the key intrinsic motivators' (McLean, 2004, p. 14).

The final driver is feedback. The teacher needs to inform the pupil on how well they are doing. This is not only about achievement but also about praising effort and the strategies they use. The personalisation of this feedback is vital in order for the pupil to feel personal success.

According to McLean, these drivers run alongside two dimensions; power and relationships. He believes that the teacher–pupil relationship is the vital component in the motivation to learn. McLean actually puts this into a classroom context. He says there are four classroom types and that a child's motivation can be affected by too much neglect or too much kindness.

This model really made me reflect when I first saw it. I immediately compared it to my own classroom. It struck me how different classes had different atmospheres. I had always put that down to the differences in student behaviour and how they reacted to what I was trying to do. When I reflected on this idea of different types of classrooms it made me think more about how I acted with different groups. Even now, many years later, I can remember looking at this diagram and thinking about classes I was teaching, where I felt their behaviour was challenging and then thought about the impact I was having on their behaviour. Rather than considering how they needed to change it made me really reflect on the changes I could make to change the climate in the classroom rather than focusing on what I thought of as poor behaviour. The relationship I had with those classes had deteriorated and they thought I did not care. When I did give them praise it really didn't mean very much to them or me and I was just trying to get through the lesson. The phrase 'plastic praise' has stayed with me. On the other hand, those classes with which I had established a good rapport showed more of the features of the motivated classroom. The trust and autonomy really stood out and the pupils wanted to learn; the learning became a collaborative act as the whole class wanted to do well.

> **Task 6**
>
> Think about a class you have taught or are teaching now where it went well, and one where the experience was not so positive. What was the difference? How does it fit into this model of the motivated classroom?

The motivated classroom is what we are aiming for but this not always easy to achieve. It means you really need to think about the class, the classroom and your relationship with both individuals and the class as a whole. What we are all aiming to create is a high-challenge, low-stress environment. When you have a motivated classroom there is a sense of what Csikszentmihalyi calls 'flow'. His seminal work 'Flow: The psychology of happiness' (Csikszentmihalyi, 1992) looked at what makes us happy in different cultures all over the world. He found that it was a state of mind rather than external factors that made people happy. According to Gilbert (2013), this idea of the 'state' we are in when learning comes up in research around effective teaching. The physical and mental state we are in when learning affects not only how we experience that learning episode but how we remember it, and how we engage with it. Csikszentmihalyi believes the ideal state being one that combines high levels of challenge with low levels of stress which is what he refers to as 'flow' (1992). If you combine that with McLean's theory around the motivated classroom then you can see the link. The motivated classroom is one that has 'flow' (see Figure 4.1). Csikszentmihalyi also noted that failure was important. Children need to know how to fail in order to succeed. This links with the work Carole Dweck has done around mindsets.

Delayed gratification

In the late 1960s and early 1970s, Walter Mischel conducted a now quite well-known marshmallow experiment where he gave children the choice of having a reward immediately or waiting a short while (15 minutes) and then being able to have a greater reward. The tester left the child in the room with the reward, a marshmallow or another treat, and the children were filmed whilst waiting for the tester to return. There are many versions of this on YouTube and I would urge you to have a look as the results are fascinating. Goleman's work around emotional intelligence also features this experiment and found that in the follow-up studies what he found was that for those children who waited were more self-assured and able to cope with the frustration in life, were better able to cope with stress, embraced challenges, were self-reliant and dependable. Their parents noted they were more academically competent, able to concentrate and more eager to learn (Goleman, 1996). This was in total contrast to those who could not wait. They were more likely to get frustrated, upset and affected by stress. It is really clear that this

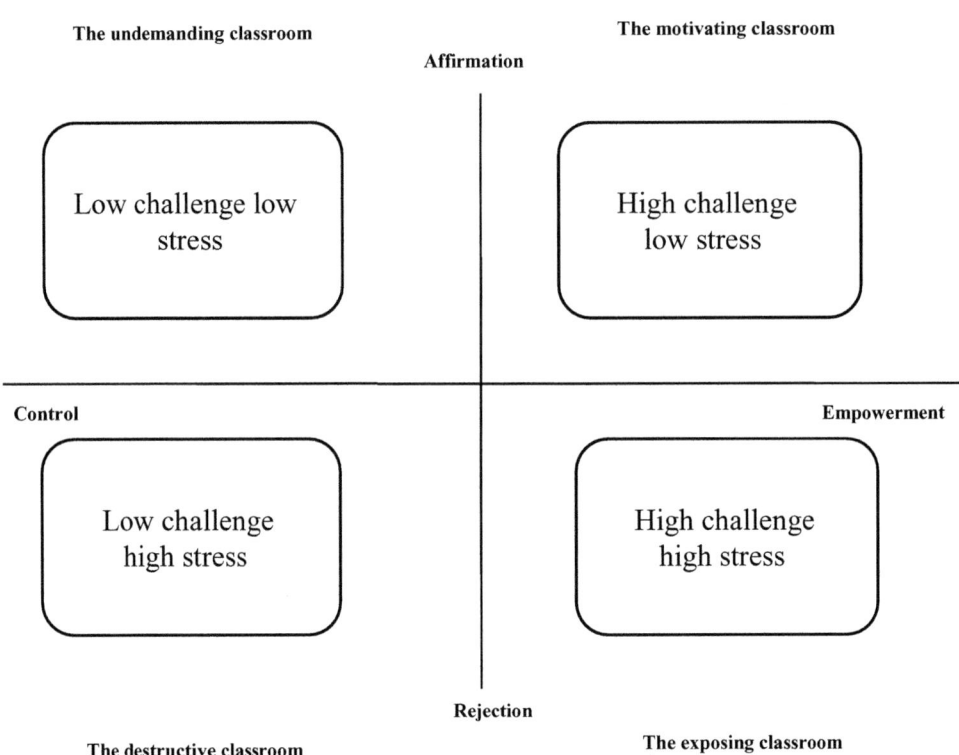

Figure 4.1 The state of the motivated classroom (based on McLean, 2012 and Csikszentmihalyi, 1992).

intrinsic motivation to see the long goal helps pupils to do better not only in school, but also in later life. What can we do as teachers? Ensure you maintain high levels of positivity and hope, ensure that your lesson planning allows everyone to succeed and try and get the 'flow' going in your classroom.

Pupil–teacher relationships

One of the most important aspects of motivation, for me, is the relationship you have with your pupils. Some of you will be little older than the pupils you are teaching and some of you might think that makes it easier, but it can make it harder. Whatever the age difference you need to find a commonality that will help you to build relationships. You need to see yourself as the teacher in the room and take on your teacher persona, whatever that might be. Spending time getting to know your class is essential; finding out what motivates them and any hobbies they might have can play dividends in the future. This cannot happen overnight, but over time it will really benefit both you and them. In order to get the 'flow' in your lessons remember to smile and greet students as you would want to be greeted. Make your classroom a welcoming environment. I don't believe in the 'Don't smile before Christmas' rule as pupils want a friendly face but you need to set your expectations high as pupils will respect you for this. What you are aiming for is that the pupils want to work hard and do well because they want to please you. At this point the 'flow' is there and you are their extrinsic motivation.

Task 7

Take one class you are teaching and discuss with them what motivates them. If you are brave enough, ask them what they think about your lessons.

Reflect on what they have said. How does this move you on in your teaching?

Conclusions

Having looked at some of the theories around motivation, and how pupils might experience your lessons, you need to really consider what role you play in motivating the students in front of you. How can you get the 'flow' into your lessons? Reflection is a large part of teaching and the more reflective you are the better a teacher you can become. Think about the classes you teach and how the theories discussed here might have an impact. One of the most valuable things I did with my classes was to talk to them. It might sound trivial but building that relationship was the most valuable thing I did in the early stages of my career. Getting to know your classes helps you to better understand what motivates them and in turn this helps you to plan better lessons for the students in front of you, and not a hypothetical class. It is why the planning of lessons is so important. In my current role as a PGCE tutor my students get fed up with me talking about it but it is about you knowing the class you are going to teach and as you get more experience you do this naturally without thinking about it so much. As a beginning teacher setting the right tone to encourage and develop your pupils is really important. There is a very fine line between motivating students and demotivating them! Consider the tasks you set, the language you use and the whole child. Don't just think about what is going on in the classroom; consider what is happening in the rest of the school, and outside of school.

Summary of ideas to promote motivation:

- Help identify the purpose and relevance of what you are teaching.

- Teach and model goal-setting strategies.

- Help children set their own individual targets.

- Encourage and adopt high, positive expectations and standards.

- Be aware of the challenges of the world beyond school.

- Let them fail in a positive way.

- Celebrate rather than reward.

- Think about the climate in your classroom as this is an important part of teaching.

Further reading

McLean, A. (2010) *The Motivated School* (2nd edn.). Trowbridge: Paul Chapman Publishing. This is a key text for reading about motivation in schools
Tileston, D.W. (2004). What Every Teacher Should Know about Student Motivation. Thousand Oaks, CA/London: Corwin Press. I would also recommend this text.

References

Bennett, T. (2016) *Developing Behaviour Management Content for Initial Teacher Training (ITT)*. London: Department for Education.
Csikszentmihalyi, M. (1992) *Flow: The Psychology of Happiness*. London: Rider.
Deci, E.L. (1975) *Intrinsic Motivation*. New York: Plenum Press.
Deci, E.L. and Ryan, R.M. (1985) *Intrinsic Motivation and Self-Determination in Human Behaviour*. New York: Plenum Press.
Dweck, C. (2015) Carol Dweck Revisits the 'Growth Mindset', Education Week.
Dweck, C.S. (2017) *Mindset* (6th edn.). London: Robinson.
Gilbert, I. (2013) *Essential Motivation in the Classroom*. London: Routledge.
Goleman, D. (1996) *Emotional Intelligence: Why It Can Matter More Than IQ*. London: Bloomsbury.
Higgins, E.T. and Sorrentino, R.M. (2016) *Handbook of Motivation and Cognition: Foundations of Social Behavior*. New York: Guilford Press.
Hughes, M. and Potter, D. (2002) *Tweak to Transform: Improving Teaching: a Practical Handbook for School Leaders*. Leadership for Learning Series. Bodmin: Network Education Press.
McLean, A. (2004) *The Motivated School*. London: Paul Chapman.
McLean, A. (2012) *The Motivated School*. London: Sage Publications.
Molyneaux, F. and Tolley, H. (1987) *Teaching Geography: A Teaching Skills Workbook*. Basingstoke: Macmillan Education.
Tileston, D.W. (2010) *What Every Teacher Should Know About Student Motivation*. Thousand Oaks, CA/London: Corwin.
Weiner, B. (2000) Intrapersonal and interpersonal theories of motivation from an attributional perspective, *Educational Psychology Review*, *12*(1), 1–14.

The importance of planning and subject knowledge in managing pupil behaviour

Richard A. Dunk

Chapter aims

- To describe common causes of off-task behaviour that may be attributed to appropriate learning activities, lesson structure and classroom organisation.

- To develop strategies to reduce the likelihood of such misbehaviour.

- To identify the significance of subject knowledge in behaviour management.

- To embed activities and strategies that promote positive on-task behaviour into your lesson planning.

Keywords: Lesson planning; pupil behaviour; pupil engagement; learning activities

Introduction

The vicious cycle of planning and behaviour management is easy to articulate; lesson activities that are too difficult, too easy, too boring or too complicated will result in pupils who do not engage in class. Pupils who are not engaged will be prone to off-task behaviours, distraction and a failure to follow instructions, which further impacts their ability to engage with the lesson. In turn, teachers may exhibit a reluctance to plan activities that allow for pupils to take ownership of learning, leading to further disengagement.

Whilst research has been undertaken in an attempt to identify causes for distraction, disruption and disengagement in classrooms in an effort to prevent such issues, this remains an under-explored area of enquiry. This 'preventing problems before they happen', at least in part, relies on proper planning and preparation, and we may be able to avoid falling into this cycle if we plan for positive behaviour alongside planning for learning and progress.

This chapter begins by looking at causality from both a pupil and a teacher perspective, particularly considering the relationship between classroom activities and pupil misbehaviour. The focus then turns to ways in which misbehaviours may be mitigated by the selection of appropriate learning activities, suitable lesson structure, and carefully considered classroom organisation and management. Threaded throughout this discussion we also find the importance of subject knowledge as a key constituent to effective lesson design.

Causes of misbehaviour in classrooms

Poor behaviour in school classrooms, as described at other points in this book, takes many forms and ranges from the common but problematic 'idleness' and 'talking out of turn' behaviours (Little, 2005) to more severe but extremely rare acts such as aggression (Sullivan et al., 2014) or drug use (Kyriacou et al., 2007). Before we begin to plan to manage the range of negative off-task behaviours exhibited in classrooms, it is important to consider possible motivations. Task 1 provides some structure for a reflection on your own experiences.

Task 1

It is likely that during your own educational experiences you may have witnessed, or even participated in, some negative behaviour.

Make a list of two or three key incidents of misbehaviour that you observed during this time. Consider both minor disruptions and more major incidents, and for each item in your list try to consider: What happened? Why were you or your peers misbehaving in this context? What other behaviours might you consider to be similar to this event? What did, or could, the teacher have done to prevent this misbehaviour?

Discuss your ideas with a fellow student or colleague and identify any similarities and differences in your experiences.

The range and variety of definitions of classroom 'misbehaviours' is not the only barrier to identifying the causes of such issues, as in-class conduct is dependent upon a multitude of interconnected social and psychological factors, many of which cannot be directly observed. Indeed, the wide breadth of causal factors may be one reason that a consideration of the causes of poor behaviour seems to absent in the government-commissioned report on behaviour in schools (Bennett, 2017). This is a shame, as with the aim to better understand the origins of poor pupil behaviour several research approaches have identified and classified causes in different ways, and utilising such research allows for a more informed approach to lesson planning to be developed.

One example of this is Gottfredson et al. (1993), who identified three areas for consideration in designing an effective whole-school behaviour management strategy: individual-level correlates, classroom-level correlates and school-level correlates. Gottfredson et al. summarise the impact of these domains by stating that

> ... research implies that misbehaviour in school has determinants at three levels: (a) Some individuals are more likely than others to misbehave; (b) Some teachers are more likely than others to produce higher levels of misconduct in their classrooms by their management and organization practices; and (c) Some schools more often than others fail to control student behaviour. Behaviour change programs that reduce risk for misbehaviour at all three of these levels are most likely to be effective.
>
> Gottfredson et al. (1993, p. 182)

In this framework individual-level correlates consist of a pupil's attitudes, prior academic success and social skills. School-level correlates tend to be related to behaviour policies, the availability of teaching resources, and the socio-economic context of the school catchment area. Whilst there is an obvious interplay between teaching practice and individual-level and school-level strands, these two correlates remain difficult for student teachers to address. Individual-level issues are pupil-specific, and often countered only through the development of relationships over an extended period. Similarly, school-level correlates are difficult to challenge without some level of recognised responsibility, or the authority of experience and/or reputation. As such, student teachers are most able to pre-emptively address issues arising from classroom-level correlates, such as working environment, organisation of teaching, and planning appropriate learning activities.

The idea of *proactively* planning for and managing behaviour (rather than *reactively* responding 'in the moment') is important, especially since 'The use of predominantly reactive management strategies has a significant relationship with elevated teacher stress and decreased student on-task behaviour' (Clunies-Ross et al., 2008, p. 693). In addition to reducing teacher stress (and therefore freeing up some cognitive load during classroom teaching while also improving overall well-being), the idea of on-task activity as a positive measure of pupil behaviour presents a strong argument for carefully considered planning. Luiselli et al. (2005) describe '... students displaying passive behaviours (for example, silent reading, listening to instruction) or active behaviours (for example, writing, delivering an oral report, asking questions) that are related directly to classroom instruction' as *academic engagement*, and consider it an '... observable and measurable behaviour that can be influenced by direct instructional approaches ... and positively-focused interventions that reduce disruption, distraction, and negative behaviours in the classroom' (p. 185). As will be seen later in this chapter, one aim of planning is to maximise engagement and positive on-task behaviours, which should mean a reduction in less desirable behaviours. This follows the work of Hofer (2007), in which '... discipline problems in the classroom are viewed as a change from pupils' on-task behaviour to off-task behaviour' (p. 28). If we are aiming to produce lesson plans that reduce undesirable off-task behaviour to a minimum, then it is important to consider the causes of such behaviour from both a pupil and teacher perspective.

Pupil perspectives on poor behaviour

Perhaps surprisingly, there has been very little research carried out into the causes to which pupils attribute negative behaviour. One such example is Bru (2006), who found that

> ... low perceived cognitive competence, perceived low relevance of school-work, and the belief that norm-breaking behaviour elicits peer approval all increase the likelihood and incidence of off-task behaviour and opposition towards teachers
>
> Bru, (2006, p. 23)

Although this study was completed in Norway, it resonates with the work of Gottfredson et al. cited above, in that it identifies an individual-level correlate, a classroom-level correlate and a school-level correlate. The individual-level correlate here is perceived cognitive competence, or self-efficacy. Whilst teachers can certainly influence self-efficacy beliefs (Pajares, 2006), this is not a concept that will change in a single lesson. Instead, continued positive reinforcement over time may produce a gradual increase in perceptions of self-efficacy. Prompts to guide planning in this area are included later in the chapter, but other strategies may offer a more observable impact.

Bru also describes pupils seeking peer approval through a whole-school culture of norm-breaking, which may be challenged and confronted by an individual teacher but is unlikely to change without collective and coherent action by all members of staff. Bru's claim above, then, allows us to direct our planning towards addressing the classroom-level issue of increasing the perceived relevance of schoolwork.

Lambert and Miller (2010) identify many behavioural correlates, and the authors are able to explore some classroom-level causes of poor behaviour identified by pupils. These include:

- Too much classwork or homework is given.

- Classwork is too difficult or pupil is bored.

- Good work is not noticed/Teachers not rewarding good work fairly.

- Teacher having a lot of time out of the classroom.

Although far from comprehensive, this list expands upon Bru's claim that a lack of perceived relevance of work can lead to off-task behaviour, and suggests specific areas that contribute to our understanding of planning to promote academic engagement. We may take these classroom-level correlates identified by pupils and compare research on teachers' perspectives of poor behaviour.

Teacher perspective

In comparison to research into pupils' perspectives on causes of poor behaviour, there has been far more research on factors that teachers think allow for distraction and disruption. Whilst there is clearly some overlap and agreement, teachers and pupils do seem to attribute different causes for misbehaviour.

In a 2002 survey of both new and experienced teachers, Mavropoulou and Padeliadu found that teachers perceived several classroom-level issues impacting upon behaviour, including class size, clarity and repetition of classroom rules, school (work) demands, teacher's attitude, and persistent academic failure. Of these, as teachers became more experienced they perceived a greater impact of school demands, classroom rules, teacher's attitude (Mavropoulou and Padeliadu, 2002).

In considering teacher attitude, Gibbs and Gardiner (2008) found that teachers were very aware that their own actions directly impact upon classroom behaviours, particularly that '… responding to children's work and behaviour … was a major influence' (p. 74). This agency over classroom behaviour is important to recognise and emphasises the power that teachers have in this respect, whilst also echoing some of the more social causes of misbehaviour identified by pupils, particularly a lack of reward for good work. Aspects of the research carried out by Miller (1995) also suggest that teachers see their attitude as playing a large role in pupil behaviour, since a lack of sympathy, a lack of incentives/rewards and an anxious demeanour were judged to cause negative behaviour, and a sympathetic approach, with rewards and the teacher feeling valued promoted positive pupil behaviour.

The role of school work demands and classroom activities on pupil behaviour cannot be understated. It is important to differentiate that it is not the perceived difficulty level of the external curriculum or exam specification that are the cause of poor behaviour, as Ogilvy points out that while

> … teachers' perception and tolerance of behaviour might be adversely affected by pressures of subject delivery and examination results, findings of this present study suggest that curricular pressures did not emerge as a distinct factor.
>
> Ogilvy, (1994, p. 74)

Instead, it is the ability of the pupils to academically *engage* with the classroom tasks set by teachers that influences behaviour. Where pupils understand an inability to engage as being given 'too much' work, or work that is too boring or too difficult, Miller's (1995) study describes the interest level of the work set, and defining clear expectations and instructions for all activities.

Having considered causes for poor behaviour as suggested by both pupils and teachers we can suggest that common factors that are related to both behaviour and planning are:

- The requirement for classroom tasks to contain a suitable amount of interesting, relevant work.

- Clear instructions on how to complete that work, and appropriate recognition for completion.

- An appropriately managed classroom, including the deployment of resources and a sympathetic but consistent application of explicit behaviour management rules.

Before we move on to consider strategies that we can use to plan lessons that take into account the above factors, you might like to complete Task 2, which gives you the opportunity to reflect on causes of misbehaviour in lessons you have taught and observed.

Task 2

Review a lesson you have observed being taught by another teacher. What misbehaviours did you note? Were there any obvious potential causes? Which causes would you classify as school-level, classroom-level or individual-level correlates? If appropriate, perhaps you could ask the classroom teacher what they thought that the causes of disengaged behaviour may have been.

Now reflect on a lesson or portion of a lesson that you have taught. Did you see any similar misbehaviours, or were different issues experienced? Would you attribute similar causes? Again, which of these causes were school-level, classroom-level or individual-level?

Considering both the observed and taught lesson, do your findings match with the research presented above, or other research on causes of misbehaviour that you may have read?

Mitigation of poor behaviour with planning

As previously discussed, reactive strategies of behaviour management contribute to teacher stress and reduce pupil engagement, showing the value of proactive planning for behaviour. Here we focus on how the factors described above may be mitigated with proper consideration during planning. The word *mitigation*, rather than prevention, is appropriate here as no amount of planning will guarantee positive on-task behaviour from all students, and ongoing active management of the classroom is essential for quality learning. However, carefully considered planning can reduce the impact and likelihood of negative behaviour, and reduces the probability of escalation.

Although aimed at English-language teachers, Farrell (2002) presents a sound synopsis of how models of teachers' planning of individual lessons has progressed over time from Tyler's (1949) rational-linear framework to more recent developments that see planning as a '… dynamic process involving teachers making choices before, during, and after each lesson' (p. 31). We must also maintain an awareness of curriculum planning that goes beyond single lessons, and consider sustained impact over time from medium- and long-term programmes of study. Romiszowski (2016) offers a comprehensive study of strategies used to '… tackle a wide variety of instructional design tasks' (p. xi). In considering lesson planning as a dynamic process stretching over a period of several lessons, the section below also draws heavily on the ARCS model developed by Keller (2010), which offers some insight into increasing motivation and engagement in pupils over time. We can use ideas from these authors, and others, to break down the three requirements from the previous section and suggest methods to develop strategies for addressing these requirements.

The requirement for classroom tasks to contain a suitable amount of interesting, relevant work

One strategy for promoting behaviours that Luiselli et al. (2005) would classify as academic engagement is to make classwork relevant to pupils in a way that will capture their attention. This aspect relies not only upon the breadth and depth of the teacher's subject knowledge expertise, but also upon a knowledge of pupils. Although it is impossible to describe all variations of classroom activities that pupils may find relevant, the ARCS model provides a series of questions that a teacher may use to promote pupil engagement in a particular topic. These questions are displayed in Table 5.1. Many of the areas touched upon in Keller's questions are mirrored in Flynn (2004), whose pupil-centred approach makes further space for curriculum standards and pupil accountability. Although it would be foolish to assume that every lesson can address all question areas, such questions can be used to structure lessons in a way that may promote engaging behaviours and move away from more procedural planning as seen in Strangis et al. (2006), where student teachers '… acknowledged the importance of standards and lesson objectives but planned in a sequence that found lesson activities before objectives' (p. 73).

However, even relevant and engaging pupil activities can result in off-task behaviour if the quantity or difficulty of work is not tailored to a particular class. Whilst the concept of 'too much' classwork is somewhat problematic (given differences in the speed of completion demonstrated by pupils, 'too much' is an entirely relative term), pupils who perceive work expectations to be unattainable may prefer to refuse to attempt tasks rather than fail to complete them. As Hofer puts it, 'After repeated failure with one task or if pupils judge the forthcoming task as too difficult, they

Table 5.1 Possible strategies to increase engagement behaviours (modified from Keller (2010)).

Relevance Strategy	Questions	Considerations
Attention Capture	What can I do to capture their interest?	Do I know what might interest this class? What aspect or application of this subject can be used to 'hook' pupils in?
Stimulate Enquiry	How can I stimulate an attitude of enquiry?	What are the mysteries of this topic that pupils could investigate?
Maintain Attention/ Variation of Experience	How can I use a variety of tactics to maintain their attention?	Have I incorporated a variety of teaching methods (video, lecture, animations, reading, etc)? Has this class had a varied diet of teaching methods in recent lessons?
Relevance/Relate to Goals	How can I best meet the needs or aspirations of these pupils?	Do I know the needs or aspirations of these pupils?
Match Interests	How and when can I provide my learners with appropriate choices, responsibilities, and influences?	Do I know their interests? What *cultural capital* are they bringing to the classroom?
Tie to Experiences/ Familiarity	How can I tie the instruction to the learners' experiences?	What are the day-to-day experiences of my pupils?

might look for a more joyful activity' (2007, p. 30). Additionally, as teachers in Warren Little (2003) describe, speed of task completion does not always mean that lasting learning has occurred, and pupils who have completed expected work may also quickly seek alternative entertainment. With this in mind the lesson planning process should attempt to make sure that all pupils have tasks that are achievable, that the goals of a task of clearly communicated, and that no pupil is left without a task to complete. This final point may be addressed by ensuring that the final portion of any task is open-ended – be that extended writing, a creative activity, or directed independent study, for example – as such activities allow for a flexibility in timing.

The requirement for clear instructions on how to complete classwork, and appropriate recognition for completion

It is unsurprising that teachers who make topics and instructions easy to understand increase academic engagement, and yet the concept of clarity itself is difficult to unpick. One of the most widely-cited studies investigating teacher clarity found that pupils understand clarity in multidimensional ways:

> Specifically, it appears to consist of a rather general dimension which involves explaining concepts and directions in an understandable manner and at an

appropriate pace, and a second dimension which pertains more specifically to teacher use of examples and illustrations in presenting material.

Bush et al., (1977, p. 57)

When planning, teachers should aim to address these ideas of clarity, perhaps by practicing explanations of concepts and tasks to ensure that the ideas and instructions are repeated, difficult points are acknowledged and highlighted, and new words are explained fully. Pupils may also be given the chance to repeat back instructions, help with worked examples of questions, and address any misunderstanding before more independent activities begin. Suitable subject knowledge is of particular import when formulating clear explanations, as an incomplete understanding of the curriculum subject content may result in unclear explanations, leading to disengagement and off-task behaviour.

As classroom activities are drawing to a close, the distribution of praise and rewards may lead to the 'reinforcement of appropriate behaviour' (Hart, 2010). Although other authors in this book outline uses of rewards most effectively, it may be useful to ensure this is indicated in the lesson planning process. The ARCS model suggests the use of questions such as 'What will provide reinforcement to the learners' successes?' to develop extrinsic rewards, 'How can I provide meaningful opportunities for learners to use their newly acquired knowledge/skill?' to consider intrinsic rewards, and 'How can I assist the students in anchoring a positive feeling about their accomplishments?' to plan to promote self-efficacy and equity (Keller, 2010). These questions can be addressed before, during and towards the end of the lesson planning process, and repeated use of such strategies can promote self-efficacy over time.

The requirement for an appropriately managed classroom, including deployment of resources and a sympathetic but consistent application of explicit behaviour management rules

When considering classroom management, it is important to plan for both the behavioural and the logistical management of inhabitants of the class alongside the management of physical resources in the classroom environment. Other authors in the book provide excellent resources with which to develop, share and reference behaviour management rules with pupils, and ensuring time is planned within any sequence of lessons to reinforce and model appropriate enactment of these rules can lead to more effective learning. Plans might consider where in a particular lesson pupils would benefit from reminders of how to behave, how routines can be established and leveraged during the lesson, or where 'trigger points' may occur during transitions between activities. Looking closely at the relationship between established rules or school policies and your lesson plan both encourages consistency and allows for issues to be proactively predicted, and considering them alongside long-term plans ensures pupils are treated sympathetically and allowed room to 'grow up' and take responsibility for their own behaviour. An ongoing consistent and sympathetic approach to interaction with pupils is integral to lesson planning, and encourages on-task behaviours.

There is a subject-specific element to the management of physical resources and the classroom environment. Chapter 9 in this book will show how practical settings such as PE require specific consideration, but all learning settings require resource management: How might the mathematics teacher plan to ensure that the calculators are taken from a drawer and one placed in front of each pupil without causing distraction? How will pupils obtain books for an English literature lesson, and be encouraged to read right away? Although such questions may appear to be 'common sense', they require an understanding of the classroom resources employed in particular subject areas, and some consideration towards management of these resources should be given during planning.

Having considered how on-task behaviours may be promoted through planning, you might like to collate your work from Tasks 1 and 2 and attempt Task 3.

Task 3

Using research evidence above, and the lists you produced in Tasks I and 2, which of the behaviours you observed could have been mitigated with careful planning? How might you have gone about this? Does the discussion above offer some sort of framework to help you consider behaviour in your lesson planning?

Use this information to create a 'cheat sheet' of personal strategies for predicting and mitigating poor behaviour when planning lessons. This could be table, a flowchart, a mind-map, or a simple bullet-pointed list.

Conclusions

As we have seen in this chapter, some causes of negative off-task behaviour attributed to learning activities, lesson structure and classroom organisation arise as a result of learning activities that pupils consider to be too onerous, or lacking in relevance or interest. Additional behaviour problems may be caused from a lack of clarity in instructions, or a lack of reward for completing work to a high standard. Such behavioural difficulties may be compounded in a classroom that is poorly organised or badly managed, or where pupils feel they are treated inconsistently or unsympathetically.

An awareness of these potential causes of off-task behaviour allows teachers to plan to mitigate potential behavioural problems. The ARCS model, for example, provides several strategies to increase relevance of learning to pupils, with the aim to subsequently increase engagement and positive on-task behaviour. Clarity of instruction, including explaining concepts and directions in an understandable manner, at an appropriate pace, and using examples, can also promote academic engagement, as can a consistent use of praise and rewards to increase self-efficacy and perceived value of classwork. Further strategies to encourage on-task behaviours stem from effective management of classroom resources, which can minimise distraction and ensure transitions between activities are smooth. Each of these areas can and should be planned in advance, and has a thread of subject knowledge running through it. Whether that is identifying interesting and relatable areas of a particular topic, ensuring clear explanation of concepts, or identifying and handling appropriate resources, the combination of effective planning and sound subject knowledge is essential to promote positive classroom behaviour. I hope that Task 4 will help you to demonstrate your skill in this area.

Task 4

Select a lesson from your upcoming teaching and consider...

■ Are the activities planned for pupils to complete interesting and relevant to them?

■ Is the quantity of work appropriate, and appropriately flexible?

■ Are your instructions clear, and have they been designed to confirm an understanding of tasks?

■ How and who will you assist during circulation?

■ What recognition will there be for completion of tasks?

■ Are pupils aware of your existing behaviour management rules? Which may they need to be reminded of in this lesson?

■ Have you considered the deployment of classroom resources?

Indicate your thinking around these ideas on your lesson plan.

References

Bennett, T. (March 2017) *Creating a Culture: How School Leaders Can Optimise Behaviour.* London: Department for Education.

Bru, E. (2006) Factors associated with disruptive behaviour in the classroom. *Scandinavian Journal of Educational Research 50*(1), 23–43. doi: 10.1080/00313830500372000.

Bush, A.J., Kennedy, J.J. and Cruickshank, D.R. (1977) An empirical investigation of teacher clarity. *Journal of Teacher Education 28*(2), 53–58. DOI: 10.1177/002248717702800216.

Clunies-Ross, P., Little, E. and Kienhuis, M. (2008) Self-reported and actual use of proactive and reactive classroom management strategies and their relationship with teacher stress and student behaviour. *Educational Psychology 28*(6), 693–710. doi: 10.1080/01443410802206700.

Farrell, T.S.C. (2002) Lesson planning. In: Richards, J.C. and Renandya, W.A. (eds.) *Methodology in Language Teaching: An Anthology of Current Practice.* New York: Cambridge University Press, 30–39.

Flynn, P. (2004) Applying Standards-Based Constructivism: A Two-Step Guide for Motivating Middle and High School Students. Larchmont, NY: Eye on Education.

Gibbs, S. and Gardiner, M. (2008) The structure of primary and secondary teachers' attributions for pupils' misbehaviour: A preliminary cross-phase and cross-cultural investigation. *Journal of Research in Special Educational Needs 8*(2), 68–77. doi: 10.1111/j.1471-3802.2008.00104.x.

Gottfredson, D.C., Gottfredson, G.D. and Hybl, L.G. (1993) Managing adolescent behavior: a multiyear, multischool study. *American Educational Research Journal 30*(1), 179–215. doi: 10.2307/1163194.

Hart, R. (2010) Classroom behaviour management: educational psychologists' views on effective practice. *Emotional and Behavioural Difficulties 15*(4), 353–371. doi: 10.1080/13632752.2010.523257.

Hofer, M. (2007) Goal conflicts and self-regulation: A new look at pupils' off-task behaviour in the classroom. *Educational Research Review 2*(1), 28–38. doi: 10.1016/j.edurev.2007.02.002.

Keller, J.M. (2010) *Motivational Design for Learning and Performance: The ARCS Model Approach*. New York: Springer.

Kyriacou, C., Avramidis, E., Høie, H. et al. (2007) The development of student teachers' views on pupil misbehaviour during an initial teacher training programme in England and Norway. *Journal of Education for Teaching 33*(3), 293–307. doi: 10.1080/02607470701450288.

Lambert, N. and Miller, A. (2010) The temporal stability and predictive validity of pupils' causal attributions for difficult classroom behaviour. *British Journal of Educational Psychology 80*(4), 599–622. doi: 10.1348/000709910X486628.

Little, E. (2005) Secondary school teachers' perceptions of students' problem behaviours. *Educational Psychology 25*(4), 369–377. doi: 10.1080/01443410500041516.

Luiselli, J.K., Putnam, R.F. and Handler, M.W. et al. (2005) Whole-school positive behaviour support: effects on student discipline problems and academic performance. *Educational Psychology 25*(2–3), 183–198. doi: 10.1080/0144341042000301265.

Mavropoulou, S. and Padeliadu, S. (2002) Teachers' causal attributions for behaviour problems in relation to perceptions of control. *Educational Psychology 22*(2), 191–202. doi: 10.1080/01443410120115256.

Miller, A. (1995) Teachers' attributions of causality, control and responsibility in respect of difficult pupil behaviour and its successful management. *Educational Psychology 15*(4), 457–471. doi: 10.1080/0144341950150408.

Ogilvy, C.M. (1994) An evaluative review of approaches to behaviour problems in the secondary school. *Educational Psychology 14*(2), 195–206. doi: 10.1080/0144341940140204.

Pajares, F. (2006) Self-efficacy during childhood and of adolescence: implications for teachers and parents. In Urdan, T. and Pajares, F. (eds.) *Self Efficacy Beliefs of Adolescents*. Charlotte, NC: IAP.

Romiszowski, A.J. (2016) *Designing Instructional Systems: Decision Making in Course Planning and Curriculum Design* (1st edn.). London: Routledge.

Strangis, D.E., Pringle, R.M. and Knopf, H.T. (2006) Road map or roadblock? Science Lesson planning and preservice teachers. *Action in Teacher Education 28*(1), 73–84. doi: 10.1080/01626620.2006.10463568.

Sullivan, A.M., Johnson, B., Owens, L. et al. (2014) Punish them or engage them? Teachers' views of unproductive student behaviours in the classroom. *Australian Journal of Teacher Education 39*(6). Available at: https://eric.ed.gov/?id=EJ1020605 (accessed 4/10/18).

Tyler, R.W. (1949) *Basic Principles of Curriculum and Instruction*. Chicago, IL: University of Chicago Press.

Warren Little, J. (2003) Inside teacher community: Representations of classroom practice. *Teachers College Record 105*(6), 913–945. doi: 10.1111/1467-9620.00273.

Working with texts: Behaviour challenges and possible solutions

Chris Hanley and Anna Olsson Rost

Chapter aims

▓ To explore how pupils can be encouraged into more productive learning behaviours in relation to textual study.

▓ To explain how teachers can adjust their practice towards better learning behaviours in two subjects, English and history.

▓ To explore some of the implications for lesson planning and content.

Keywords: Textual study; pedagogy; scaffolding understanding; learning behaviours; English; history

Introduction

This chapter considers pupil behaviour from the perspective of two subject disciplines that require frequent and detailed work with texts: English and history. It is argued that behaviour is likely to improve in tandem with an improved pedagogy. The chapter focusses on lesson planning that determines the format, sequence and content of textual study tasks. It is argued that lesson ideas can be deployed more or less effectively in sequences of tasks that influence pupil behaviour. Suggestions are made about how to link robust pedagogic ideas with classroom tasks that support more independent pupil inquiry. These suggestions are supported with theoretical material intended to stimulate further inquiry in these areas. Possible solutions are examined in the respective subject disciplines.

Part I: Working with texts in English classrooms

This section explores links between pedagogic ideas, planning and task development and classroom behaviour. The key idea is that textual study is informed by different assumptions about how texts function. Exploring these assumptions can lead to clearer conceptualisation of single tasks and sequences of tasks. Pedagogy and classroom behaviour are not separate issues. It is illustrated how approaching the former differently also brings about improvements in the latter. Confusion about the nature of non-literary and literary texts is highlighted as a pedagogic issue that can develop into behaviour difficulties. An alternative view of English practice is offered, emphasising firstly the centrality of the *learner* (pupils) in the generation of textual effects, secondly, the *genre* or *type* of text, and thirdly, the ways in which the text fulfils its *purposes*.

Introduction

Frequently in English classrooms knowledge is generated across a *sequence* of activities. For example, a *questioning* routine, beginning with 'what' questions, leads to 'how' and 'why' questions, leading to 'explore', 'reimagine' questions, and so on. Such pedagogic routines can be tremendously important for supporting both the pupils' and student practitioner's understanding of how knowledge is acquired. Reliable pedagogic routines also provide the student practitioner with a *way of being* with the class – both practitioner and pupils recognise a common language and sequence of activity. However, routines can also become stale (Ellis, Fox and Street, 2007), stifling the aspects of language that encourage flexibility and responsiveness.

This *pedagogic* tension between 'reliability' and 'staleness' can manifest as a *behavioural* issue in class. As a teacher educator I observe many lessons by beginner practitioners in school. Recently, several lessons were on the topic of non-fictional persuasive writing, focussing particularly on the language of advertising. Next is a summary of the pedagogic approach and the behaviour issues it created. The approach by several practitioners was sufficiently alike to warrant a general description.

The beginner practitioner introduced to the class a list of key language or 'persuasive devices'. These included: lists of three, use of exclamation marks and other punctuation, use of statistics or facts versus opinion, creating a positive tone, use of the 'inclusive' pronouns *you* and *we*, being 'personal', use of descriptive or emotional language. Together, the whole class was tested to ensure the devices and their definitions were recognisable by everyone. Next, a different persuasive text was introduced to the pupils, sufficiently similar to what they had already seen for the same persuasive features and effects to be recognised in this new context.

Behaviour was good at the beginning but drifted in the middle and worsened in the lesson's later stages. Talking to pupils and reading their work indicated they were struggling to go beyond identifying the language in its new context. Effective language use requires comprehension as well as pattern recognition (Harrison, 2004). I believe the behaviour difficulty originated in the requirement for pupils to explain the *effects* of language features in the new context (*what is the effect of this rhetorical question in this text*?). Pupils were unsure, became distracted and less compliant or resorted to *repeating the definitions*. The reason pupils did this, I believe, was because the task implied that language generates the same effects irrespective of context – a difficulty that will be explored in some detail below.

The main points so far about behaviour management are, firstly, mini-structures and routines help to create a coherent image of the knowledge to be attained; they can scaffold pupil responses and support an inclusive culture in the classroom. Secondly, behaviour can be problematic when mini-structures and routines do not create smooth sequences of learning, but create problems seemingly connected with the very nature of the routine itself. In the example just given, the intrinsic problem is overreliance on the innate capacity of language to determine its context of reception (as if, by virtue of its linguistic properties, an advertisement is, *by definition*, persuasive). Next, these insights will be theorised to show how pedagogic dilemmas might be differently understood and, crucially, to help re-evaluate the figure of the 'misbehaving pupil'.

Theoretical development and practical implications

A famous diagram by M.H. Abrams, in his study of Romanticism *The Mirror and the Lamp* (1958), depicts the 'basic co-ordinates of critical orientation' (Freund, 1987, p. 1). We are given a model of the interrelations of author, audience, text and world. Elizabeth Freund describes Abrams' diagram as follows:

> At the centre is the work or the artefact itself. In orbit around it, at equidistant points, are the other three basic elements that constitute the object of critical investigation. These are the work's producer, the state of affairs ('nature' or the universe of existing things) which the work reflects or signifies, and the audience to which it is addressed (1987, p. 1).

Figure 6.1 is influenced by but also extends Abram's work to include the theoretical vocabulary employed in this chapter.

The pedagogic issues reported above indicate that the *work* is emphasised at the expense of the other elements. There is perhaps too much focus on *language* and not enough on *who* is reading. I believe it is crucial to identify a text's *target audience*. Often this will not be the pupils who are reading the text, and a gap will be created between the text's 'target' response and the pupils' actual responses (e.g. *this advertisement is not aimed at me and I am not persuaded*). Analysing this gap can help pupils to understand how and why texts influence their readers, but readers may or may not respond as they are supposed to.

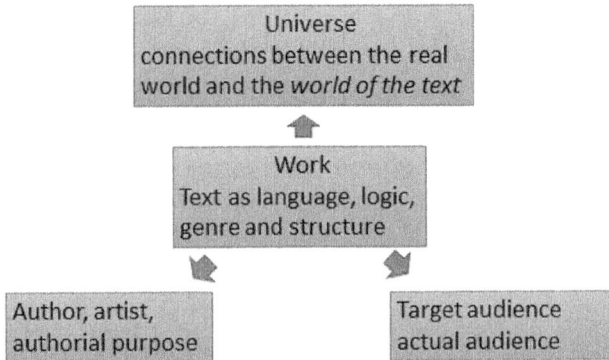

Figure 6.1 A model for textual analysis in English (Adapted from Abrams, 1958).

It is crucial for the term *audience* to be understood not as an abstraction but as referring to *actual pupils who are reading the text now*. It can re-direct disruptive behaviour towards better outcomes if pupils believe they have a stake in the text under discussion. By this I do not mean pupil responses are equally perceptive or accurate, but they are still treated as helpful in revealing what the text is trying to achieve. Even if the text is described by pupils as 'pointless' or 'boring', it indicates the distance between the pupil's reaction and the text's 'target' reaction and reveals something about what the text is trying to achieve. The key pedagogic recommendation here is for pupils to be addressed as *actual potential audiences*.

The diagram also suggests that the concepts *purpose* and *genre* might be emphasised over linguistic structure. It is useful to connect these concepts, with *purpose* linking both to the author and to the work's *genre*. This means that while a text produces linguistic effects to fulfil certain purposes, these purposes are products of the writer's intention as governed by the text's genre. One cannot gauge the quality of a linguistic effect without analysing its *intended product* or purpose. For example, advertising texts often exude positive energy and optimism, but they do not necessarily excite these states in the audience. The effects can fail, while negativity and fear can also be powerful advertising tools. It is insufficient to argue that a text is persuasive because it contains positive emotions. The target audience might be expected to respond with 'positivity', but the pupils may not respond in that way. The analysis needs to consider whether or not a linguistic effect *fulfils the text's purpose*.

Genre and world of the text in *Lord of the Flies*

The key pedagogic recommendations are, firstly, language should be analysed not as a disparate series of effects but in terms of how effectively it *fulfils the text's purposes*. Secondly, this approach can help the teacher to weave a higher level of intellectual challenge into the lesson content, particularly where pupils are *not supposed to be the target audience*. Thirdly, different genres of text create different effects and should not be analysed the same way. The third point is further explored in this section.

Fictional and non-fiction texts do not function in the same way, but it is tempting to teach them as if they do – for example, by emphasising the presence of linguistic textures and structures in both kinds of text. Of course, teaching pupils about language is crucial, but the diagram reminds us that language gives access to different domains of readerly experience (writer, audience, world of the text) in addition to structural effects. A concern with the *world of the text* raises the question of how the text produces a world we recognise (the 'mimetic approach' (Freund, 1987, p. 1)). Clearly, novels and advertisements do this in very different ways.

Novels enable imaginative projection by readers. To adapt Terry Eagleton's description, novels bring 'life closer to us rather than raising it beyond our reach' (Eagleton, 2005, p. 8). Pupils can talk about characters *as if they are real people*, so that vocabularies for purposive human action (intention, feeling, attitude, belief, etc.), apply in realistic, non-ironic ways to the actions of characters. This seems significantly different from the snapshot, hyperbolic characterisations of a television advertisement, but some of the difficulties with teaching advertising, mentioned above, still apply to literature. Often, pupils find fictional worlds difficult to relate to. The pedagogic recommendation here is for teaching to consider the various ways in which pupils can be enabled to access the *world of the text*, whose strangeness can create behaviour issues, but it can also be the focal point for rich and satisfying learning experiences, particularly those linked to imaginative projections by readers into the lives of characters who seem speculatively real.

Before this point is developed, it is worth noting what can happen when novels and other fictions are treated mainly or exclusively as linguistic artefacts. Pupils can miss out on one of the most enjoyable aspects of sustained reading – namely, having that familiarity with a situation that allows them to experience and assess it as if it is real. For instance, a narrator may describe a character in a positive or negative way, or both (in *The Great Gatsby*, Nick Carraway's attitude to Gatsby himself alternates between the two). The reader's job is not merely to accept the description, but to *evaluate* it. (*Is it fair? Is it justifiable? What is its motivation?*) To make this kind of evaluation, the pupils need to be able to make an *independent* assessment of the character, which requires them to read the novel *as if* the character is a real person whose actions gather significance over time.

In contrast, if the textual analysis is overly linguistic, the behaviour can dip rapidly. My observations suggest this happens for similar reasons to those highlighted in the earlier example. Behaviour is good earlier in the lesson, when learning activities are well structured and map out a clear route to the end of the lesson. Behaviour drops in the middle sections, when pupils are trying to attach significance to the language they have identified. It is useful for a practitioner to anticipate behaviour difficulties by *modelling* how fiction is analysed. In my view such modelling is particularly challenging for the practitioner, as it is reliant on her or his judgement about how pupils will perceive and relate to the *world of the text*.

William Golding's *Lord of the Flies*

The following discussion of *Lord of the Flies* (1954) indicates how a teacher can analyse a scene while building layers of interpretation about the *world of the text* (which also tells us about *our* world). The key pedagogic point here is that particular words or images do not occur in isolation; they are focal points for what we have been thinking and feeling so far. Reading in this productive, constructive way, is more akin to an act of *writing* (Freund, 1987).

The novel is set during a war. An aeroplane carrying British boys crash-lands on a tropical island in the Pacific Ocean. The boys try to make a 'reasonable society for themselves' (Golding's letter to Jonathan Cape, quoted in Carey, 2009, p. 150), but it is destroyed from within by the boys themselves, some of whom have been conditioned into domineering destructiveness, while the others are too inexperienced or ineffectual to resist.

The fair boy (Ralph) and the fat boy (Piggy) are sympathetic to the reader and significant actors in the boys' initial attempts to construct a workable, cohesive social unit. When they meet for the first time and discuss the circumstances of the crash, the text hints at how their respective personalities will later unfold. Ralph seems less aware of the other boy, he speaks little and seeks to pull away from Piggy towards further adventure. Piggy tries to establish the friendship and reveals a more observant, practical attitude towards their current predicament. He is conscious that he and the other boy belong to a wider group of boys, about whom he is also concerned.

Analysis

Next are two alternative accounts of how this meeting between Piggy and Ralph could be analysed. The first deals with the explicit *messages* of the text, while the second tries to relate to the *world of the text*. For the sake of clarity, the readings are presented as if they are completely separate from one another; in practice, they would probably overlap.

Reading the text for explicit messages

The scene can be analysed for *information* about the novel's two main characters. The challenge is to find out about the characters: who they are, how they are different, what is likely to happen to them, and so on. Pupils might be asked to identify significant words or phrases. There are some linguistic markers of their difference ('the fair boy', 'the fat boy'), some idiomatic speech markers of social class ('it wasn't half dangerous'). There are signs that foreshadow future disaster for the fair boy ('he tripped over a branch and came down with a crash') and that the fat boy is going to be vulnerable later in the story ('I was the only boy in the school what had asthma').

The information is certainly useful, but this might not be the best approach for modelling to pupils how to conduct a substantial, stimulating analysis of a literary text. It might be relatively straightforward for pupils to identify quotations supplying various kinds of information about the characters, but difficulties arise when pupils are asked to analyse the quotations' *effects*.

Often, pupils struggle with the idea of *effect*. This may be because the word *effect* implies *someone being affected* – i.e. a *reader*. When asked to identify an *effect*, pupils often think they are being asked to locate something lurking beneath the surface of the text, so they end up locating not an *effect*, but merely *additional information*. For example, the pupil is asked to locate *foreshadowing* in the text and explain its effect. The pupil identifies Ralph's tripping over a branch, and explains that this stumble *foreshadows* future calamity, brought about by Ralph's hasty judgement. The pupil then explains the *effect* of this narrative device <u>by</u> <u>repeating the initial point</u> – saying that the *effect* is to foreshadow the future disaster brought about by Ralph's poor judgement.

The *world of the text*

A better approach is to help pupils enter the *world of the text*. The passage can be read speculatively, as if the fictional world and its concerns are *real*, in the sense of being subject to the same natural laws and causal logic as our world, making it imaginatively habitable. The characters' meeting can be read as a representation of a meeting between two strangers. The pupils could be asked what is being *shown* about each character, or what do we *learn* about each character. This would take the emphasis off what the text *explicitly* says, highlighting the need for independent thought and interpretation. We can see that for Ralph, being stranded means freedom from grown-ups. For Piggy, the absence of grown-ups signifies threat and disorder, while Piggy himself will later become a surrogate parent to the group. Piggy reveals *without intending to reveal* that his thoughts immediately turn to adult authority and the rules they entail ('My auntie told me not to run'). Meanwhile, both characters are reacting to a sudden uncertainty about what to do next. The reader can see Piggy's response is personal and collective ('What's your name … more of us scattered about'), while Ralph's is more individualistic and escapist ('Ralph shook his head and increased his speed'). The key pedagogic point is that pupils can use their own experiences of other children as building blocks in the imaginative reconstruction of the psychologies of two fictional characters. Carefully handled, this can enable the teacher to convince the class that they are already in possession of significant resources that will enable them to understand and interpret the textual dynamics of a piece of fiction. Here, the teacher could *begin* the analysis by modelling how to identify key points whilst emphasising that interpretation takes place within *a range of possibility*, based on the assumption that fictional characters are a bit like us – and in this sense, within limits, everyone can understand them.

Part 1: Conclusions

This section's key argument is that classroom behaviour might benefit from pedagogies that recognise the importance of *reader response*, *genre* and *fictional worlds*. These concepts and their associated pedagogies can be helpful for scaffolding pupil understanding and directing pupils towards more productive activity. Particularly with the benefit of teacher modelling, pupils can learn how to use their own reactions and responses as a basis for *evaluation* (not just *recognition*) of linguistic effects, which can be very useful in terms of fostering pupil independence, particularly in more challenging (and potentially disruptive) lesson phases when pupils are tasked with applying, interpreting and analysing ideas.

Task 1

Review a lesson in English that focussed on literature or language.

With the above diagram in mind, consider which aspects of language or literature were being emphasised (world of the text, work of the text, authorial intention, audience).

Consider how and why particular parts of the lesson were successful or unsuccessful, particularly in respect of pupils' independent ability to fulfil the lesson objectives.

Part 2: Working with texts in the history classroom

Compared to the examples from the English classroom analysed above, there certainly are key differences in the way in which we analyse texts in the history classroom. However, there are also tangible similarities when we look at how subject pedagogy can influence issues related to classroom management. Rightly or wrongly, compared to in the English classroom, we tend to pay less attention to the linguistic devises contained in texts when teaching history, although there is certainly a place for such analysis in history too (Smith, 2001). When pupils study texts in the history classroom, we are just as likely to come across confusion in regards to the nature of texts as in the English classroom. Drawing on lesson observations, as well as on my own teaching practice, it is also noticeable that issues sometimes arise when we, as history teachers, try to employ routinised teaching strategies or mini-structures without reflecting more deliberately on their suitability for pupils' work with texts of different natures, genres and contexts. Therefore, student teachers and NQTs who teach history can also benefit from looking at how subject pedagogy, in the form of routinised teaching strategies, might sometimes act as barriers to deeper learning, understanding and, crucially, engagement among pupils. In turn, this also provides an opportunity to consider how unproductive learning behaviours might be pre-empted through lesson planning.

Textual study: more productive learning behaviours?

When planning history lessons for the purpose of encouraging pupils to evaluate texts, it is easy to fall into what we might call the 'provenance trap'. By this, I mean routine questions and tasks that are devised to analyse the provenance of texts, but that might not always take into consideration the role and importance of different key areas of consideration that pupils are required to master in order to start to make sense of the provenance of a specific historical text. This includes a contextual understanding and the substantive knowledge required for such an understanding, an appreciation of contemporary attitudes and values, and an understanding of the nature and limitations of different genres of texts. For example, just because pupils have completed a GCSE-style answer related to interpretations in a previous lesson, this does not automatically give them the tools to answer a similar question about two other interpretations today – they might need additional subject knowledge and understanding, relevant to these new texts, to be able to answer the question posed.

Unproductive learning behaviours can sometimes occur if pupils have (possibly quite quickly and superficially) commented on pre-determined criteria, such as the author, purpose, date of the text. They might then consider themselves to be finished with the task that, on the surface, appears quite simple. However, superficial comments, such as 'he/she is Norman so they are biased' or 'it was written at the time so they would know what happened', is not uncommon, and the knowledge and understanding garnered from such analyses does not sufficiently prepare pupils for the possible extended writing phase of the lesson, which might require them to use the evidence to answer, for example, a question on the utility of a text, or maybe even of the utility of a number of texts as group. Similarly to the observations made in the English classroom, therefore, behaviour might become less productive as lessons progress. If some pupils are uncertain of how to approach the more challenging analyses, which they might feel underprepared for, this can lead to an unwillingness to undertake the task – hence impacting on engagement and classroom management.

There is, of course, merit in asking pupils to evaluate texts by considering their provenance, but without the required tools to do this effectively, pupils can become disengaged. This can turn out to be particularly troublesome if lessons are frequently planned along a similar pattern where pupils are required to evaluate the usefulness of texts against rigid criteria, and in very similar ways – regardless of the nature, context or purpose of the text studied. As explored in relation to the teaching of English above, routines can be effective pedagogical as well as classroom management tools. However, by habitually starting lessons by listing aspects of the provenance of texts that pupils are expected to analyse, the specific value of the text, and the purpose for which it is being investigated, become less obvious. In turn, this can lead to less engagement among pupils, and the routine analysis of the provenance become less purposeful if applied to a text generically. This is where more specific direction from the teacher can make a big difference. It is well worth thinking about how you can make it clear to pupils why you have asked them to read a particular text. Asking them to think about what might have prompted you to ask them to read this text? Why would you think it is valuable for them to read? And so on. Furthermore, consider which key aspects, in terms of the text's provenance, might be notable and therefore worth taking into account when analysing this particular text. By developing your subject pedagogy in this respect, you can start to move beyond the 'provenance trap'.

Theoretical development and implications

Figure 6.1 is helpful for planning lessons on textual study in history, as well as in English, since it compels us to consider the interrelationship of 'author', 'audience', 'text' and 'universe' more deliberately. Whilst the 'text', 'author' and 'audience' are relatively often emphasised in history teaching, 'universe' often remains relatively unexplored. This is perhaps unsurprising since this is arguably the most complex aspect to comprehend, and it can undoubtedly seem quite daunting to try and approach this with secondary school pupils. When considering texts in this way, however, it becomes more evident why approaching textual study in a routinised manner can be problematic since it might not allow for taking more nuanced complexities into account. This notion of 'universe', in relation to studying historical texts, has sometimes been described as a 'sense of period'. History teachers have grappled with how to tackle the development of a sense of period among pupils, emphasising the importance of pupils considering factors beyond the regular questions of who, when and where. For example, Ian Dawson has highlighted how it is important for pupils to consider the ideas and attitudes of the period the text is from, and also what people would have known and understood at the time (Dawson, 2009, p. 50).

When thinking about how to approach a more nuanced reading of historical texts, Wineburg's (2001) analyses of the very advanced reading skills required for historians to make sense of historical texts can be useful. Wineburg explains that historical texts need to be viewed as both rhetorical and human artefacts (2001, p. 65), and looking at texts in this way can be very helpful when considering how to approach lesson planning for textual study in history. If we are serious about teaching pupils to read historical texts as successfully as possible, this inevitably has to include an aspect of recognising potential sub-texts. Wineburg argues that apart from viewing texts as a rhetorical artefacts, where the purposes, intentions and goals of the author are considered, a historical reading of the text needs to move:

> ... beyond the use of language as a linguistic technology for persuasion. In fact, many subtexts include elements that work at cross-purposes with authors' intentions, bringing to the surface convictions authors may have

been unaware of or may have wished to conceal … [this] frames reality and discloses information about its author's assumptions, world view, and beliefs.

Wineburg (2001, p. 66)

Just as in the case of textual study in English, pupils are rarely the intended audience of the texts studied in the history classroom. However, the reading of historical texts can be viewed as a process where the audience, in this case your pupils, are the essential ingredient in constructing meaning from the reading of texts. From this vantage point, the gap between the intended audience's potential response to the text, and that of your pupils, can become an engaging and enriching learning opportunity (Huijgen et al., 2015). By treating the complexities of developing pupils' understanding of 'universe' in relation to historical texts as a potentially engaging learning opportunity, and planning lessons with this in mind, subject pedagogy can have a positive impact on pupils' engagement and, by extension, classroom management.

There exists a false dichotomy, purporting tensions between considering the discipline of history to be either a subject that is all about facts, subject knowledge and content, or, on the other hand, that it is all about skills. Of course, this stance is too simplistic in that it completely disregards the fact that substantive and procedural knowledge and understanding are intrinsically linked. Christine Counsell (2017, p. 80) has argued that substantive knowledge is 'emancipatory' for pupils learning history, and she has further observed that:

> … knowledge about period values and textual traditions will help pupils to interpret the text. Knowledge of political context, chronology and cultural diversity will also support pupils' work on source evaluation. Likewise, the critical, reflective or evaluative work will result in transformed or extended period knowledge.
>
> Counsell (2004, p. 1)

This clearly illustrates the interdependence between contextual knowledge and understanding historical texts. Counsell also writes about 'period-sensitivity', and the importance of allowing pupils the time to get immersed in debates and practices of the time they are studying (Counsell, 2004, p. 1) if they are to be fully engaged with historical texts.

Reconsidering approaches to textual study in history: avoiding the 'provenance trap'?

For example, fictional writing from the period under study can generate interest and reveal quirky insights into contemporary habits, customs and beliefs. Such texts can be very powerful as introductions to new periods of study and, with some coaching, pupils can start to develop valid enquiry questions to be explored further. Mary Woolley (2003) accounts for her use of Thomas Hardy's *The Withered Arm* for this exact purpose; reading her article will give you a starting point for how to undertake such an enquiry in your own classroom. This approach can certainly be adapted for other periods or topic areas, for example, Charles Dickens or Elizabeth Gaskell might be tempting choices for industrialisation during the nineteenth century. This kind of enquiry can become a stepping stone towards developing pupils' awareness of the 'universe' aspect of textual analysis. As previously argued in relation to textual study in English, the fictional genre can allow pupils to engage with the reading in a more imaginative way than might be the case in other genres of texts that pupils engage with in history lessons. This can provide different types of opportunities to relate to, and discuss, human actions as they relate to the characters of the novel.

Another way to try and avoid the 'provenance trap' is to turn lessons on their head. By this, I mean to get pupils to think about the context and nature of a text *before* asking them to engage with the actual text itself. The fact that history rarely provides certain answers, but rather a myriad of evidence and interpretations, is one of the reasons why it is so fascinating, but this is also why pupils sometimes become exasperated and complacent – what is the point if we will never know what really happened anyway? We might as well just guess or make it up! As history teachers, we somehow need to counteract this mentality, and by paying closer attention to the nature of historical evidence, we can start to address this. In practice, this can include studying the authors of texts in some depth, prior to introducing the sources at all. Ian Dawson's thinkinghistory website (Dawson, 2017) provides a range of different suggestions of how we can begin to approach this. For example, we can present pupils with an enquiry question and then ask them to rate a range of evidence in relation to how helpful the evidence is likely to be in view of the overall question – before reading the texts. Pupils can also be asked to predict what they think specific texts are likely to say before they even look at them – basing this on their knowledge about the authors (Dawson, 2009). This type of activity becomes not just purposeful in regards to the learning of history, but is also engaging since pupils have got a stake in finding out whether their predictions were accurate or not.

Similar techniques can certainly be used the other way around too: by looking at texts where the details of the provenance have been intentionally removed. Although if you have coached your pupil well, this might generate some outrage – how are they supposed to be able to evaluate a historical text without its provenance?! However, by approaching it this way, pupils can start to use their contextual knowledge and sense of period to analyse the text with a view to guessing the author, the timing (might it originate from before or after a particularly significant event), the views and attitude of the author, and so on. In this way, by turning what we regularly do in our history lessons on its head, we can start to help our pupils to become active and skilful readers of historical texts.

Part 2: Conclusions

This section has argued that the routinised approaches to textual study that can be detrimental to learning behaviours in the English classroom, can also present very similar issues in the history classroom. By reconsidering pedagogical approaches to textual study, we can begin to scaffold pupils' learning to build their competency in detecting subtexts, develop their understanding of the importance of having a sense of period, as well as thinking about how we can start to imbue such a sense of period in our pupils. Essentially, this chapter hopes to provide a starting point from which student teachers and NQTs can reflect upon the pedagogies they apply in relation to textual study in their classrooms. By starting to reflect upon how subject pedagogy can have an influence on learning behaviours among pupils, it is possible to develop approaches that can underpin classroom management.

Task 2

Scrutinise a few of your lesson plans where pupils were required to undertake textual study. Also, scrutinise your evaluations of these lessons.

A. To what extent have you relied on routinised approaches for textual study? Do you recognise the 'provenance trap' in your own lesson plans?

B. Referring to your evaluations of these lessons, do they reflect the issue of unproductive learning behaviours related to textual study, as discussed in this chapter?

C. Keep the above reflections of your own practice in mind. Plan a future lesson where textual study is required with a view to avoiding the 'provenance trap'.

D. Evaluate the alternative approach you used: what implications did this change in pedagogical approach have for classroom management?

Recommended reading

For further reading to inform your understanding of the links between textual study and subject knowledge: Counsell, C. (2017a) The fertility of substantive knowledge – in search of its hidden, generative power. In Davies, I. (ed.), *Debates in History Teaching* (2nd edn.). Oxon: Routledge, pp. 80–99.

For practical advice on designing tasks to enhance pupils' reading of historical texts: Counsell, C. (2004a) *History in Practice. History and Literacy in Y7: Building the Lesson around the Text*. London: Hodder Murray.

For a useful overview of debates around the formation of subject knowledge in English, see Green, A. (2006) University to school: Challenging assumptions in subject knowledge development. *Changing English: Studies in Culture and Education*, *13*, 111–123.

References

Abrams, M.H. (1958) *The Mirror and the Lamp: Romantic Theory and the Critical Tradition*. New York: Norton. (First published 1953). Cited in Freund, (1987), p. 1.

Carey, J. (2009) *William Golding: The Man Who Wrote Lord of the Flies: A Life*. London: Faber & Faber.

Counsell, C. (2004) *History and Literacy in Y7: Building the Lesson around the Text*. History in Practice. London: Hodder Murray.

Counsell, C. (2017) The fertility of substantive knowledge – in search of its hidden, generative power. In Davies, I. (ed.), *Debates in History Teaching* (2nd edn.). Oxon: Routledge, pp. 80–99.

Dawson, I. (2017) Helping Students Think about the Provenance of Sources. Online http://www.thinkinghistory.co.uk/ActivityBase/HelpingStudentsWithProvenance.html [accessed: 13 December 2019].

Dawson, I. (2009) What time does the tune start?: From thinking about 'sense of period' to modelling history at Key Stage 3. *Teaching History, 135*, 50–57.

Eagleton, T. (2005) *The English Novel: An Introduction*. Oxford: Blackwell.

Ellis, V., Fox, C. and Street, B. (eds.) (2007) *Rethinking English in Schools*. London: Continuum.

Freund, E. (1987) *The Return of the Reader*. London: Methuen.

Golding, W. (1954) *Lord of the Flies*. London: Faber & Faber.

Green, A. (2006) University to school: Challenging assumptions in subject knowledge development. *Changing English: Studies in Culture and Education, 13*, 111–123. doi: 10.1080/13586840500347475.

Harrison, C. (2004) *Understanding Reading Development*. London: Sage.

Huijgen, T. and Paul Holthuis, P. (2015) 'Why am I accused of being a heretic?' A pedagogical framework for stimulating historical contextualisation. *Teaching History, 158*, 50–55.

Smith, P. (2001) Why Gerry now likes evidential work. *Teaching History, 102*, 8–13.

Wineburg, S. (2001) *Historical Thinking and Other Unnatural Acts: Charting the Future and Teaching the Past*. Philadelphia, PA: Temple University Press.

Woolley, M. (2003) 'Really weird and freaky': Using a Thomas Hardy short story as a source of evidence in the Year 8 classroom. *Teaching History 111*, 6–11.

7 Your voice and your classroom management

William Evans

Chapter aims

- To explore the ideas of how your voice is crucial in the management of your classroom. It is one of the main forms of communication and inextricably linked to your non-verbal communication.

- To give a better understating of what we consider to be a 'good voice'.

- To develop your understanding of your own voice and give you some practical ideas of how you can further develop your voice for use in the classroom.

Keywords: Voice; practice; communication; air; classroom; breathing; warm-up

Introduction

Why is your voice so critical in communication and thus a vital tool for your classroom and the management of the pupils in it? As you trained as a teacher, or may be training as a teacher, you have most likely thought about what you would say, what instructions you might give or perhaps even planned for the type of questions you will ask in lessons, but have you thought about *how* you will say it? Do you consider or plan for this or more likely react in the moment, using your voice in a limited number of ways?

Task 1

Before reading on make a few notes about how you and others around you use their voice. This could be in a classroom or other situations. Can you analyse this? What changes in people's voices as they communicate in different ways? Start with obvious points like the volume they use (dynamics) and then try to analyse more complex uses of the voice. Perhaps changes in pitch, timbre, when they breathe, or other things you can hear or notice with your eyes.

Why are our voices important, as human beings?

Our voice and language are key to us as humans. As part of the global tribe we now live in. We put so much time into planning our curriculum and lessons, into organising our rooms and resources, into ensuring that we have thought about the learning and assessment. But if we can't communicate and manage our classroom, will any of this matter? Alexander notes the pervasiveness of talk:

> Of all the tools for cultural and pedagogical intervention in human development and learning, talk is the most pervasive in its use and powerful in its possibilities.
>
> Alexander, (2008, p. 92)

Harari (2011) argues in his book *Sapiens* that somewhere between 70,000 and 30,000 years ago the brain of *Homo sapiens* changed. He describes a journey from humans as hunter-gatherers to living in small, then larger groups. The changes in our use of voice and thus types of communication could be argued to link into this change of our living circumstances. Studies into animals have shown that they can communicate and use sounds, or language, to do this. They also use variation in the 'voice' to communicate different situations.

For example, green monkeys use calls of various kinds to communicate. Zoologists have identified one call that means 'Careful! An eagle!' A slightly different call warns 'Careful! A lion!' (Harari 2011, p. 24).

So, if language is used by animals to communicate and to aid survival it could be argued that there is nothing special about it. But, as humans, we use our language for far more than this. Even if we extend our consideration to more complex sounds these can also be seen (and heard) in other animals such as whales and elephants. Many common birds have the ability to mimic our language, copying every sound but this again is not special or real communication. However, what is quickly apparent is that *Homo sapiens* developed language systems that are considerably more complicated in their range of sound and meaning than other species. As Harari puts it:

> Our language and communication evolved to not only help us to survive but also to help us communicate complex and interesting ideas. Over time, we have evolved in our abilities to share these imbued with meaning and nuance. Amongst a huge variety of things, it has enabled us to share fantasy lands, abstract ideas and build shared belief systems.
>
> Harari (2011, pp. 22–25)

This leads to Harari's second theory about our communication, that our language evolved to enable us to talk about us:

> ... the most important information that needed to be conveyed was about humans, not about lions and bison. Our language evolved as a way of

gossiping. According to this theory [we] are primarily a social animal. Social cooperation is our key to survival and reproduction. It is not enough for individual men and women to know the whereabouts of lions and bison [thus to survive and behave like monkeys]. It's much more important for them to know who in their band hates whom, who is sleeping with whom, who is honest and who is a cheat.

(Ibid., pp. 25–26)

The most common answer is that our language is amazingly supple. We can connect a limited number of sounds and signs to produce an infinite number of sentences, each with a distinct meaning (ibid.). We use this complexity through supple and simple development from an early age, without really ever knowing. We are surrounded by 'professionals' right from our first moments, we are encouraged to make mistakes, to practice outload and develop our communication. We become expert speakers without even knowing it.

But what do we need to consider as we use this communication in the classroom? What do we need to consider supporting our communication? What is the difference between being an expert speaker and an expert communicator to large groups or classes? Embracing the brilliance of the monkey calls to the complexities of subtle human tones.

Task 2

What sort of voice do you think you have? Is it deep, high? Light, strong? Do people compliment you on your voice? Do you speak too fast? Do you use a range of pitches?

Again, take a few moments to analyse your own voice. Do you know how you make the sound you make? What are you earliest memories of making sound? Even, singing?

Your voice is a key part of you and your identity. If we look around our society, we see so many people who are famous for their voice, from Brian Blessed to Chris Evans, from Richard Burton to Karen Carpenter, their individual, characterful, voices support their livelihoods and careers.

For many, our earliest memories of using our voices, for more than just general communication, can often be quite negative. From speaking aloud in class at an early age or perhaps being part of a school choir, we do not always have the most positive start with our voices. We would, of course, have been using our voices for years before these experiences, but these key moments may have been the first time we would have really thought about using our voices as a 'tool'. We may have been told to speak slower, to emphasise certain words, or to sing clearer or more in tune, but most of this feedback will have been in criticism, intended to 'improve'.

It would often, as it does in teacher feedback, reinforce worries or concerns we have about our own voices.

In our research there seem to be few people who have a positive story to tell about their first memories of using their voice. This, of course, can stay with us forever. Have you felt nervous about speaking in a large group or in front of a class? Where do these feelings of nerves come from? Are they related to early memories and worries about your voice?

Even in my work with degree-level musicians, few of them ever volunteer themselves as good singers. If I ask in a lecture of 30 students, who can sing?, rarely more than 5 hands will be raised. In fact, many will rate themselves as 'tone deaf'. Let's dispel that first – only around 1 in 5,000,000 people are really 'tone deaf'. If you can answer your phone and recognise the voice on the other end as your mum, sister or friend, you are not tone deaf! You recognise tones. Truly tone-deaf people can't even listen to music; it would bother them, they don't recognise sounds or tones or have an ability to distinguish them well.

So, you may not think you have a good voice, a good singing voice or even a good voice for teaching or classroom control but you can develop this. It is just practice. It is not a gift. Later in this chapter, I will go on to suggest what you might practise and think about, to build both your confidence in your voice and understanding and why this is so important for you as a teacher

As a teacher it is vital to consider that your voice is crucial to all of your communication. Not just what we are saying but what underlying messages our speed of talk, pitch, dynamic is conveying to the pupils in your room. We will need to go on to consider what different voices we need to use in our classroom if we want to manage it effectively and how true understanding of how we can practice and develop this has an impact on our pedagogy.

Good teaching cannot be reduced to technique; good teaching comes from the identity and integrity of the teacher. This is linked closely to how we use our voice and body at all times (Palmer 1998). And a key part of your identity to pupils is how you sound. How we communicate. Do we sound in control, relaxed and confident? What in our voice conveys this underlying message?

The basics of your voice

Earlier in the chapter there were two tasks which asked you to consider your voice and the voice of others. Have a look at those notes now. What did you consider were the basics of your voice? Did you think about how you make sound? What about *you* controls this sound? How do you change and control these sounds so that you can make them more useful to you as a teacher?

There are three key things in your production of sound. The fuel of your voice, or the AIR, the production of the sounds, or your VOICE BOX, and the resonance of this sound, the RESONATOR.

Air – the fuel of your voice

So, breathing in, is the first key thing in not only staying alive but producing sound. You will breathe very naturally but have probably never used your lungs, diaphragm or air as well as you could. You may have been told to breathe properly or to breathe with your diaphragm but may not have done anything more with this unless you're an expert wind or brass player.

Breathing exercises will not only be good for your voice but **they will be good for you**. Developing your breathing will not only allow you to use your voice much more effectively but will also contribute to relaxing you, giving you a moment of peace in a busy teaching life and supporting you to do all you do more effectively. There are lots of videos on sites such as YouTube where you could look up some breathing exercises but let's go over a few basics here.

Perhaps find a place where you can be on your own. Stand up and try to stand central to your body weight. Do stand in a relaxed manner – feet will normally be about shoulder width apart but don't force this; try more to sense how you stand naturally. Counter-intuitively, trying to stand naturally is not natural so it may take a little time to relax into this. You could even try gently bending forward to your toes and then slowly rising into a 'natural' position.

Try going through a short exercise of tensing your body to understand the feeling of relaxed, or normal to sense this. Stand up … tense your toes, hold, add tension to your calves, thighs, bum, tummy, shoulders, hands, teeth, jaw … then release. Do this a couple of times to feel that moment of release.

Now, standing, imagine a band around your waist and just breath in and out slowly. Try to count in for 4 and out for 4. Then do this to a count of 8. Try to work with your natural way of breathing. Work with this but try to understand a little more what your body is doing and how you can support or develop this.

It's worth taking a few minutes at the start of each day to do this. It will warm you up much more effectively and help relax you in preparation for your day in the classroom. It is also key that you warm your body and voice up. Many teachers develop voice problems over a long career and this could be related to lack of warm ups and care taken over their voice. It is important that you don't start each day by shouting, by stressing your voice without ever thinking about warming up first.

Place your hands on each side of your waist and repeat the breathing exercise. Try to sense your waistband trying to expand your hands as the air enters your body. This is the feeling of your diaphragm moving downward to pull the air into your body. This is supported by the muscles around your lower abdomen. Take a few minutes each day to do this, to relax yourself and to get the air going. Try to support the air as it leaves your body in a constant flow, it may be worth pursing your lips slightly so that this is audible. Try to keep the noise this makes consistent by supporting it with the muscles in your lower chest. For many years, it was taught that the air leaving your body was about diaphragm support; more recently, however, this has been disproven and breathing out is about the stomach muscles.

This is incorrect, as Jacobson notes, 'the diaphragm has no nerve endings or sensation. Additionally, the diaphragm is primarily a muscle of inspiration and consequently plays very little role in exhalation rendering the idea of "diaphragmatic support" to be without basis in scientific fact' (Jacobson 2015).

Try to experiment with moving your shoulders up and down and sense how the position of these affects the air flow. The throat and upper chest need to stay as relaxed as possible to allow the air to flow.

You may even want to try some 'box breathing'. Imagine a rectangle in front of you, with the short side vertically. Try visualizing moving your eyes around the perimeters of this box. Breathe in across the top edge as you move slowly across. Hold the breath as you go down the side. Expel the air from your body as you go across the bottom edge. Then again, hold your breath as you go up the side. Try this a few times slowly to understand more how you are breathing and how you can develop more control.

It is also important to warm up the face and throat ready for a busy day of teaching and talking! Try some gentle yawns to go with your air support. Sense again what this does in stretching muscles in your face and neck. Try some gentle coughs to open the throat. Try raising the shoulders and dropping them. As part of your warm-up in the early morning it may also be useful to have a gentle hum along to the radio on the way to work to allow the voice to awaken.

Take a few moments to sit upright in a chair. Use the back of it to align your spine. Move your head to either side slowly, lowering the side of your head as close as you can to the top of the shoulder.

Go back to standing and try the breathing exercise again. This time as you count out 4 or 8 or even 16 add a 'Tsssssssss' sound to the air. Do this a few times. Try to do this quietly, as though you are just making the noise for yourself. Then do this again, thinking that you are trying to get the noise to travel about 6ft. Then try it once more and try and get the sound to travel to the back of the room.

Over time you want to be able to sense that you can get more air from your body. This is about controlling the air leaving the body, making it slow and also keeping the throat open to allow a lot of air to leave the body at one time. This will make your voice much bigger and is essential in filling a large space or for teachers working outside. Air speed, fast air, will make your voice louder, you use this when you shout, but to get a big voice you need a lot of warm air. The exercises for controlling the air speed and support from your stomach muscles will help with this.

To try and sense this we're going to experiment with a technique I got from the virtuoso euphonium player, Gary Curtin – he has videos on YouTube if you'd like to look up more by him. He suggests that you need to lick your hand and blow on it. Blow with fast air. This should feel cold on the back on you hand. Then repeat this but yawn onto your hand. Slow the air down. This should be warm. Warm air. You should also be able to allow more air to leave your body. This is the air you want to talk with. This amount of air will make your voice fill a space – it will sound much stronger and carry further. Also, because you are breathing more effectively, more slowly, you will calm yourself, you will come over as calmer and your powers of communication will improve. There is such a crucial link here with behaviour management. So much of what pupils will react to will be non-verbal signals. The pupils will sense that this is a bigger and calmer voice without necessary knowing this. They will sense, without knowing, that your body language and non-verbal signals are so much calmer. You will already be in better control of your whole classroom.

To take this further go into an empty space, even your classroom.

Try the 'Tsssss' exercise this time with your hand in the air flow. Wet your hand and try to reach the back of the room, but with 'warm air'.

Practice talking as though at the start of the lesson, but sensing the warmth of your voice. You need to start practicing slowing the air and speaking with warm air. Put your hand in front of your mouth again – is the air warm? This will also help you to slow your words down, to speak more clearly and be less likely to rush. Many teachers talk too fast. Video yourself, get others to listen to you. Try varying your speed

The voice box – making sounds

Now you are thinking about the air speed you also need to consider what makes produces the actual voice. Your voice box, or larynx, is much like your lips. Flaps of skin which 'buzz' by air passing through them, tensioning them will change their thickness and change the sound. Like tensing your lips when you blow air through them, as you do to play a brass instrument this vibration changes the pitch and quality of the sound.

As you pass air through the voice box, you can vary the tension and thus the thickness of flaps of skin. This allows you to produce the different sounds the human voice can make. It allows you to adjust the pitch, intonation and quality of sounds in an infinite number of ways. So it is important to experiment with this; to practice making a more interesting sound.

Going back to being relaxed and standing naturally your head position is key in the production of sound. As Jacobson explains:

> The larynx hangs from the hyoid bone which is slung from the mastoid processes on the skull. If the head is pulled down into the spine, the neck and throat muscles will be tense and the torso will become rigid. Excess tension kills vibrations and will produce a sound that is tight and strained.
>
> Jacobson (2015)

So avoid 'odd' positions for your head. Plan not to be writing on a board or explaining a video and twisting your head to communicate with your pupils.

This has the potential of damaging your voice and will not support effective communication in many ways. Think about how you can vary your position in your room or space to help your voice. Linking to other chapters in this book it will also help you to consider how teaching position can be key to classroom management.

The sound that then is produced in your voice box is resonated in your chest, throat, sinuses and your mouth and tongue become key in forming the sound. Watch any good singer and just observe how much facial movement goes into producing a clear sound. I would recommend Michael Bublé or Karen Carpenter. Have a listen to some slow, warm air which is produced so well. Listen to their articulation of words.

The throat, nose, chest, mouth, tongue and sinuses will all have a major effect on the sound you produce and how your voice is heard. Just try saying an 'eee' sound and then an 'oooo' sound. Can you feel or spot where those sounds are made? Where they resonate? Where they simply cause vibrations?

To make the 'eee' sound raise your tongue to the upper part of your mouth. It resonates in the sinuses and nose. To make the 'ooo' sound, as you drop your tongue the sound more readily resonates in the chest. Try also varying the pitch of these 'eee' and 'ooo' sounds to try and feel where they happen and where you can position them.

Go back to the exercise in your classroom. Not only do you want slow air from the body, articulation with the lips and mouth, but you also want it to resonate more in your chest than your head, simply, it's a bigger resonator. Go back to the 'eee' and 'ooo' sounds. Get the sound to move in your body from head to throat to chest. This will come with some practice. Don't force this, just try to sense more where your sound is coming from and where it is resonating.

To be clear, we are trying to go for slow air which you can feel in your upper chest. Try also not to hold any tension in your shoulders, chest or neck. Speaking well should feel easy. It may be very useful at this point to get some video footage of yourself teaching so that you can take time after a lesson to reflect critically on this data.

Task 3

Try to analyse your voice.

Do you breathe well? Do you use fast or slow air? Can you vary this? Do you vary the pitch? How do you stand when you talk? Does your position in your teaching space support good communication.

From this make a short list of ideas to practice. Things you can change to start to consider better classroom communication and control.

In my many years in teacher education it is clear that there is a voice you don't want to adapt. I have so many times watched student teachers work and their whole lesson is affected negatively by their vocal communication. A combination of nerves … wanting to control the pupils … wanting to get through the lesson plan turns their voice into a ***slightly high pitch semi-shout.*** It also never changes. Pupils are confused whether they are being instructed, questioned or 'told off'. It soon turns to pupils struggling to listen and often not. I even struggle myself sometimes.

So, you need to consider what can make your voice more interesting. Perhaps even start with a few famous people of singers who have 'interesting' voices. I'll guess they use slow, warm air that is well articulated. But try and develop some understanding for yourself. To begin to vary and develop your voice. Think of at least four voices for starting off if you are a student teacher. If you are more experienced get video or reflect on these four, 'different' voices as a starting point.

What sort of voice do you need for:

1. bringing students into the classroom and getting attention;
2. engaging pupils in questioning and the task;
3. talking to pupils one to one;
4. controlling whole class feedback or discussions;

Make a quick list under these headings of what theses voices sound like. Not just what you might need to say it, but analyse how you say it. What is the difference in tone of voice where the teacher sounds like they know the answer or a question which is about the pupil offering the answer. How should the volume or dynamic vary for each voice? How do you do this?

How much air do you need for each voice? How can you support this with breathing? Do you give yourself time to breathe in? Do you run out of air or sense you are straining your voice?

How should the pitch vary in these voices? Should it even change within this?

How much do you use your tongue and face to articulate your words? Do you give yourself time to do this?

Where should pauses be built in? Do you pause enough?

Certainly, as a student teacher you must consider at least a few different voices and how this affects communication in your classroom and thus everything else that happens.

Shouting

There are many reasons you should avoid shouting. But, if I'm honest, as a student teacher and newly qualified teacher it was one of my few effective tools. You may not have the variation in your voice, vocal range or real understanding of effective communication in your classroom.

So, try to keep your shouting voice for very short affects:

'**YEAR 9 ...** [pause], so we are all looking at the board and Mark is reading our first task for today ...'

You must. Warm your voice up before attempting any big sounds. This is vital for the long-term health of your voice.

It is also vital to consider what happens in the brain for learning, and how this can be affected by shouting. It is likely to demean not only the pupils but also the teacher. Is shouting necessary? Is that the teacher you want to be? It is also more likely to engage a chemical reaction in the brain, moving towards the use of the amygdala, something that teenagers are very good at! This emotional part of the brain is responsible for the flight, fight or freeze part of the brain. None of this will be conducive for learning, for concentration or in the end for good classroom management.

Task 4

Think about how you use your voice and a lesson that you are going to teach in the next few weeks. Draft an explanation of the concept that you could use within the lesson. Try and ensure that that the total explanation is no longer than two to three minutes. It is important to make sure that you have completed a full written draft of the explanation in order to do the next parts of the task.

Make sure you warm up your voice and consider practical ideas mentioned earlier in this chapter.

Phase 1: pauses and breaths

We all naturally talk too fast for presentation so consider feeling as though, in your head, you are talking slowly.

Work through your text and identify pauses. Use a single slash (/) for a short pause and a double slash (//) for a longer pause.

Read through your text, testing the pauses. It would be useful to try this in your teaching space and to video yourself doing this.

Phase 2: stresses

Read the explanation through a couple of times and identify the key phrases or words that need to be stressed. Identify at least one word in each sentence and underline the chosen word in pencil. How will your voice contribute to this? How does the pitch or pace need to change?

Read the explanation again aloud. Record this so that you can try different ideas and listen more

Phase 3: intonation

Work your way through the explanation and identify where possible changes of intonation might occur. A good way of doing this is to try and pick out keywords or phrases that capture the key impressions within the explanation that you are trying to convey. Examples here may include you wanting to 'motivate', 'encourage' or 'enthuse' your students. Write your chosen words in the margin of your explanation as a reminder of the need to change your intonation.

Again, rehearse and record your explanation. Can you feel a difference? Can you hear a difference?

Think about how you breath and use the air. Your body and head position. Your position in your teaching space.

Read the speech aloud again, but on this occasion exaggerate and heighten the shifts in it.

Try the exercise after going through the earlier breathing and vocal warm-up. Use 'warm air'.

Again, say it as though for yourself. To someone about 6ft away, then to the back of the room.

It is estimated that between 5–10 per cent of the workforce are 'heavy occupational voice users' (Titze, Lemke and Montequin 1997). This group includes a very wide range of occupations, including those working in telesales, members of the clergy, tour guides, actors, singers and lawyers. However, it is teachers who represent the largest group of professionals who use their voice as a primary tool of their trade (Evans and Savage, 2018, p. 144).

So, it is essential that we consider this for the longevity of our careers.

Some simple dos and don'ts might help here:

Do

- Warm up your voice each day.

- Take breaks and give yourself pauses.

- Talk less, do more.

- Keep yourself and voice hydrated with water.

- Talk with good posture.

- Take time for yourself during the day to relax.

- Warm down at the end of the day.

- Seek help if your voice changes suddenly or becomes weak. Don't ignore issues.

- Wash your hands regularly to avoid colds and flu.

Don't

- Shout.

- Drink lots of caffeine.

Try to

- Avoid spicy food.

- Avoid smoking.

- Get good sleep.

- Relax yourself into your teaching each day.

Take time to consider your physical environment and what you could change. Consider things that can help your voice:

- classroom noise and acoustic;

- varying activities;

- visual cues;

- air quality;

Your voice needs to last a long time, as long as you, so think about not wearing it out.

Conclusions

To sum things up, there is no fixed point to start from and everyone's voice is different. Do not be misinformed into thinking that you do not have a good voice though and you cannot develop it. Yes, it may seem as though some people do have a 'natural' voice; we live in a culture that extends a belief in gifted people. There been a popularised belief in many areas that people who just can, they were born with that voice. It is important over time to just develop ideas of deliberate practice, not just practising or reinforcing mistakes you might be making.

We all know what practice is. I do it all the time. Odds are good that you do it in a similar general way, regardless of what you're practising. When I practice golf, I go to the driving range and get two big buckets of balls. I pick my spot, put down my bag of clubs, and tip over one of the buckets. I read somewhere that you should warm up ... [ ] ... I hit quite a few bad shots. My usual reaction is to hit another ball as quickly as possible in hopes that it will be a decent shot, and then I can forget about the bad one.

Colvin (2008, p. 65)

Think about how much of this can relate to your teaching and your use of voice. Even your classroom management. To break the mould, to change things, consider breaking ideas down as the chapter has described and bringing in routines of deliberate practice.

… deliberate practice is a highly structured activity, the explicit goal of which is to improve performance. Specific tasks are invented to overcome weakness, and performance is carefully monitored to provide cues for ways to improve further. We claim that deliberate practice requires effort and is not inherently enjoyable. Individuals are motivated to practice because practice improves performance.

Ericsson et al. (1993, p. 10)

This will take time though, like becoming a good teacher, but this is a good thing. I have always felt the day that I feel I am any good at this 'teaching lark' I should give it up because perhaps that's the day I won't be. I must be open to continually improve through what I do.

The point of deliberate practice is not to make something perfect but to develop more effective routines so that you continually improve. The teachers who are most successful are those that see their work as continual development, as having no set end point other than to keep enjoying what they do and improving.

Evans and Savage (2018)

Teaching is not an easy career, but it is so very worth it and fulfilling. Developing good vocal skills and classroom management takes time and like other skills of pedagogy never ends.

It must be so. If the activities that lead to greatness were easy and fun, then everyone would do them and they would not distinguish the best from the rest. The reality that deliberate practice is hard can even be seen as good news. It means that most people won't do it. So, your willingness to do it will distinguish you all the more.

Colvin (2008, p. 72)

Further reading

Colvin, G. (2008) *Talent is Overrated: What Really Separates World-class Performers from Everybody Else.* London: Penguin Books.

Evans, W. and Savage, J. (2018) *Using Your Voice Effectively in the Classroom.* London: Routledge.

Further resources

There are lots of good online resources, but consider going to a singing workshop to develop some vocal confidence. I can recommend contacting your local music hub, they're all over the country, they will provide support, recommend courses or even deliver whole-school CPD.

For further ideas and practical examples also find 'The Breath Guy'. https://www.thebreathguy.co.uk/

References

Alexander, R. (2008) *Essays on Pedagogy*. London: Routledge.

Colvin, G. (2008) *Talent is Overrated: What Really Separates World-class Performers from Everybody Else*. London: Penguin Books.

Evans, W. and Savage, J. (2018), *Using your Voice Effectively in the Classroom*. London: Routledge.

Ericsson, K.A., Krampe, R. and Tesch-Romer, C. (1993) The role of deliberate practice in the acquisition of expert performance. *Psychological Review 100*(3), 363–406.

Harari, Y.N. (2011) *Sapiens: A Brief History of humankind*. London: Penguin.

Palmer, P. (1998) *The Courage to Teach: Exploring the Inner Landscape of a Teacher's Life*. San Francisco, CA: Jossey-Bass Inc. Publishers.

Titze, I., Hunter, E. and Svec, J. (2007) Voicing and silence periods in daily and weekly vocalizations of teachers. *The Journal of the Acoustic Society of America*, *121*, 469–478.

Websites

Jacobson, P. (2015) 9 Things Singers Need to Know about their Bodies, http://www.totalvocalfreedom.com/9-things-singers-need-know-bodies/ (last accessed 30/1/2019).

Magic of Voice (2013) 'Your voice can change the world'. https://magicofvoice.wordpress.com/2013/08/29/posture/ (last accessed 19/5/17).

Technology to support behaviour management

Eleanor Overland

Chapter aims

- To consider how technology can impact both positively and negatively on behaviour management and teacher workload.

- To explore the impact of computerised systems in addressing the complexities of behaviour management.

- To consider how pupil use of technology can have both positive and negative effects on behaviour.

Keywords: Behaviour apps; Bring your Own Device (BYOD); computerised systems; General Data Protection Regulation (GDPR); mobile phone ban; rewards and sanctions; screen time; social media; technology; workload

Introduction

Effective use of technology in education exists in pockets. Some schools are quite developed in the use of technology. Other schools may be less so or rely on the developments and enthusiasm of individual members of staff. I have often had school-based mentors delight in telling me how much they enjoy having student teachers in their schools as they bring the latest ideas and uses of technology. Your new energy and enthusiasm will be welcome and can provide an opportunity to make a real contribution to the school, but it is important to consider carefully before you implement anything new.

This is a story about Katie, a geography Newly Qualified Teacher (NQT). She starts her school year full of enthusiasm and loves using technology, particularly social media, as part of her teaching. When she arrives in school she creates a geography department Twitter account. The head of department does not use technology much themselves but is happy for Katie to do so and approves of the new Twitter account. The Twitter account is also approved by the Senior Leadership (SLT) and checked that it follows the school e-safety policy and General Data Protection Regulation (GDPR) requirements.

In September, Katie tweets regularly; resources, examples of good work and general geography news. Parents, pupils and colleagues start to follow the account. She creates #starofthelesson where she tweets some great work completed by a pupil each lesson. The pupils are proud of this and keen to have their work selected. #starofthelesson has a positive impact on behaviour in the lesson and pupils are more focussed and motivated. Word spreads and Katie is asked to include work from other classes across the department.

As the term progresses, Katie starts to become overwhelmed with other work and her geography tweets become less regular. The pupils start to notice: when asked to improve on a piece of work, one pupil even says 'Why should I bother? You don't care about it anymore'. The head of department also notices and asks her to return to posting the department tweets as staff found it motivated their pupils. No one else in the department is able to access the account or knows how to use Twitter. Katie is exhausted and feels unable to manage this additional workload.

Task I

Consider Katie's story and reflect on these questions:

- What were the successes of the new Twitter account for the pupils, Katie and the department?
- What were the drawbacks of the new Twitter account for the pupils, Katie and the department?
- Could Katie have started the Twitter account in a different way to make it more manageable?
- What should Katie do now she finds herself in this difficult situation?

Teacher tools and workload

New technologies and systems are introduced with the promise of solving a problem. Teachers who remember life before email talk about the delay in receiving information about pupils, the lack of access to information when in the classroom and the endless time spent wandering schools to find the right colleagues to speak to. Email has certainly revolutionised communications within schools, but it is not without issues. In response to a report on workload, the Education Secretary asked parents not to contact teachers during evenings or weekends as it was a contributing factor to excessive workload (Hinds, 2019). Teachers' lines of communication are now open for parents, leaders and even pupils to get in touch, often with non-urgent queries or to question the teachers on homework, detentions or even classroom incidents. For some, the 'good old days' of being uncontactable and having to wander corridors to actually speak to colleagues would be a welcome regression.

As a student teacher or NQT it is important to decide when and where you are going to access and answer emails, particularly those relating to behaviour incidents. Before responding to sensitive emails, it may be worth chatting to your mentors or peers first to ensure a considered response. If you are spending time planning (or reading a book!) it is your time away from email as they can just become a distraction. If you have email notifications switched on (or any other teaching-related apps) they can invade your personal space, especially if they are linked to behaviour incidents, as some of these can trigger an emotional response and will often take your mind away from what it is you were doing. Also have similar expectations for email responses from your colleagues, mentors and tutors as an 'out of hours' working culture is not necessarily a productive one.

With the focus on reducing workload, many education technology tools are designed to support teachers with their general administration, assessment and often behaviour management. Some of these focus on information management, such as collating and analysing data, and others on communications, such as issuing homework. Where these are effective, they can make a teacher's life much easier and improve consistency across the school, but they can also have their drawbacks. Some teachers find they have additional administrative burdens or feel they are under greater scrutiny as school leaders can easily identify staff who may not have set homework on time or have not followed up on behaviour incidents. The Education Technology Action Group have made a recommendation to government that it should be a statutory requirement of schools to justify their use of digital technology across the school within their policy documentation (ETAG, 2015).

Task 2

Identify the technological tools that are linked to behaviour management in your school. For each, consider the ways the technology reduces teacher workload and also how it may increase it. If you had to justify the use of these tools in the school behaviour management policy would you be able to?

Computerised systems and the complexities of behaviour management

As you may well have just identified, many schools have adopted automated systems to support the reporting, sharing and following up on behaviour incidents. They aim to reduce teacher workload, improve communications, both within school and with parents, and to ensure resolutions can be found. You may well find yourself using these systems to log incidents, issue rewards or raise concerns. If you are a form tutor, you may also find that you are required to review some of these records as part of your pastoral support.

The statutory advice on behaviour and discipline in schools (DfE, 2016) outlines a clear list that headteachers need to adhere to around their requirements for a behaviour policy in school. The guidance makes it very clear that consistency is key, alongside appropriate rewards and sanctions, ensuring pupils complete the required work set and that liaison with parents and other agencies is critical. In many cases, computerised systems can tick many of these boxes and are used across the school to log, monitor and address a significant majority of issues. As you will now have realised, however, behaviour management is a highly individual and complex process that often requires personalised approaches and a high level of skill to be able to address.

Task 3

Read the three scenarios below. These outline common computerised systems used in schools and the individual stories of three pupils' experiences of the systems. Although names have been changed, each of these stories is real and not uncommon. For each situation consider these questions: What is the behaviour needing to be addressed? How does the situation make the pupil and their parents feel? How does the process reflect on the staff in the school? Could a different approach have changed the outcome?

Suzanna's story

Suzanna feels anxious going into lessons. Her mum drops her on time at school every day. She attends registration and receives her attendance mark for the day. Registers are also completed for, each lesson throughout the day Suzanna is frequently marked absent or late to lessons. Sometimes she is hiding out in toilets or roaming corridors to avoid attending the lesson. At other times she sits in the library or sits in other lessons with her friends where she feels more comfortable. Despite attending school every day last term, her attendance was 72 per cent.

The attendance system is linked to parental texts. The first time Suzanna was absent from a lesson but in school, her mum received an automated text informing her of the absence. She telephoned the school immediately, really concerned as to Suzanna's whereabouts and thinking she had left the school premises. After over 40 minutes, the school phoned the parent to let her know that Suzanna had been located and was back in lesson, an anxious wait for a concerned parent.

The texts to the parent gradually became more frequent. The first few times she telephoned the school immediately. The receptionist gradually became quite blasé: 'I'm sure she'll turn up, I'll call you back when she appears.' As the texts became more frequent, the parent stopped telephoning the school. During the last week of term the parent received 12 such texts during the school week, she did not respond to a single one.

Ryan's story

Ryan is at a school with a system of 'merits and demerits'. Teachers have a list of pre-scribed reasons to issue demerits and merits are awarded on a basis of effort. If pupils receive more than 25 demerits in a term, the Head of Year invites the parents in to a meeting to discuss the issues. In his first term of Year 7 Ryan gained over 50 merits. He also gained 26 demerits so his parents were called in as he was identified as a 'cause for concern'.

Both parents were understandably concerned about Ryan being identified as a cause for concern in his first term at secondary school. At primary school, he had always had positive reports, was a 'bit disorganised' but always worked hard and enjoyed school but it was clear the transition for him had not gone well. The parents both took time off work to be able to attend a meeting with the Head of Year. The Head of Year down-loaded the list of demerits in the meeting so both he and the parents could see what the incidents were and how they could address them. Of the 26 demerits, 3 were for 'inci-dents in lessons' (mainly talking and not listening), 2 were for not having his planner and 21 were for not having a pen.

Mo's story

Mo is in a school where rewards are given out every lesson. Consequences are also given out and logged on the system (Cs). If pupils receive more than 3 Cs in a week an automated email is sent to parents. An automated email is also sent out to inform parents each time their child has received 5 rewards. Teachers are required to give out a minimum of 2 rewards per lesson. The system has been in place in the school for four years.

Mo is in year 9. He has never received a 'C' in any lesson. He has also received only 4 rewards in his secondary school career. His parents have never received any auto-mated emails.

Having thought about these systems and these pupils' experiences, you may have realised that a 'one size fits all' approach may not be the ideal solution.

Implementing a system into a school can be quite a large undertaking, often with considerable expense. Sometimes systems are introduced without any piloting or research to find if they are actually going to improve on systems that were previously in place. As a student teacher or an NQT, it is not your responsibility to source or implement such systems but it is important to consider how they are used and where the 'human touch' might actually have a greater impact or a faster response than mindlessly making use of algorithms. Whilst systems and consistency is important in behaviour management, it is important to be reflective, consider the individual nature of each situation and identify the times when your personalised intervention as a teacher may have greater or faster impact on pupil behaviour.

Selecting apps and technologies to use in your classroom

The previous section discusses technologies and processes implemented at a whole-school level but educational apps and software is a growing market and teachers are in constant receipt of advertisements for products they could adopt for their own individual classrooms. As with any resource you select for your classroom it is important to think about the purpose. There are apps for giving praise, asking questions, making seating plans, printing feedback, awarding badges, monitoring time spent on task, peer assessment – the list goes on. In fact, if there is an app that teachers think might help them it will not be long before an entrepreneurial app developer has designed one. With this market-driven approach, the apps vary hugely in quality and functionality. It is important to do your research and to understand the needs of your pupils before you introduce the tools. It is also important to evaluate their use and ensure that there are no unintended negative consequences.

Researching the app can often find reviews and information from other teachers who have also used it. There may also be information about the research and theories behind the design. For example one app, currently used by three million teachers globally, supports the theory of growth mindsets, based on the work of Dweck (explored in Chapter 4). It is designed to encourage behavioural traits, including participation, perseverance and helping others. If this is appropriate for your class this would seem ideal but there are further considerations to be made, especially where and how the data on your pupils is stored and used. Williamson argues the app is being used to support the rise of behavioural psycho-policies and may actually be a way of adding a level of surveillance of psychological characteristics in the classroom, currently harnessing the data of 35 million children (Williamson, 2017). It is essential any app you introduce complies with the school policy on GDPR and e-safety, but there may more fundamental questions to consider such as the funding source and developers behind the app – is Silicon Valley attempting to determine your classroom practice?

The use of data and a view of apps being used as 'surveillance' is a consideration. For some pupils, the perception that they may be constantly monitored, or data shared with parents, may create additional pressures and anxiety. Some apps or technologies introduced at a classroom level may replicate tools already in existence across the school so it is important to be discerning in your choice and implementation.

Pupil use of technology and the impact on behaviour

In 2018 President Macron of France made a big announcement to ban mobile phones in schools. The law affects millions of children up to the age of 15 across France and makes it illegal to use mobile phones on school premises. The parliamentary debate of the time bought about some interesting discussions and concluded that all children had the 'right to disconnect' from digital pressures during the school day and were to concentrate more on their studies. Some politicians even argued for the ban to extend to teachers and all school staff, but the final legislation did not go that far. Globally, there has been much discussion about children and their 'screen time', particularly the use of smartphones, and the impact this has had on their lives, including behaviour, mental health, safety and time dedicated to studies (UNICEF, 2018).

In the UK, there is no such national legislation and schools are free to develop their own policy on the use of digital devices in school. Some schools have a blanket ban with strict rules and pupil use of devices leading to confiscation. At the other end of the scale some schools embrace a 'Bring Your Own Device' (BYOD) policy with children actively encouraged to bring their own devices to school, connect to the school Wi-Fi and use their own technology whenever appropriate in their lessons. As a student teacher or an NQT, you may find yourself in a school with quite a different policy and you will need to adapt your practice accordingly. With experience, you will no doubt develop your own views on whether banning or embracing devices supports the behaviour of pupils in your classroom, but it is useful to consider the range of approaches.

Ask experienced teachers about some of the current challenges with managing behaviour in their classroom and many will cite mobile phones, especially pupils trying to use them when they shouldn't be (Ofsted, 2014). We will all be familiar with those texting messages under their desks (the modern-day equivalent of passing notes?), having that sly headphone peeping from a pocket or a sleeve or even more blatant use where the sudden need to take a selfie or use the camera to adjust one's hair takes priority over any other task in the lesson. Where the school has a clear binary policy this should be relatively straightforward to deal with by following the appropriate warnings and sanctions. Where the policy is consistently implemented across the school, as long as you are clear as to the policy and procedures and follow them, disruption should be limited. Once pupils are aware you are following the policy very few incidents should ever arise as they will probably be at the ultimate risk of having their device confiscated.

Where schools are inconsistent in the use of the policy or sanctions this becomes much more of a challenge for the individual teacher: 'Put your headphones away', 'But Miss lets us listen to music when we're doing our work'. This now becomes more problematic to deal with. It is now a distraction from the lesson and an unwanted debate. Once teachers start to deviate from whole-school policy this can become part of the culture of the school and the ground rules for your own individual classroom become critical. When observing colleagues in school it is worth noting if they vary their practice and how this is managed. You then need to develop your own views and expectations for your classroom. Are there going to be occasions where the use of technology is acceptable? How will you determine when this is? At other times, how will you manage the situations when pupils do use their devices without permission; how will you ensure the expectations and consequences are made clear?

In schools where pupils have devices to use or are encouraged to bring their own in, again consistency and clear expectations are important. In the longer term, many in education consider pupils having their own devices as an inevitable progression for schools. With school budgets being under pressure, and many pupils having more processing power in their smartphone in their pocket than many school PCs provide, it is seen as a logical move with schools just needing to resource the pupils who do not already have devices rather than having to fund universal provision (ETAG, 2015). Also, as technology becomes smaller and more sophisticated it is getting harder to simply ban devices. My smartwatch currently does most things my phone can and when this is reduced to the size of a contact lens or skin implant confiscation is going to be quite a challenge. This is a continuing debate but, regardless of your views on this, pupils still need to understand how to behave, both when they have a device in a classroom and when they are online. Where schools ban the use of mobile devices, block social media and, in some cases, do not even provide pupils with email accounts, how will pupils learn appropriate etiquette of when and how to use devices? Should this be the responsibility of the school or the home?

Where schools work in partnership with families they have the greatest success in developing pupils' online behaviour on conduct relating to technology. You may find a pupil in your lesson is overly tired due to playing computer games for long periods of time, pupils who report situations linked to social media or get told pupils have been behaving inappropriately online. Many of these may also impact on pupil's mental health (see Chapter 12). Your school may well have information for parents and carers on supporting their children to use technology safely; when incidents do occur, it is important to be aware of the procedures to ensure families are fully informed and supported (Childnet, 2018).

Task 4

Consider the use of devices by pupils in your school setting in the lessons you have observed and during break/lunchtime. Does it follow the school policy?

Do you feel the policy is appropriate for the pupils within the school? What are the implications of the policy for your own classroom environment? Does the policy have implications for pupil use of technology outside of lesson time or at home?

Technology instead of teachers?

Development of digital teaching resources, free online courses, live online broadcasts, online discussions and general access to a wide array of digital content, could actually drive more teaching to be online and reduce the need for teachers at all. Artificial Intelligence (AI) could use data in a sophisticated way to direct learners to appropriate resources 'learners with similar answers to you found this activity to be helpful', a bit like your online shopping selections. You may have already found this developing in some of the subject-specific packages you use. A number of educators are currently exploring the future role of teachers and how technology may actually reduce the need for the presence of teachers in classrooms (Coleman, 2012).

So far, much of this rhetoric about technology replacing teachers has been around personalising learning, assessment and directing learners to resources, but what if technology was to be harnessed in similar ways but to influence behaviour in the classroom? Technology is already being used in more and more sophisticated ways to influence human behaviour: fitness watches telling users to get up and walk around; social media that tracks locations and links people in the same place; digital timers and calendars to organise events and set reminders; voice-controlled devices that recognise instructions and (allegedly) record conversations in the home. It does not take the wildest of imaginations to consider ways of combining emerging technology into a 'behaviour management device'. This may sound like a work of science fiction, almost Orwellian, but the technology is already there, some parents are already tracking the location of their children, some classrooms are already fitted with CCTV, we can issue detentions and inform all parties who need to know in one single touch. As the new generation of teachers, this use of technology will evolve as your career progresses. This chapter has already encouraged you to be discerning in your selection and implementation of new technology and it is important you continue this approach throughout your teaching career.

Conclusions

Throughout this book, authors explain the importance of relationships within the classroom, the important processes of decision-making and planning when it comes to behaviour management and the significance of the personalised approach. This chapter is no different as, although technology cannot be used to enforce behaviour management, it can certainly be used to support aspects of it but only in the hands of skilled, thoughtful and adaptable teaching professionals. It is also important pupils understand how to behave themselves when using technology and how they can harness it for positive purposes. The most effective teachers understand the needs of pupils and develop the correct environment for pupils to learn (Gilbert, 2014). It is often looked to student teachers and NQTs to have the latest ideas, especially when it comes to technology, so there is actually quite a responsibility on your shoulders. You will have the opportunity to shape the uses of technology in current classrooms and input into future school policy – proceed with enthusiasm and caution!

References

Childnet (2018) Teachers and Professionals. Online https://www.childnet.com/teachers-and-professionals (accessed 21/12/18).

Coleman, J. (2012) Digital Technologies in the lives of young people. *Oxford Review of Education, 38*, 1–8.

DfE (2016) Behaviour and discipline in schools: guidance for headteachers and school staff. https://assets.publishing.service.gov.uk/government/uploads/system/uploads/attachment_data/file/488034/Behaviour_and_Discipline_in_Schools_-_A_guide_for_headteachers_and_School_Staff.pdf (accessed January 2, 2020).

Education Technology Action Group (ETAG) (2015) Education Technology Action Group: Our Reflections. Online http://etag.report/ (accessed 21/12/18).

Gilbert, I. (2014) *Why Do I Need a Teacher When I've got Google? The Essential Guide to the Big Issues for Every Teacher.* London: Routledge.

Hinds, D. (2019) Press Release: School Leaders Should Ditch Email Culture to Reduce Workload. Online https://www.gov.uk/government/news/damian-hinds-school-leaders-should-ditch-email-culture-to-cut-workload (accessed 24/1/19).

Ofsted (2014) Below the Radar: Low-Level Disruption in the Country's Classrooms. Office for Standards in Education, Children's Services and Skills. Online https://www.gov.uk/government/publications/below-the-radar-low-level-disruption-in-the-countrys-classrooms (accessed 21/12/18).

UNICEF (2018) *The State of the World's Children 2017: Children in a Digital World.* New York: UNICEF. https://doi.org/10.18356/d2148af5-en.

Williamson, B. (2017) Decoding ClassDojo: Psycho-policy, social-emotional learning and persuasive educational technologies. *Learning and Media Technology, 42*(4), 440–453.

Behaviour management in a practical setting and outside the classroom

Jedde de Vries

Chapter aims

- To understand and appreciate the positive learning experiences for pupils in practical educational settings.

- To appreciate the change in classroom dynamics in regard to pupil engagement, pupils' placement and consequently behaviour management issues that might arise.

- To understand the need to plan for behaviour management interventions for non-classroom and practical settings.

- To appreciate and apply the school behaviour management policy in non-classroom environments; begin to plan for effective behaviour management in practical settings within your subject.

Keywords: practical learning; outside the classroom; experiential learning; adolescence; relationships; organisation; preparation; intervention; sanctions; rewards; teaching assistants; phase transitions

Taking behaviour management outside the classroom

Behaviour management does not finish when pupils leave your classroom, are out of sight or leave the school grounds. Pupils' experiences in corridors between classes, in dining halls or playgrounds can affect their daily school experience and their disposition when they enter your classroom; as such, there are significant behaviour management challenges for subjects engaged in practical settings outside the traditional classroom. A good example of this would be orienteering, where pupils are expected to complete tasks outside teacher supervision during geography or physical education (PE).

It can be argued that there are three "phases" of behaviour management:

1. *preparation (pre-empting possible behaviour management issues before they arise)*: creating a safe school environment based on good organisation, activity planning, risk assessment and management;
2. *experience*: behaviour management issues actually arising in a lesson outside the classroom, during lesson transitions or in break time;
3. *intervention*: strategies for low-level and serious incidents, exploring inclusive or exclusive behaviour management strategies.

The behaviour management strategies can be said to derive from three different perspectives:

1. the pupils' experiences;
2. the responsibilities as a student-teacher or teacher;
3. institutional/school paradigms, such as behaviour management policies, which support effective behaviour outside the classroom.

Learning outside the classroom

The pupil perspective

Learning outside the classroom makes learning relevant to pupils (Ofsted, 2008). It gives pupils opportunity to gain knowledge and develop understanding of concepts learn from concrete experiential events (Beames et al., 2012) which can contextualise and rationalise the purpose of the learning content.

The adolescent

Knowing your target group is essential for effective behaviour management. Although every individual pupil needs to be taught in relation to their individual learning needs and potential, the journey through adolescence has some common traits that can affect behaviour and engagement in learning (Hayman et al., 2002). One of the main features is an increased need for autonomy. Consequently, learning through practice can benefit pupils' experience of ownership of their learning journey. However, giving pupils increased freedom of physical movement and social interaction through reduced direct teacher supervision can create an opportunity for pupils to take advantage of this freedom. There can be a range of reasons pupils cause behaviour management issues outside the classroom:

■ the learning environment might seem a less 'serious' teaching context than the regular classroom environment;

- reduced direct supervision might empower some pupils to engage in more 'entertaining' activities, than pursuing learning content and outcomes;

- social groupings or tensions between pupils might become more prevalent in a less structured environment, with pupils showing excluding behaviour towards peers.

However, adolescents are also critical and reflective; in the same way as adults, they will respond positively to an environment that is well-organised and lesson content that is safe, attractive, purposeful, well-paced and pitched at the appropriate differentiated level.

Relationships

The key concept for good behaviour management is good relationships with the pupils. When pupils need to work individually or in small groups out of direct aural or visual supervision of the teacher, there needs to be a level of trust between the teacher and pupils. From a pupil's perspective, this means that they need to feel both safe and valued in the learning context. There are a number of elements that can negatively influence safety and feeling valued:

- poor organisation;

- dangerous physical environment;

- poor-quality/malfunctioning equipment;

- challenging social environment;

- lack of lesson structure;

- poorly-differentiated task setting;

- lack of target-setting and formative assessment;

To build trust, pupils need to feel that teachers have *genuinely* invested in their learning experience. This means that the sequence of learning events are well structured and supported with ample, high-quality equipment, that the learning environment is appropriate and that resources are attractive and well-designed.

Task I

Identify the practical learning experiences outside the classroom that are specific to your subject.

Which activities do they entail?

Why are these activities valuable as a learning activity?

What are the specific environmental needs to facilitate an excellent learning experience?

Teaching outside the classroom

In contrast to the classroom environment, teaching outside the classroom often includes physical movement and displacement of students. Organisation of tasks and plenaries have to be adapted to the needs of the students in the particular learning environment.

Preparation

Preparing for behaviour management is key to success. Moreover, knowing your pupils, good organisations, forward planning and pre-empting possible behaviour management issues are generally key to avoiding behaviour incidents to happen and allow both pupils and teachers to enjoy a positive learning environment.

Registers

All teachers are responsible for the pupils in their lesson and in their department. Ensure that registers are prepared and at hand before pupils enter the department. Registers should be taken before the lesson commences so any non-attendance or irregularities can be followed up immediately within the school. Most schools will have electronic registers so ensure that electronic equipment is ready to be used when pupils enter the department. Depending on the activity, mid-session and post-session registration might be appropriate to ensure all students are completing expected learning tasks and that all pupils are accounted for during and after the lesson or trip.

Equipment

Before preparing lessons ensure that a comprehensive equipment list is available. Equipment should be:

a. safe, clean and in working order;
b. safely and logically stored, easily accessible and transportable for pupils and staff;
c. sufficient to facilitate all pupils as well as differentiated learning tasks.

Learning environment

Before preparing lessons, ensure that there is a good knowledge of the teaching environment:

a. safe, clean and with appropriate fire procedures;
b. travel time and procedures to and from the activity area;
   example 1: Do pupils need to cross a public road? What are the procedures?
   example 2: when possible avoid walking past classrooms of colleagues as this might disrupt their lessons.

c. understand possible hazards or aspects of the environment that can lead to unwanted behaviour.

example 1: Are there areas where pupils hide from teacher supervision?
example 2: Are there aspects of the environment that invite for disruptive play?

Moving to the working area

As you will often be the last person to leave the classroom/bus/assembly hall, to lock up and check that all pupils have left, it is imperative that pupils know what is expected from them when they enter a practical learning environment. If there are no specific tasks set or routines in place, pupils will generally find ways to entertain themselves until the moment you will start the first plenary or learning task. This would be valuable learning time wasted, which could be used effectively for pupils to engage in a starter activity or to the main task. Every department or teacher might have its specific preferences; for pupils, the most important thing is the clarity of instruction and the expectation that these will be followed. Routines can help raise expectations. Table 9.1 displays a few organisational options.

Equipment

Dealing with equipment should be part of the learning activity in the lesson; it develops pupils' ownership of and responsibility for both equipment and the environment. Furthermore, as a teacher you cannot carry all the hockey sticks, collect all the worksheets spread out over the field, neither should time be spend in putting pencils back in boxes or sorting out coloured discs. Pupils have to follow clear instructions, cooperate and develop understanding of how and why equipment is

Table 9.1 Active and non-active approaches to learning

Non-active learning approach	Active learning approach
Pupils are requested to:	*Pupils are requested to:*
• sit on the benches; • stand/ sit on a line; • sit in a specific area; • line-up outside storage area.	• engage with relevant starter activities. *Example 1: Find certain flora or fauna.* *Example 2: Find geographical clues in the environment.* *Example 3: Warm-up as a group, pairs or individual.* In these circumstances, only specific pupils are requested to take out and carry equipment whilst other pupils are engaging in starter activities.
These types approaches of more, might be necessary to take registers, organise mixed-gender/ability classes, ensure pupils are available to carry equipment or as a behaviour management strategy, slowing down the pace of the lesson.	These approaches and more can be effective as pupils are able to take responsibility for a quick and active start of the lessons. The teacher has the opportunity to adjust tasks, raise expectations and create leadership roles throughout the teaching units.

stored in a specific way for safety, easy access and maintenance. The idea of the **6Ws** gives a good structure for organising equipment and pupils.

Who? *Teacher,* teacher *assistant, pupils in general or specific individuals*
The teacher should at all times be able to observe the pupils carrying equipment and preferably also the rest of the class. A good habit is to stand strategically in the door opening of the storage, in order to supervise storage and monitor the rest of the class.
Identify which pupils take equipment. Ensure that there is a good balance between physical capacity and social cohesion. Pair pupils who will work well together.

What? *Equipment or task*
Identify which piece of equipment pupils will need to carry and look after

Where? *specific place in the activity area/storage facility*
Ensure that pupils know where they need to place equipment in the learning environment, using goals, fences or environmental demarcation such as a treeline. A comprehensive diagram on the whiteboard can clarify this and can be returned to for consultation.

When? *The order of taking out and returning equipment*
The order in which equipment is taken away can affect the efficiency and pace of the lesson.

Which way? *How is equipment carried/transported?*
Lifting, carrying and correctly storing equipment is vital for pupil safety. It will also affect the wear and tear of the equipment. Explain these expectations clearly to pupils.

What after? *Where do I go or what do I do when I am finished?*
This is a key element of effectively managing pupils and equipment. What do pupils do when they have completed their initial task? There are many options and teachers will have their preferences. A key principle should be that equipment is not left for either the teacher or just a few pupils to carry. Consider some of these tips:

- after task completion, pupils sit in view of the teacher, so they can be asked to assist with equipment;
- equipment is carried by those that are the first/last to move to or from the activity area, depending on the position of the teacher and tasks of the pupils;
- pupils can move to the classroom/ changing rooms/ assembly hall/ bus after they completed their task.

Poor Practice

- carrying the equipment as a teacher: you will tie yourself into this single task and be unable to deal with other issues arising;

- allowing pupils to leave before all equipment is removed from the learning environment;
- allowing pupils to carry/move dangerous or attractive equipment unsupervised;
- allowing pupils to leave the activity area before checking if all equipment and/or rubbish has been cleared.

Knowing your pupils

The variety of pupils and behaviours in lessons is one of the factors which makes teaching attractive but also challenging. Teaching outside the classroom means that pupils have much more freedom to move around and determine their personal and learning space; therefore, pupils' individual needs and strengths must be considered particularly carefully. The following accounts illustrate the critical importance of not only being well-planned and prepared – particularly for learning beyond the school grounds – but also of knowing your pupils.

> Early September, my first permanent job as a PE teacher, Year 9 hockey. Following the lead of the head of department, I handed out hockey sticks to every pupil in the storage and took the hockey balls down myself. Two pupils came late out of the changing room so I was slightly delayed arriving at the hockey field. When I arrived at the field, pupils had set up their own game of 'Who can hit the goal post with a hockey stick from the edge of the 18 yard box?' The next session designated pupils carried six hockey sticks under my supervision, whilst the rest of the class organised themselves into even teams, set-up pitches and organised their warm-up.
>
> Secondary NQT PE teacher

This group of Year 9 boys needed quick engagement and supervision until a new relationship based on trust and expectations developed between pupils and the teacher.

> We went on a school trip to a historic city. When everybody set off with their pieces of paper to answer questions about architecture and the city's historic development, we stepped on a tram, sat outside a cafe to have a drink whilst we completed the tasks randomly. When we returned the teachers did not have clue.
>
> Pupil

The pupils in the example above were known to abscond from lessons, but their history does not seem to have influenced their teachers' choices. With better-informed decision-making, a more rigorous approach to supervision would have ensured full pupil participation and certainty of pupil location.

Task 2

Reflect on your own learning experiences outside the classroom as a secondary pupil.

Identify a positive practical learning experience and highlight why this was successful.

Identify a negative practical learning experience and describe the main reasons for this poor learning experience. What changes would you have made as a student teacher?

Behaviour management: interventions

Interventions for behaviour management issues range from effective 'idiosyncratic' teacher strategies to applying whole-school behaviour management policy and strategy effectively.

Task 3

Consider the school Behaviour Management Policy in your current/most recent school and consider the following questions:

Does the Behaviour Management Policy specifically support staff with any issues that might occur during teaching outside the classroom?

Which Behaviour Management Policy steps are applicable outside the classroom and which ones will be less effective?

Minor behaviour incidents

Many experienced teachers will agree that if you deal effectively with small incidents, they do not escalate into major issues. Low-level disruption, as it is commonly termed, describes behaviours which disrupt the flow of the class and the individual progress of a small number of pupils. These behaviours can include quiet chatter with a friend or physical behaviour, such as poking or tapping others, sending notes etc. Dealing with low-level disruption at an early stage can avoid small incidents leading into more complex and time-consuming incidents.

Minor behaviour incidents during plenaries outside the classroom

Organisation

It is key to have oversight of your pupils at all times. Ensure that you can make eye contact with all pupils and that all pupils can hear you without raising your voice.

The moment pupils stand behind each other or are outside your line of sight, you cannot ensure their focus, nor address any disruptive behaviours effectively. Furthermore, as we have already seen, it is more likely for pupil to be disruptive if they feel unsupervised.

During instruction, pupils can be lined up in a semi-circle or at a 90-degree angle. Sitting pupils down is another option, depending on the surface. When outside, ensure you are not in front of the sun (leaving you in silhouette) and, if possible, ensure any strong breeze is behind you, to carry your voice.

Intervention

We have seen above that low-level disruption can be verbal or physical, such as friendly chat or distracting another pupil. It is *essential* to deal with these appropriately, based on the teacher's understanding of the pupils in the class. The following interventions are quick and effective ways of dealing with these:

- make eye contact with specific pupil(s), alerting them that you are aware and would like them to pay attention;

- move towards the pupils disrupting the plenary whilst continuing instructions;

- mention specific pupils' names through the plenary;

- stop mid-sentence and continue when pupils are quiet again.

Once pupils are back on task, address the specific pupil(s), make them aware that any disruption is not appreciated and emphasise expectations and school ethos. If necessary, apply the school's Behaviour Management Policy, such as a first warning.

Whilst minor incidents must be tackled, it is also important to remember that the vast majority of pupils will be paying careful attention to the teaching and so as the teacher, you will want to try to reduce any break in the flow of the lesson by using quick, effective strategies.

Persistent low-level disruptive behaviour during plenaries can be addressed accordingly:

- send a pupil to the end of the line, preferably next to an attentive pupil so he/she has minimum influence to interfere with the plenary;

- split pupils (sometimes friends) during the plenaries;

- during question and answer sessions, pupils can refocus by having to respond to a peer's answer. It will alert them that they were not paying attention;

- if possible, pre-emptively engage disruptive students in a model performance of the next task.

Poor intervention practices:

- singling disruptive pupils out and reprimanding them in front of the group;

- asking disruptive pupils to reiterate instructions, when you know they will not be able to;

- stopping the plenary to start a whole-class lecture about expectations and school ethos;

- asking a disruptive pupil to stand next to the teacher during plenary. This may well lead to further disruptive, even defiant, behaviour.

Minor behaviour issues during learning tasks

Organisation

Again, key to good behaviour management is your ability to have clear oversight and recognise poor engagement and disruptive behaviour at the earliest moment. By scanning (Mawer, 1995) the group, unwanted behaviour should be recognisable immediately. There is a range of possible ways you can address pupils who are misbehaving and you will develop your own repertoire. The following methods are a starting point:

- clearly identify the working area. Fences, sports pitch lines, cones or markers. Colour-coordinated areas make it easier for pupils to identify their task environment;

- organise tasks in such a way that, as a teacher, you do not have to travel far to intervene;

- let pupils work in a similar direction when completing the tasks, so that you can easily scan a calm, clear environment;

- ensure that pupils have enough space not to interfere with others' working areas.

If your pupils have to conduct tasks outside the view of the teacher, or at further distances, immediate behaviour management intervention might not be possible. The expectation that your pupils engage with and complete tasks to the best of their ability, is based on mutual trust and confidence that the teaching content and environment are challenging, attractive and stimulating. You might consider the following methods to enhance teacher control of the environment:

- ensuring pupils know where to go to if they cannot complete their tasks, a central instruction point (CIP);

- creating checkpoint to ensure pupils are on task within timeframes;

- pupils regularly returning to the CIP with outcomes, to allow for AfL, Q&A and feedback;

- use of an audio cue (such as a whistle) to aid with time-keeping and meeting deadlines.

Example from practice highlighting organisational challenges

A few years ago one of my good friends explained how she managed to sneak home for every cross-country lesson (30 times over 5 years), and watched television for an hour before returning to the PE base, pretending to be out of breath. Teachers tended to send pupils on the same cross-country circuit around the school and never checked if pupils arrived at the halfway point. Although the particular student abused teachers' trust, there was a lack of organisational strategy by the teachers. In this particular case, there is also a safeguarding issue.

Former pupil

Intervention

To facilitate the best outcomes for pupils, learning contexts and tasks are well organised, instructions are always explicit, pupils' levels have been assessed and tasks have been differentiated according to needs. However, even after all this is in place, certain pupils might still decide to disrupt your lesson and tasks, taking forms such as:

- refusal to engage with the learning task;

- poor engagement and/or effort to complete learning tasks;

- changing the learning tasks to something they prefer to do;

- verbally disturbing other pupils on task.

By preparing, exploring and practising interventions, you will eventually discover the most effective ways to deal with these minor disruptions; we must ensure we remain true to our own 'self' as a teacher. However, without exception, early intervention in poor engagement is essential. This ensures that:

- low standards do not become the 'accepted' norm;

- school ethos is considered in all aspects of school life;

- learning of peers is not affected;

- minor behaviour issues do not escalate into major incidents.

Many experienced teachers will have their individual preferences to deal with minor behaviour incidents. A systematic guide is suggested below, to ensure that any teacher interference has the least effect on lesson flow and pace and thus on pupil progress:

1. mentioning a pupil's name can be enough to make them aware that you have spotted them and make adjustments to their behaviour;
2. take a pupil out of a task and question him/her on the understanding of the task and outcome. If possible, use other pupils' behaviours as examples, affirming that task engagement is a normal lesson expectation. This allows the teacher to address any misconceptions that might have caused the behaviour issue;
3. take a pupil out of a task and let them walk with you, whilst you are scanning the class. This takes them away from the situation, allowing space for a calm conversation, which can guide them back into practice;
4. if there is a group of pupils disrupting the task, it might be necessary to take all pupils away from the task. Either the task can then be re-set, or the pupils can relocate to groups that are functioning well;
5. when returning pupils to task, reiterate expectations and outcomes and make pupils aware that you will check their progress shortly.

Rewards

Besides the school-based institutional reward system, pupils can also experience more 'subtle' rewards and find them stimulating. Praise and appreciation of their work, engagement and progress is, at all times, critically important. However, practical learning settings can bring a variety of social dynamics to the fore, as they can provide a rare opportunity for friends or groups of friends to work together, upon which the teacher can capitalise. Although working in friendship groups can cause disruption, desired behaviour can also be rewarded by letting pupils work in their preferred social groupings.

Major behaviour incidents

Whilst dealing with minor behaviour incidents requires you to be effective in subtle ways, major incidents are often more challenging outside the classroom/school building, as support from colleagues or senior management is generally not immediately available.

Major incidents can be identified as persistent/severe defiance of teacher instructions, school rules and school ethos. This is behaviour that disrupts the learning of others in your lesson through persistent disturbance, not following instructions and/or refusal to engage with learning tasks.

When dealing with major behaviour incidents, you need to allow the strength and effectiveness of the school's Behaviour Management Policy to work for you.

Appropriate application of what pupils normally expect should ensure a much more positive response.

Preparation

Key to dealing with major behaviour incidents, particularly in a practical environment, is preparation. Developing a toolbox of short-term solutions will help you tackle serious behaviour issues without interrupting the lesson or getting into personal confrontation – particularly if the class are engaged in practical activities requiring your supervision. Try to familiarise yourself with potential time-out areas and to consider strategies for quickly recruiting support from colleagues, including senior management.

High-level behaviour incidents can involve the following generic behaviours:

- persistent low-level disruption;
- persistent task refusal;
- significant disruption of the learning of others;
- defiance, refusing any sensible instruction or request from the teacher;
- verbally abusing peers or the teacher;
- physically endangering or abusing peers or the teacher;
- absconding; leaving the working area, supervision of the teacher and/or school grounds.

For obvious safeguarding reasons, it is always preferable to keep the pupil/s concerned within supervision of the classroom teacher or an alternative responsible adult. However, this may not be an option if the learning of others will be severely disrupted. Similarly, whilst it is important to follow the school behaviour management procedures, it may be necessary when teaching in a practical setting to skip certain steps to avoid more challenging or dangerous situations to occur later in the lesson.

When dealing with major behaviour incidents outside the classroom there are four generic options:

- *A mini-exclusion from the lesson.*

  a. This can be an effective strategy for persistent low-level disruption. Pupils are requested to sit out for a limited amount of time, in a designated space, within the vicinity of the teacher; when dealing with multiple pupils, it is advisable to spread the exclusions out. Pupils have the chance to reflect on their behaviour and then re-engage with the learning content and you can check on learning needs and make adjustments if necessary.

    b.   However, for pupils who *persistently* refuse to engage in learning tasks, this may be less appropriate as it can serve as an exit from task engagement.

▪ *A full exclusion from the lesson.*

▪ If your pupil/s *persistently* fail to engage positively with their learning, disrupt the learning of peers and/or are persistently defiant, they can be asked to sit out of an indefinite amount of lesson time. This is generally a less attractive option, as pupils are not engaged in any task and might continue to show similar, alternative and/or increasingly challenging behaviour issues. However, if this is the only way to remove a pupil from his/her peer group, it can be called on.

▪ *Removal from the lesson.*
For behaviour incidents including persistent defiance, verbal abuse of physical abuse or endangerment removal from the lesson might well be the only option. You should follow arrangements for such incidents based on departmental and school behaviour management policies. The effectiveness of these policies rely on the organisation, infrastructure and staffing in the school or department.

    If you are teaching within the sight of the school and have a member of staff who can supervise an exclusion area, you have the opportunity to send pupils directly away from the lesson. This is often effective as it means the incident can be dealt with by the specific department, without additional senior management support. However, this must be facilitated by *clear and prior agreement* with departmental colleagues. This would also assist with the practical question of pupils changing back into normal school uniform.

    Excluded pupil/s pupils may well be sent straight into the agreed exclusion area, such as the entrance of the PE department. At this point, by prior agreement, a member of staff can receive and supervise the pupil/s until the class teacher can follow up on the behaviour incident.

    In the rare case when a pupil behaves defiantly *beyond* the view of the school or possible exclusion area for pupils – and especially if safety might be compromised – three generic interventions can be called on, to reduce the teacher's vulnerability, depending on the school Behaviour Management Policy and the situation:

    a. use the teaching assistant, if available, to supervise the pupil to an agreed exclusion zone;
    b. have some form of communication available, such as a mobile phone or internal mobile communication equipment;
    c. finish the class early. Take the whole class back to the classroom or department and organise the withdrawal from the pupil(s) once back in the school.

Note: it is not advisable to send a pupil for assistance with major behaviour incidents. It can put this pupil in an awkward position with his/her peers, which may lead to subsequent issues.

Terminating the lesson.

If it is not possible for you to remove a pupil from the learning environment and particularly if pupils' safety is at risk, terminating the lesson and going back to either the classroom or another teaching area in the school might be the best option.

Task 4

Think of a major behaviour issue that you have experienced with a pupil as a student teacher during a practical teaching setting (you can also use a school experience from when you were a pupil):

■ Were the behaviour issues effectively dealt with?

■ Did the school Behaviour Management Policy effectively support the teacher to deal with the incident?

■ Did normal teaching continue after this behaviour incident?

Behaviour management during lesson transitions and break times

It is important to recognise that lesson transitions and break times are pupils' 'own time' and they should be allowed to enjoy their break with a certain amount of freedom. However, the unstructured environment can also be a cause of anxiety and tension for some pupils, as it more easily facilitates bullying behaviour.

> They are just shouting abuse to me from a distance in a group. It's just because of my religion, because I am Jewish.
>
> Year 8 pupil

This type of behaviour is more typical of unsupervised educational environments and is thus more challenging to manage. However, there are some effective ways to address behaviour management issues during transition and break times.

Staff supervision is one of the main tools available to deal with any behaviour issues. Staff presence should thus be the main deterrent to prevent issues arising. Where necessary, the school's Behaviour Management Policy should give sufficient leverage, as a preventative measure, to ensure that unwanted behaviour does not occur. Behaviour issues observed by staff should be dealt with appropriately, when recorded and reported.

Transition between lessons

Task 5

Engage with the school Behaviour Management Policy and consider the following questions:

- What are the schools' strategies regarding supervision during class transitions and break times?
- Does your department have specific routines? Are they effective?
- Do other departments have different routines? Explore why?

Moving from classroom to classroom can be quite an adventure in some schools, firstly, because of the distance between teaching spaces and secondly, by the fact that perhaps another 2000 pupils have to use the same space at the same time, to get to their next class.

Logistics

Ensure that all the movement pathways in the school are logical and safe. Avoid two-way traffic on stairs or in small corridors. Pupils are less likely to physically bump into each other and engage in avoidable confrontations.

Supervision

Ideally, teachers should be waiting at their classroom door to meet and greet pupils but also to monitor the corridors of their department (usually, senior staff supervise areas that are not covered by class teachers outside their teaching room). Sometimes staff might have to deal with some aftermath of the previous lesson, but this can be minimised if other teachers in the department are taking their post outside the classroom.

Behaviour management strategies

1. When in the corridor, acknowledge pupils as they walk past, creating a positive but affirmative staff presence.
2. When minor behaviour issues are observed, calling a pupil's name can already be sufficient deterrent for pupils to adjust their behaviour.
3. If necessary and if possible, asking a pupil to come and stand next to you or in the classroom for a short period might be effective, particularly if the problem is peer-related. The adversaries will have moved on to their next lesson. However, do not keep pupils too long as this might disrupt the start of their next lesson. If necessary, follow up on any issues during break or lunchtime.
4. Unfortunately, when unwanted or challenging behaviour occurs in the corridors, especially by unfamiliar students, there can be little time to actually deal

with the situation there and then. The pupil concerned might have ignored you and/or moved on, whilst you are receiving pupils for your next lesson. Thus, follow-up on these incidents is essential to make pupils aware of teacher supervision and to maintain a safe environment. The incident should be recorded, reported and consequences should be aligned with similar behaviour in the classroom, with regard to school policy.

Break times

Pupils should experience break times as an opportunity to relax and have the freedom to choose their own environment and peer group. Whilst most schools will have continuous supervision in dining halls and playgrounds, it is not possible to observe all pupils all the time everywhere. Subsequently, when considering behaviour management strategies, both contexts should be considered.

The supervised break-time

Again, supervision in dining spaces, corridors and playgrounds should be meaningful and support a safe environment for pupils to have a pause from learning, enjoy social networks and participate in organised activities. Pupils should feel free from the direct supervision they experience in the classroom; supervision around school is an opportunity to build relationships with pupils, as well as, be a deterrent for unwanted behaviour. A few positive and pre-emptive strategies can reinforce the impact of supervision:

- strategic positioning. Ensure that the whole area can be viewed even when speaking to a pupil or other member of staff;

- be kind and assertive, greeting pupils and acknowledging them without being over-familiar or becoming distracted;

- consider social dynamics and make pre-emptive contact with pupils who are either overly loud or boisterous.

When necessary, a sanction-based approach can be used, according to the specific Behaviour Management Policy:

1. Informal warning;
2. Formal warning;
3. Behaviour points and relevant consequences;
4. Removal from recess area.

Option number 4 can be rather extreme but necessary if instructions are ignored, or pupils are in verbal or physical conflict. Most pupils appreciate firm and resolute intervention from staff, particularly if there are serious behaviour issues, as it makes them feel safe. You need to ensure that you know information, procedures and sanctions for dealing with these situations:

- Where are pupils going? Time-out room/Exclusion area/Reception/Senior Leadership Team?

- Who is looking after the pupils, once they have arrived?

- Who is supervising the break/lunch area whilst pupils are escorted from this space?

Usually, busy, high-usage communal areas will be supervised by two or more members of staff. Depending on the school's dynamics and the layout, the use of audio communication through walky-talkies or mobile phones to receive additional support quickly when necessary.

Unsupervised break-time

Although not recommended because of possible safeguarding infringements, pupils can find themselves outside the range of observation of any member of staff during break-times, such as at the far end of the playing field. Pupils will usually be aware that the school's Behaviour Management Policy will apply to any infringements of these expectations, whether reported verbally or extracted from CCTV footage.

Conclusions

We have seen, from the preceding information, that the teaching and behaviour management of pupils in outdoor settings requires forward planning, careful preparation of resources and keen vigilance to ensure the safety of all. The good news is that a *great deal* of success, in all these areas, can actually be guaranteed with good organisation and common sense; an advance visit to the area concerned, good knowledge of the needs of your pupils and a thorough awareness of the school's Behaviour Management Policy will forewarn you for many eventualities. Occasionally, unexpected circumstances can arise and, as a new or recent entrant to the profession, seeking help and support from more senior colleagues *as soon as possible*, always reduces complexities later.

Outdoor learning, physical education and extra-curricular activities beyond the school grounds, form a crucial aspect of young people's educational journey; for some children, it will be their only chance to experience these wonderful activities. It is, therefore, incumbent on us, as teachers who wish to see *the whole child* flourish, that we ensure these opportunities continue. As your teaching skills develop, so will your behaviour management; by being firm, fair and consistent, it will improve exponentially. This will quickly enable you to confidently lead successful, fun learning activities and create memories that many pupils will treasure forever, as a precious part of their school career.

References

Beames, S., Higgins, P.J. & Nicol, R. (2012) *Learning Outside the Classroom: Theory and Guidelines for Practice*. London, New York. Routledge.

Hayman, L., Mahon, M. & Turner, J. (2002) *Health and Behaviour in Childhood and Adolescence*. New York: Springer Publication [Online]. http://www.dawsonera.com/depp/reader/protected/external/AbstractView/S9780826197641.

Mawer, M. (1995) *The Effective Teaching of Physical Education*. London: Longman Group Limited.

OFSTED (2008) Learning Outside the Classroom [Online]. http://www.lotc.org.uk/wp-content/uploads/2010/12/Ofsted-Report-Oct-2008.pdf.

Before the system: The importance of building relationships with your pupils

Joe Barber and Michelle Noble

Chapter aims

- To illustrate opportunities to embed respectful and just expectations and nurture positive and productive classroom relationships.

- To recognise that unwanted pupil behaviours may belie more complex needs and problems which the behaviour management system may not fully address.

- To appreciate that, by understanding these paradigms, there will be a reduced need to call on the school's behaviour system.

Keywords: Behaviour management system; behaviour management policy; relationships; pastoral care; respect, fairness, choice, consistency, communication, behaviour as a language; zero tolerance

Introduction

For teachers at the beginning of their career, it is typical to experience something of a rage for order; a need to bring within the span of their control and understanding a complex and wide-ranging body of skills, knowledges and competencies. The area of behaviour management is one of these and in our experience, the one which dominates the thoughts and feelings of most student and Newly Qualified Teachers (NQTs). Ahead of starting your course or before meeting classes for the first time, the fear of not being able to manage behaviour looms large. It eclipses all other important factors, such as: is my subject knowledge strong enough? What is the difference between an aim, objective and an out-come? Does my philosophy of teaching and education have a place in this pro-cess? Rather, the nightmare scenario of not being able to manage a 'difficult' class or resolve conflict or ensure a 'triumph' over an awkward pupil plays itself out until you begin to realise that as more experience comes your way, this is, in fact a highly unlikely scenario.

However, it is worth reminding yourself, when you feel like this, that the major-ity of pupils arrive at classrooms understanding that there is an expectation that they engage with learning, make an effort and accept a common set of expectations. Those expectations are yours, their peers', other teachers' and the school-wide community's. Expectations are inscribed, embedded and recited in every corridor, lunchtime queue and classroom. Not every pupil will embrace or even accept those expectations all of the time, but you should keep them at the forefront of your mind so as to remind, repeat and reinforce whenever necessary, even to yourself. To begin with, this simple mantra seems too easy and too good to have any effect, but it really isn't. Grounding yourself in this clear context should be the touchstone for your belief in yourself as an effective classroom teacher as well as a starting point for addressing behaviour issues.

From the off, you should see yourself as part of the school and as having a role in upholding expectations for the sake of all pupils and teachers. This means find-ing out, at an early stage, what expectations exist in the school, of pupil behaviour and conduct. Gaining a thorough and clear understanding of these at an early stage will provide the bedrock of the climate and expectations in the corner of school over which you have complete responsibility: your classroom. Equally, accepting and embracing lifelong development of skills in managing pupil behaviour is vital. This skills set is not something which can be 'finished' in your Post-Graduate Certificate of Education (PGCE) or NQT year. Nor should it. Your PGCE aims to kick-start your learning as a reflective teacher-practitioner, so that you will hone your craft in managing a classroom and to begin to understand the behaviours of your pupils.

Successful learning via a positive classroom: bricks and mortar

Whilst there is a range of successful, tried-and-tested behaviour management strat-egies (see below) your overall demeanour and consistency as a human being – the driving force of the classroom – are the cornerstones on which to pin these. Considering how it would feel to be one of your own pupils, in your lessons, is a very helpful way to appreciate the ethos and atmosphere you are creating.

We could think of the learning process as bricks and mortar. If the bricks rep-resent the segments of curriculum, through which a significant amount of sub-ject knowledge is built, then we can imagine the mortar as the classroom ethos, with strategies and discourses of success and positivity, cementing the learning. Without the mortar, the bricks may stand a little while and the wall (subject knowledge) may be superficially maintained; but with a gust of wind on the pupils – other subject pressures, personal difficulties, summer holidays – that precarious structure will immediately be lost. Through a happy, emotionally-safe environment, learning is embedded, ready to be revisited and built on at any time.

Your character, your expectations and your boundaries are what pupils are looking to see from you. The 'mortar' is why you will hear pupils racing to Mr Jones' lesson, because, '… history is ace'. In reality, it may be that the pupil actually didn't think history was 'ace': rather, the teacher's fairness and humanity – the mortar of their classroom – has switched the pupil on to the subject itself.

What does good behaviour management look like?

Observing teachers who are rated as good behaviour managers is a very worthwhile project. One of the tasks in this chapter assists you in focusing your observations on what kinds of behaviour management techniques, approaches and strategies are used by different teachers. Some of them may work well for you and your emerging style and teacher persona; others less so. We want to stress, however, that any teacher who is effective at managing pupil behaviour has first created a classroom environment which enables all pupils to feel valued and involved, where respect is circulated amongst all people in the room and where high expectations of self and others is paramount.

Perhaps naturally, as part of the 'rage for order', student teachers and NQTs often seek simple solutions to what can be complex circumstances. A common pitfall for the teacher is often to assert control over pupils, creating ordered and even silent classrooms. Behaviour management systems can seduce less experienced teachers into believing that they are these 'simple solutions'. With the Teachers' Standards (DfE, 2011) forming the basis of QTS, it is understandable that Standard 7, Managing Behaviour, plays a key role in any trainee's concerns. However, in this 'ordered' scenario, pupils are, in fact, often in a passive state, managed by the teacher, rather than demonstrating a conscious awareness of themselves and what they are doing at any time during the lesson. This relates back to our initial point about the basic acceptance on the part of your pupils to behave according to the school's systems and expectations. The best classroom managers are those who recognise the nuances of human behaviour, meet need but maintain the highest standards – and seldom, if ever, require assistance.

For instance, a rule that everyone arrives on time for each lesson will be widely understood, even if some pupils choose to reject or ignore it. That said, there will be times when pupils have good reason for being late, and the best thing you can do is prompt them to start work and state publicly that you'll talk to them at the end of the lesson. At the end, you can ask them if they have an explanation whilst bearing in mind the common expectation you both share, that they will all arrive to lessons on time. The pupil's explanation is likely to tell you much about their culpability and decision to ignore the expectation, but allowing them a chance to explain is important here. If the pupil blames another teacher for making them late, you can check with that teacher at break. In other words, the resolution can be deferred until you have more information. Finding that the pupil was telling the truth means you have avoided an unfair judgement and possible sanction of the pupil as well as disrupting your lesson and putting them off engaging with the learning you have planned. Equally, discovering that the pupil was being dishonest puts you in a position where, with your expectation touchstone in place, you can address the matter in full possession of the facts and with an expression of reasoned and reasonable disapproval, disappointment or sanction. This ultimately brings the pupil's decision to be late, and to lie about the causes, back to themselves and ask them to consider if their actions were the right ones, as well as to ask them, in the context of expectations, how it should be dealt with. Such an approach also provides opportunity for the pupil to share with you, reasons why they may be avoiding the lesson. Choice is a powerful tool, and invites the pupil to assess their behaviour even further. In a situation like this, your expectation of reasonable behaviour is modelled by your own reasonable behaviour (Garner in Capel, 2016), which is difficult for any pupil to dispute. You have been in control throughout and role-modelled fair and reasonable decision-making.

When embarking on a teaching career – particularly in our highly performative culture – it is understandable that you feel you must show complete control in your classroom, responding immediately to situations, with the courage to use sanctions. Thirty children, some of whom may be testing your resources, can also contribute to these impulses. However, the example above shows the difference between a 'controlling' teacher and a teacher who is in control.

Many schools have 'zero tolerance' approaches to pupil behaviour and will claim that they work well for eradicating 'poor' behaviour. In our opinion, this approach should be handled with some critical distance and judgement. Such systems satisfy a need to state rules without any acceptance that pupils will break them, often, knowingly and willingly. The teacher who uses their knowledge, skill and understanding to discuss the pupil's choices to behave one way or another is, in our opinion, likely to have a greater impact on the pupil's understanding of themselves, respect for others, and contribution to the school community. It also helps to ensure that a pupil knows that it is their behaviour which is unwanted but that they are still important, wanted and valued. As we explain later, behaviours are proxies for other things: feelings, thoughts, the need for attention, a desire to rebel. Behaviour becomes the language used to express them.

Case study 1: zero tolerance approaches to behaviour management

Take the experience of Pupil X, in a school with a 'Zero Tolerance' policy, placed in detention one day after school. This is the latest in a long list of detentions for non-completion of homework, poor effort and attitude. Set a writing task to complete (as a side note, should writing be used a punishment?), she realises she has no pen. Rather than raise her hand and ask the teacher who is supervising the detention (and who issued it), she signals to another pupil for them to loan her one. Spied by the supervising teacher, she is removed from the detention and suspended for two days. This was the next stage on the escalatory behaviour management and sanctions system and so the teacher followed it. Whilst this is logical, it seems that asking the pupil what she needed and supplying her with a pen would have secured a better outcome for her, given that at that stage she appeared to have every intention to accept her punishment and complete her detention. There can be little doubt that the pupil would, herself, have been asking the same question and been confused about her exclusion. So, how did this experience improve the pupil's attitudes towards learning, discipline, the school's system or its staff? If we cannot say it did, then what was, ultimately, the point of the sanction?

As we mentioned earlier, a useful way to think of pupils' behaviour is as a form of communication – a language – which may well be the only one at their disposal. If you were planning to visit a cosmopolitan, fast-paced city, you would expect to hear a variety of languages spoken. You would probably be looking forward to embracing varying cultures, beliefs and values as part of your trip, as an outward-looking, inclusive human being; in other words, you would recognise difference and diversity. Our behaviour as human beings is another one of these languages and, just as in the fast-paced city, your classroom presents a range of experiences, backgrounds, cultures and socio-economic profiles, manifesting as behaviour with which we deal effectively as classroom teachers.

Even as adults, many of us find it easier to act out how we are feeling, rather than to explain it; this is particularly true for young adults, who are refining their emotional filters and learning how to synthesise the behaviour and responses of others. The pupil who kicks over the chair and claims they 'Couldn't care less,' actually cares a very great deal; enough to kick a chair over in anger and frustration. The point is that they simply do not know how to show you that they care. This scenario, complete with expletives and physical threats, is every new teachers' worst nightmare, followed by the eternal question, 'What will I do about that?' The more constructive question to ask oneself is, 'How will I make sure that never happens in my classroom?'

Whole-school behaviour systems in today's settings are now both varied and sophisticated, with a wide range of levels, warnings and sanctions. As a student teacher or NQT, you will have been graded, against the Teachers' Standards (DfE, 2012), on your ability to understand and apply the school systems to your own classroom. This will continue into your NQT year and beyond and whilst there is no doubt you should adhere to policy, for a host of reasons, a more proactive way to manage behaviour in your classroom is to think about the strategies which minimise your need to ever call on a whole-school behaviour system.

Case study 2: Alex and a year 11 pupil

To illustrate this further, take the example of Alex, an experienced English teacher who was praised for her behaviour management in the very challenging setting in which she worked.

Having been in the school for a number of years, Alex was particularly fond of her Year 11 English class, enjoying a very positive relationship with all pupils. As they continued with their individual work on this particular day, a group of culturally-awakening boys, sitting dotted around the room, were once again sharing their observations on life. Always intelligent and entertaining, the boys could, nevertheless, easily dominate and distract the class. Keen to encourage her pupils' own learning beyond the classroom, Alex had become adept in balancing the need to support and encourage these boys with a firm hand of keeping them on track.

Reining them in for the second time that lesson, Alex asked them firmly to refocus on the task in hand more assertively, reminding them of the looming deadline. Simon, however, the slightly less compliant member of the gang – and viewed by many other teachers as difficult and uncooperative – looked up and quibbled, though speaking quietly enough that Alex could not make out his exact words.

Smiling, with tongue-in-cheek, Alex calmly responded, 'Simon, that's enough arguing back; or you know I will send for Mr Jones, who'll whisk you away up that corridor.' The class – including Simon's friends – chuckled at the gentle warning and quietened down.

Looking up steadily, however, and without smiling, Simon replied to Alex, 'You wouldn't do that.'

The entire class gasped. Interpreting this comment to mean that, for the first time ever, Simon was refusing to work, Alex's tone of voice and physical stance changed. In spite of herself, and in some shock, she asked: 'I beg your pardon, Simon?'

'I said, you wouldn't do that. You'd never send for someone to come in here. You would sort it out yourself,' Simon explained, with a smile.

Completely wrong-footed, Alex smiled and looked round. A number of other pupils nodded and continued working. The class fell silent to concentrate on their work, with no further chivvying required. Clearly, the other pupils had been in equal shock at Simon's comment too, underlining the positive, happy ethos of the room. How had Alex created this dynamic with a boy who had been given a school-wide label as argumentative and challenging – even with the most senior staff?

The key to this lies in what the 15-year-old pupil had spotted for himself: Alex was the manager of her own classroom. She was consistent and fair, with a sense of proportion and humour. Whilst she had an eye to the school's behaviour policy and procedures, she had used it on only a handful of occasions – even in a highly challenging setting – because, in her lessons, the need rarely arose. Alex describes this incident as one of her most important achievements; it was a moment of shared metacognition with the pupils she adored, who recognised her worthy of their respect, with no need to rely on a school behaviour policy.

Relationships

In our view, the teacher should see 'the system' as an end point on a spectrum of behaviour management strategies. All too often, there is a very real risk that it is viewed as a starting point. It should be viewed as a destination reached when pupils will not and cannot engage with you as their teacher and the expectations you share, embody and practice in each and every lesson. Before you reach the stage of utilising the system, there is a range of simple, low-level behaviour management strategies which follow on from the simple strategy of getting to know your pupils. However, it's crucial to bear in mind that learning with a checklist of tips is simply relying on another system. What we advocate is attempting to develop relationships with pupils which allow for trust, fairness and consistency. This means that getting to know and understand your pupils, explaining why you may be dissatisfied with their behaviour and giving them a chance to put it right, can be much more effective in the long term than escalating an issue to another sanction or issuing a praise point or other reward. In both cases, what is missing is the strength of the relationship between the pupil and the teacher. A reliance on systems can not only stymy relationships, but also negate them entirely.

The school policy

All schools will have a policy and a set of procedures for addressing, labelling, stratifying, managing, rewarding and punishing pupil behaviours. Most teachers and pupils would concur that poor standards of behaviour impact greatly on pupil achievement, attainment and progress, not to mention feelings of emotional safety, enjoyment and motivation. Therefore, the ubiquitous appearance of the behaviour management system is understandable when considered in light of the above. Systems which are based around sanctions and rewards are generally characterised as escalatory, providing pupils with verbal and written warnings and graded punitive responses ahead of a consequence. This might take the form of a name on the board, followed by a detention if pupils fail to respond to an initial request, instruction or sanction. If used well, the system will be communicated to all staff throughout the school and all will execute it with consistency as far as is possible and reasonable. In an ideal situation, this would be part of whole-school culture rather than just being confined to classrooms.

So, given the reasons for its rightful prominence in the school's culture, is it a problem to simply rely on the behaviour management system in most situations, allowing it to do the hard work for you? If we take the instance above as an example, then it would certainly appear that the need to control pupils' behaviour begins to overshadow the job of helping children make decisions about what kinds of behaviour are appropriate, socially beneficial and without risk or harm to themselves or others. Instead of it acting as an instrument which performs the job of managing pupil behaviour and ensuring an orderly, productive classroom, it could well undermine the power that you have to develop strong relationships and routines as well as pre-emptively and positively minimise disruption which, longer term, ensure that pupils do as you expect of them.

In other words, we want to argue that there is a risk in becoming overly reliant on 'the system' to manage unwanted behaviours at the expense of the teacher's skill in working with their pupils to ensure their shared classroom space is built upon clear expectations and routines which pupils come to know providing there is consistency and positive relationships and also that there is care and clarity. The recommendation of Tom Bennet (DfE, 2017) is that each classroom teacher should embed the 3 Rs of relationships, routines and rewards within their classroom. There is much sense in this approach and although this is nothing new, the enduring sense and efficacy of the approach is, for those who practice it, highly evident. Wright (2017) describes the school's behaviour management policy and system as 'extrinsic', distinguishing it from the 'intrinsic' aspects of what teachers do in their classrooms to ensure that the potential for learning is central, and embedded in the cultivation of positive relationships, consistent routines, clear expectations and effective and considered planning. In order to stand the very best chance of nurturing classrooms characterised by agreed understanding of rules, pupil–teacher and teacher–parent/carer relationships which are built on trust, transparency and fairness, teachers really must work to build them. In Case Study 2, Alex believed deeply in democratic classrooms, determined to provide her pupils with something better than the culture of fear and blame she had herself experienced at school. Relationships with her pupils were strong, positive and meaningful; she worked hard every day to make pupils believe she cared for them. This care equally included the strength to chivvy, chastise and sanction if necessary.

But what exactly do we mean by a 'democractic' classroom? Is this code for a situation where every pupil gets what they want? No. A 'democratic' classroom is one where fairness and consistency rule above all else;

The 'Democratic Classroom' is one which considers:

■ pupils' backgrounds, including social and cultural capital;

■ pupils' domestic circumstances;

■ barriers to learning;*

■ learning styles and preferences;

■ boosting higher-ability pupils;

■ a baseline of fairness, equity and consistency regardless of the above.

* This phrase is taken from a paper, *Removing Barriers to Achievement* (DFES, 2004), and urges consideration of those factors which may affect pupils' learning but may not be classed as an SEND.

> **Task 1**
>
> What is the impact of fairness in a classroom?
>   Who determines what fairness is?
>   How is fairness enacted and embedded?

Case study 3: a visibly-fair teacher

A pupil who is told that their name is on the board once identified as not paying attention, or speaking when they ought to be listening, is not necessarily going to view their teacher's authority and confidence as strong, nor will they begin to understand reasons for the sanction or the teacher's rationale for applying it, especially if it was not a deliberate attempt to break with a classroom rule or to undermine the teacher's authority. Rather, they will most likely view the teacher's recourse to the system as unfair and respond with, at best, some slight loss of trust or worse, with contempt or with disregard. It may even be viewed as something to contest, publicly, with an audience. In this scenario, the teacher has to be seen to counteract the pupil's wilful challenge. The need to have the final say becomes the teacher's principal objective. In this situation, it is the teacher who has opened up an opportunity for a public showdown.

Teacher authority

This starts to take us towards a consideration of the ways in which teachers can establish authority in classrooms and which might make the most significant contribution to managing pupil behaviour so that the outcomes are positive and the impacts expedient. We can say that a teacher's authority develops from three different factors:

- Roles
  Using your position as a teacher and member of an organisation. Belonging to and upholding the rules of a community plus recognising the responsibility you have for students' learning, development and well-being.
- Knowledge
  Using your subject knowledge to demonstrate expertise and secure your pupils' confidence in you.
- Relationships
  Treating pupils fairly, with respect and dignity, role modelling excellent relationships through interactions with colleagues.

Discovering and applying your classroom principles

Having established your authority in the classroom, it is imperative to demonstrate it through a clear set of rules and principles. As you embark on your teaching career, you will come to understand the 'framework' of your classroom and of your teaching style more and more; the pillars which uphold this include:

(i)   Consistency:
      Be the teacher on Thursday afternoon that you are on Monday morning. If titles need underlining, then they are underlined every day of the week. If ties should have a knot, then knots should be in place, at any point of the day. Think back to inconsistent bosses you may have worked for; how frightening is the feeling that they will have different expectations, different moods and different responses from day to day?

(ii) Setting a high bar of expectation and aspiration:
      Making pupils believe they can achieve well is extremely infectious and motivational. Consider the objectives and outcomes that you set. Do you expect all pupils to use and develop the same knowledge and skills within the subject in a learning episode? Praise the class for tackling and understanding that very difficult text, and tell them you will bring an even higher challenge next week, whether they are students with SEN or those aiming for Grade 9. Convey and repeat that the sky is their limit: 'good enough' should never be good enough.

(iii) Sense of humour and proportion:
      Do you smile when you see pupils? Do you look pleased to see them, welcoming them at the door in a fun, professional manner? Are you prepared to have a joke with them in the right way? Remember how you have felt when bosses or even teachers from your own past, 'welcomed' you with stony-faced silence. No one learns when they are afraid and anxious; we simply go into survival mode, hoping to escape at the end without having been in trouble.

(iv) Caring:
      This can be shown in myriad ways. Telling them you care, dropping off a book at home, attending matches, staying late, working individually with pupils. Build up a reputation as a teacher who cares – remember you need to build a reputation with parents too. If the parents respect you, they will support you, rather than just believing their child. This is particularly helpful in times where you have to reprimand; the respect you have built up as someone who truly cares for them gives you 'permission', in their eyes, to be upset or disappointed with them when they get it wrong.

(v)   Assertive management techniques:
      When you do have to reprimand a pupil, separate them from their 'crime'. Explain why you are disappointed. Offer the pupil the chance to apologise – and accept it graciously, however it is said. Never reject or refuse an apology. Assure them the matter is over and that we are moving on. And then stick to it! Allowing students a chance to reflect on why their behaviour is an issue in the context of the school's rules as well as your expectations and established sense of fairness, is very powerful.

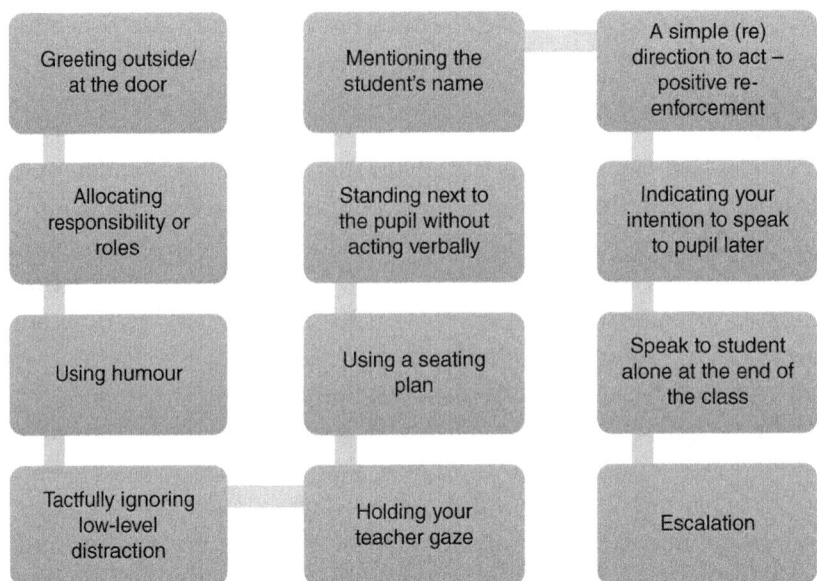

Figure 10.1 Managing behaviour at the lowest level.

(vi)   Tackling 'low-level' behaviour proportionately:
       It's worth considering what you interpret as a low-level behaviour issue. One
       teacher's productive noise is another teacher's chaos. Have you considered
       and established working conditions for your pupils, especially around talk,
       discussion and collaboration? Stick to your high standards and tackle low-
       level disruption with sense and proportion. Offer chances and choices to do
       the right thing. (See Figure 10.1 for examples of tackling low-level behaviour
       proportionately.)

(vii) Choices and chances:
       Far from putting the student in control, this actually works on a 'lifeline'
       principle. You are offering the student a chance to rectify their behaviour
       through making a good choice. For example:
           'John, this is the second time I have asked you to stop talking. If it carries
       on, you know what the next step will be. Would you prefer that to happen,
       or prefer to stop talking? You know I would prefer you to stay here and
       carry on with your learning, because I want you to do well. What do you
       prefer?'
           This example also shows the power of using rhetoric positively rather than
       in the time-honoured teacher tradition of negatively (classics such as 'What
       time do you call this?' and 'Who do you think you are talking to?' can still
       occasionally be heard drifting around!). It is hard for anyone to say they would
       prefer not to be included in their safe environment and, by doing so, succeed.

This kind of rhetoric reminds the pupil that you want them to be in the classroom, you want to teach them and you want to see them fulfil their potential; in other words, you care (see below).

(viii) Positive reinforcement:

Tell pupils how well they are doing, how proud you are of them, how much you enjoy teaching them, on a regular basis. Celebrate in individual, group and class achievements, wherever possible. Reward pupils for getting things right, particularly the 'small' things. These are not small things at all; the pupil praised for finally applying semi-colons correctly will blossom and bloom under the success, gain confidence in using punctuation generally and start to take risks with it. The pupil who is praised – without sarcasm or 'edge' – for handing in homework on time, will appreciate your recognition and want to please you again. Remember, very, very few people do not enjoy praise.

This diagram shows a number of simple strategies which concludes with calling upon the school behaviour policy and sanctions system.

Behaviour as a language

Knowing your pupils well and being familiar with their circumstances and temperaments is crucial in helping you decide if each will accept being challenged or admonished in certain ways in particular contexts. A child whose Monday morning is typically chaotic because of home circumstances may be less accepting of a public challenge to wear the appropriate items of uniform and an ensuing sanction according to the school system. Rather, a quiet word at the end of the lesson could avoid embarrassment and permit learning to take place in the lesson itself. An upset, angry or frustrated child is unlikely to learn or even cooperate with a teacher who seeks to make an example of them for something they have little control over and may feel especially sensitive and self-conscious about. Doing nothing at all is not an option and you must address the matter with the pupil once affording them some privacy and a chance to agree on a solution before informing any other staff who will come into contact with the child that day.

As we said earlier, pupils' behaviour is a language they use to communicate, not always consciously, to the outside world, how they are feeling, what sort of morning they have had or what fears and worries they may be experiencing. There is, of course, a risk that oversimplifying causes much worse problems, especially where longer-term relationships between pupils and teachers are concerned. Let's take the simple situation of a pupil who arrives late for a lesson, has forgotten their exercise book, planner and has no pen to write with. The teacher responds by asking in front of the whole class, 'Where are your things?' and 'What do you mean, you have forgotten them?' (notice the negative rhetoric at work). There's a good chance that the pupil will feel embarrassed, or even quite pleased that they have managed to cause a distraction and draw attention to themselves. Either way, the pupil's response communicates something – be it fear of revealing that they are living between two homes or that they want some attention for it is lacking elsewhere in their lives. Opening either of these scenarios up for public airing and scrutiny is asking for the pupil to react in a way you would rather they did not.

The solution is twofold:

1. Firstly, know your pupils and any circumstances of their home and personal lives which have been shared with the school. Form tutors, heads of year and SENDCOs are critical links to this information. This means that in being an effective teacher, well-planned and organised with expert subject knowledge under your belt, you must also know your pupils so that you can understand a little of the person behind the learner. This can take time, but find out early on what information is available about the pupils you teach.
2. Secondly, handling issues such as the one above in front of an audience is likely to create an adversarial scenario with the pupil resenting being embarrassed or else determined to show you they are unafraid to challenge you.

Case study 4: behaviour as a language: a familiar analogy?

The following example might help to illustrate how behaviour communicates a set of feelings – and how powerful these actions can be. This case study reminds us of all-too-familiar traits we have seen in adults. Imagine working for the following boss; what does the following scenario tell us about how the boss is actually feeling?

On Monday, she sets you a task about which you are not sure. You don't feel you can say this, as she has a 'Zero Tolerance' policy towards what she regards as mistakes. You are now afraid of her.

On Tuesday, she arrives in a foul temper and tells you not to 'bother' her with 'silly' questions, even though you are really struggling with the task. Her behaviour has intensified your fear.

On Wednesday, she is extremely nice and brings in sticky buns for you both; but in the two hours that pass before that break, she roars at you for something with which you were not involved.

On Thursday, she talks about the task again; it becomes clear to you that she now wants something very different to what she had originally outlined. Her office door remains closed for the day, with a 'Do Not Disturb' message on the door.

Friday's deadline arrives. No mention is made of the original task. You have completed all your other work very well, but have received no praise or recognition for this.

Task 2 How would you interpret this behaviour?

The experience of interpreting another adult's behaviour as a signifier of how they feel or think is familiar to us all. We often accept that adults carry 'baggage' and express their feelings in negative ways; with friends and loved ones, we actually give permission for this and often empathise with the person's inner struggles.

Ironically, children are the ones without the fully formed filters; yet, when they display their baggage, we refer to this as 'acting out', 'acting up', being difficult, disruptive or simply 'stroppy' and give little permission for them to vocalise this.

Conclusions

Your goal in successfully managing pupils' behaviour should not just be an end in itself, but – as we have seen – to support successful, deep learning through your Continuing Professional Development. The emotionally-safe, successful classroom, where content is delivered through fair and consistent ground rules, is one where the most rapid and successful academic progress occurs. In the best classrooms, this seems to happen almost by osmosis, but actually, it does not. It is in the positive and happy classroom, with learning delivered powerfully and imaginatively, that learning is retained, pupils are enthused and, therefore, logically, behaviour is good. Learning cannot take place when uncertainty and anxiety preside; at best, all that can happen in those conditions is content coverage, a far cry from independent and purposeful learning. Inconsistency and an unwillingness to manage low-level behaviour will result in a disaffected pupil body – which will respond accordingly.

This chapter has examined the importance of realising that any school behaviour system should be regarded as a final destination, not a first response. We have seen, from various examples and principles, the importance of managing your own classroom, building up a fair and reasonable approach to tackling behavioural issues and, as a result, developing excellent relationships with pupils. As the oft-quoted Haim Gillot states, you have the power to make the weather in the classroom (Ginott, 1972). Planning for behaviour, managing behaviour and intervening are as straightforward and as necessary as planning, managing and intervening in learning.

> **Task 3**
>
> Familiarise yourself with your school behaviour management policy and procedure. Who are the key players in this process?
>
> Observe three lessons with teachers rated as good behaviour managers. With their permission, tally the amount of positive to negative comments used in the lessons and calculate the percentages.
>
> What peripheral and subliminal messages does your room give to pupils? How do the walls suggest an emotionally-safe classroom?
>
> How do you use praise and rewards to positively manage behaviour?

References

DfE (2011) Teachers Standards. https://www.gov.uk/government/publications/teachers-standards.

DfE (2017) Behaviour in Schools. https://www.gov.uk/government/publications/behaviour-in-schools.

DFES (2004) Removing Barriers to Achievement. http://media.education.gov.uk/assets/files/pdf/r/removing%20barriers%20to%20achievement.pdf.

Garner, P. (2016) Managing classroom behaviour: Adopting a positive approach. In S. Capel, M. Leask and Younie, S. (Eds), *Learning to Teach in the Secondary School: A Companion to School Experience* (8th edn). Oxon: Routledge.

Ginott, H. (1972) *Teacher and Child: A Book for Parents and Teachers.* New York: Macmillan.

Wright, T. (2017) *How to Be a Brilliant Trainee Teacher.* Oxon: Routledge.

Being human: Compassionate education rather than behaviour management

Mark Sackville-Ford and
Sarah Baggaley

Chapter aims

- To explore alternative perspectives that challenge the notion of 'behaviour management'.

- To understand the ways that humanism offers an opportunity to support teachers and learners in schools.

- To reflect on Nonviolent Communication and Restorative Approaches as mechanisms and structures towards a compassionate education.

Keywords: Behaviourism; humanism; guidance approaches; restorative approaches; non-violent communication; relationships; compassion

Introduction

The main purpose of this chapter is to explore a more compassionate and human stance towards 'behaviour management'. We invite you to think more about the pastoral aspect of your role and how this relates to behaviour. We consider the ways that your interactions and relationships with your students may attempt to connect you at a deeper level. Noddings (2003) reminds us in the following quote of the ways that homes and school may have more shared values than one might initially consider:

> The best schools should resemble the best homes … The best homes provide continuity of caring relations, attend to and continuously evaluate both inferred and expressed needs, protect from harm without deliberately inflicting pain, communicate so as to develop common and individual interest, work together cooperatively, promote joy in genuine learning, guide moral and spiritual development…, contribute to the appreciation of the arts and other great cultural achievements, encourage love of place and protection of the natural world, and educate for both self-understanding and group understanding. The best homes and schools are happy places.
>
> Noddings (2003, p. 260)

Noddings's quotation is fascinating when framed within the current dominant discourses and ideologies around what constitutes a 'good education', particularly in English schools. Neoliberalism manifests in educational policy through a technical rational approach, reducing teaching and learning to a singular process, seeking to promote economic productivity. One premise is that if teachers teach the correct content in the correct way, this will lead to high standards and a strong economy. Schools have become increasingly driven by performativity, leading to a narrowed curriculum and a culture that sees a 'good education' as one that focuses on examinations and attainment, often diametrically at odds with some of the conditions that are advocated in the above quotation.

Within this neoliberal school context, 'behaviour' is similarly framed within discipline discourses, pertaining to a set of tools to control and manage behaviour. As Noguera (1995; cited in Porter, 2014, p. 35) suggests, 'the economic function employs controlling discipline, where students are taught obedience while teachers deposit knowledge into them'. This can lead to authoritarian relationships in schools and an unequal distribution of power between the teacher and the learner. This emerges in UK policy through approaches such as Tom Bennett's (2017) 'Creating a culture' document which, although presenting some sound ideas, is wholly based around controlling discipline and underpinned by behaviourism. The learner is reduced to a commodity that is managed through a business model of education, as knowledge workers being prepared for jobs. As Freire (2000, p. 60) argues, 'the oppressed, as objects, as 'things', have no purposes except those their oppressors prescribe for them'.

Within this bleak picture that we paint at the start of the chapter, we want to show that there are other ways to view behaviour within education. Imagine that everything that you had previously thought about behaviour (and its management) was unhelpful, even some of the ways that it is described elsewhere in this book. Imagine that there are alternative ways to support young people and respond to disruptiveness. We argue that such approaches exist beyond the imagination. Many schools are currently approaching behaviour in holistic and creative ways.

This chapter seeks to theorise around these and offer ways for you, as a student or newly qualified teacher, to reflect on and consider these different approaches alongside your own current responses to behaviour within your classrooms.

We acknowledge that at this stage of your career, it will be difficult to reject the dominant discourses described above. You are still in the shadow of the teachers' standards which perpetuate the discourses. However, you are at the perfect time to reflect upon your current teacher identity and the values and beliefs that you hold. By looking at more progressive viewpoints we hope that it supports you to become the type of teacher you would like to be. Professional identity is an organic entity, growing and responding to the dynamics that surround teachers (Coldron and Smith, 1999; Beijaard et al., 2004). Hsieh's (2015) study identifies the unique perspectives we bring to our professional roles and how our identity as teachers often has some foundation in our early experiences as pupils. What are the key influences that you bring to the type of teacher you wish to be? What are the values and beliefs that are central to your understanding of 'good education'? These are important questions for all teachers to ask, but particularly those at the early stages of their careers.

Task 1 What type of teacher am I?

Write a short paragraph around the 'type of teacher you want to be'. Try to write in a fluid and personal way without thinking too hard about it. Attempt to capture the reasons and emotions that led to you pursuing a career as a teacher. Include the ways that you think you will engage with unwanted classroom behaviours.

Humanity in teaching: a compassionate approach to behaviour

Through many years working as educational professionals supporting our most vulnerable young people in schools, we have developed a philosophy that views behaviour as a form of communication, advocating a compassionate response to behaviours that interrupt teaching and learning within classrooms. Where young people exhibit behaviours that are challenging, they are communicating an unmet need. This is already explored elsewhere (see Porter, 2014; Sackville-Ford, 2018) and such positioning aids this growing interest in schools that are thinking about behaviour differently, proposing a 'compassionate educational response'. Carl Rogers founded humanist theory, which recognised the importance of behaviour being connected with need, rather than consequences (see Rogers, 1951; Rogers, 1978). Such theory has been taken on by others who share the belief that all individuals have an equal right to having their needs met.

Maslow's 'Hierarchy of Needs' recognises that human needs are pivotal to life, including when learning. Maslow and Murphy (1954) stated that people are motivated to achieve certain needs and that some needs take precedence over others, impacting on our behavioural responses. Our most basic need is for physical survival, including access to water, air, food and sleep. Maslow considered these physiological demands the most important, with all other needs coming secondary until these requirements are met. Next is safety, sought in the form of protection from elements, security, order, law, stability and freedom from fear.

After physiological and safety needs have been satisfied, Maslow identified the third level of human needs as social, involving feelings of belongingness. Here the need for interpersonal relationships starts to motivate behaviour through seeking friendship, trust and acceptance. Following this we seek esteem needs. Maslow classified these into esteem for oneself (dignity, achievement, mastery, and independence) and the desire for reputation or respect from others. Maslow indicated that the need for respect or reputation is most important for children and adolescents and precedes real self-esteem or dignity. This may be something that you can relate to when reflecting on behaviours that you have seen within your classroom of adolescents.

Maslow suggests it is only with all these needs established that we are able to realise our personal potential; to be able to learn to be our best; 'to become everything one is capable of becoming' (Maslow and Murphy, 1954, p. 22). We would argue that a compassionate educational approach is one that recognises that it is unmet needs that drive the unhelpful behaviours that we see within our classrooms. 'If our physical and emotional needs are met we are able to function at our best – and if they are not, we are under-resourced and less able to cope – especially in challenging situations' (Hopkins 2015, p. 25).

Taking a 'needs-led' approach sits comfortably with Noddings's quote at the start of this chapter. What are your thoughts? As the teacher within that room, what responsibility do you feel you have towards that unmet need? What are the values that govern your response? Is your priority towards enforcing systems and processes, responding via regulations and rules? Or is it to see and respect the individual situation before you? Do you 'seek to understand before being understood' (Covey 2004, p. 236) and see building and maintaining relationships with your pupils as a central part of your teaching style?

Humanity in teaching: relationships and the importance of connection

'Life is, by nature, highly interdependent' (Covey 2004, p. 51). We are all impacted upon by the people around us and few of us would argue against the benefits of building strong relationships.

> Every child deserves a champion; an adult who will never give up on them, who understands the power of connection and insists that they become the best they can possibly be
>
> Pierson (2013)

Who has positively connected with you and helped you to become the best you could be? It may well have been a teacher in your past who has led to your decision to become a teacher yourself.

Task 2 Who helped me to be the best I can possibly be?

Consider a person who positively influenced you, preferably someone outside of your family circle, possibly an adult or teacher from your school days or university. Recall the relationship, the things this person did and said and how this left you feeling.

When reflecting on this relationship consider...

- How fair were they?

- Did they praise you?

- Were they interested in you? How did you know?

- How firm were they?

- Did they have boundaries?

- Did they have high or low expectations of you?

Write down a selection of words that describe them and the relationship they had with you.

Return to your paragraph from Task 1. Do you see any similar themes or values between your view of the type of teacher you wish to be and this person whose relationship with you has had positive influences?

Humanity in teaching: a values-based approach to your classroom management

We are all involved in making hundreds of decisions every day; these are a study of our values and are directed towards the specific purpose of satisfying our individual and/or collective needs. Our values have a major influence on our thoughts, feelings and behaviours. It is our beliefs and values that inform how we feel about our actions (Baggaley, 2018). A more explicit understanding and recognition of what form we believe our role in behaviour management should take can help inform our behaviours, and our response to others' behaviours. This can help us to make decisions that are based on our values, helping us to teach with integrity.

When we use our values to make decisions, we make a deliberate choice to focus on what is important to us. Hence, explicitly identifying with our beliefs and values around what makes a 'good teacher' can help us to become the teacher we would like to be, helping us create the future we want to experience within our classrooms. Did you enter teaching because of your interest in the curriculum or due to interest in teaching children? Where does your value base lie? Is it with your relationship with your subject or with your children?

A compassionate approach to education would encourage explicit focus on the relational dynamic inherent in teaching, seeing each individual in your care first as a child, and then as a pupil. We would suggest class management isn't so much about having the right rules as having the right relationships.

We as teachers are 'Humans first. Professionals second' (Myatt 2016, p. 15). We know that quality relationships with our colleagues influences the levels of compassion and kindness between us, allowing us to feel safe and understood on those days when we are not our best selves. This is the same within our classrooms. 'Relationships are at the heart of children's wellbeing. When children talk about what is important in their lives, they highlight their need for love, support, respect, fairness, freedom and safety-concepts that are central to what it means to be human, social beings' (Pople et al., 2015, p. 14). In addition, relationships are key to the learning we seek to enhance. Hattie and Yates (2014) highlighted the importance of interpersonal relationships between teachers and students, identifying effective relationships between students and teachers having a positive impact on learning, where trusting relationships facilitate students in taking risks and increasing effort in their learning.

So humanity, with its features of empathy, compassion, feelings and kindness, has a clear connection to teaching and a 'good education' and many schools have humanity at the core of their teaching and learning ideology. Here we explore two approaches, Restorative Approaches and Non-violent Communication, that are being adopted in different educational settings to achieve a compassionate educational community.

Restorative Approaches

The core beliefs of Restorative Approaches (RA) exist within the domain of building and maintaining healthy relationships. Stutzman Amstutz and Mullet (2005, p. 18) describe working restoratively as 'giving attention to how we learn to live and work together'. RA is not a programme of interventions to be followed, rather it is 'a compass' (Zehr, 2002, p. 10), which emphasises the importance of investing in the relationships around us. This builds up 'social capital' through making and then enjoying the 'ups' together, which then provides currency that can then be used to help us survive the 'downs'. Working restoratively is both firm, in terms of standards of behaviour, and fair in terms of nurturing and supporting others in changing their behaviour, thus supporting and developing pro-social skill sets and outcomes.

This is best illustrated in Figure 11.1 from Thorsborne and Blood (2013: 32), which is an adaption of Wachtel's (1999) representation of the Social Discipline Window:

The Social Discipline Window offers a way of reflecting on our way of being; helping us to view our actions towards an event and whether what we do or say helps to foster changes in behaviours and how our response affects our

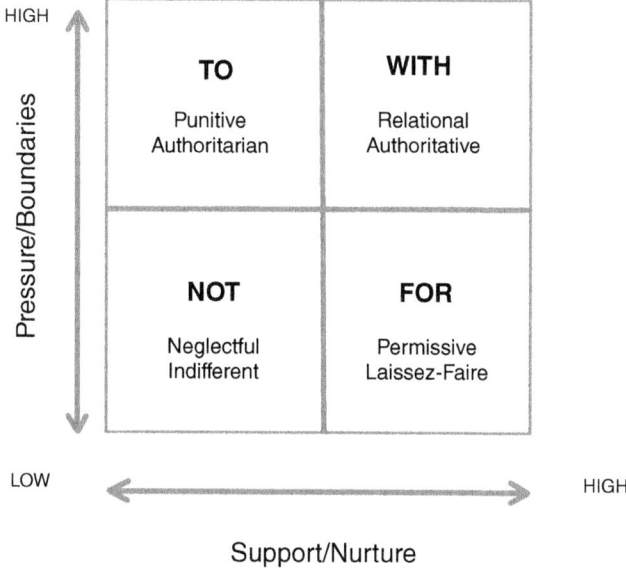

Figure 11.1 Social Discipline Window (adapted from Wachtel, 1999).

relationships with the people involved. The vertical axis determines the intensity to which behavioural expectations are applied and the horizontal axis the depth of support and nurture that is offered. These axis create four distinct 'ways of being'.

The 'TO' window: The upper left-hand window represents the context where we are offering high challenge with low levels of support towards a situation that we wish to change. In its purest form this response is identified as punitive and authoritarian, with the words that our response is done *TO* or 'do what I tell you', rather than 'do what I do myself'. So whilst there can be some positive change achieved from this approach, the learning developed here is in the form of compliance rather than ownership and often at the expense of negative impact on the health of the relationship of those involved.

The 'FOR' window: The lower right-hand window represents the context where we are offering high nurture and support with low levels of challenge towards a situation that we wish to change. In its purest form this response is identified as permissive and excusing, engendering overprotective and excusing behaviours. Here we are rescuing or doing things *FOR* others, rather than fostering learning, resilience and ownership. Whilst there can be positive outcomes relationally with regard to offering understanding towards an individual's needs; others' needs can be seen to be overlooked and there is no change in behaviours as there is no challenge to change or learning to cope or take responsibility.

The 'NOT' window: The lower left-hand window represents the context of low levels of challenge and support towards a situation we wish to change. In its purest form this response is identified as neglectful and is best described as *NOT* meeting the needs of anyone involved in the situation. This is often the box where, due to circumstances, we are indifferent or unable to offer any support or challenge to a situation, resulting in no learning and negative impact on our relationships.

The 'WITH' window: The upper right-hand window represents the context where we are offering high challenge with high levels of support towards a situation that we wish to change. In its purest form this response is identified as authoritative, the relational and restorative approach, when high expectations of behaviour and learning are practiced within an environment of understanding and empathy. Here we are working *WITH* each other, a firm and fair approach where the emphasis is on acknowledging we all make mistakes, fostering responsibility to repair harm and to seek to learn from each other. This window fosters collaboration, the development of resilience and independence and focuses on achieving the best from all within the context of building and maintaining of healthy relationships.

Introducing the terms *not, for, to* and *with* can quickly lead to reflective discussions around 'ways of being with others' at home and in the workplace. As commented by Vennen (2015, p. 129), 'the window engages our 'internal working model' for understanding relationships and moves it towards becoming explicit. And, once explicit, our way of being in relationship with others can change.'

In our experience the benefits of the *with* approach are often appreciated and enticing; however, the move to use this in practice is less straightforward. Discussions regularly return to focusing on the benefits of taking a more authoritarian approach, using the *TO* box. Many teachers observe the direct punitive approach to solving a conflict can lead to fast and efficient results. The focus is on the rule broken, with clear and often well-worn systems of consequences designed to act as deterrents and to reduce re-offending. The lure of a 'quick fix' is appealing with students seen as objects to manage, and rules used effectively to serve out established consequences for wrongdoing.

In our experience this is typical of the punitive systems used within schools, where rule-led procedures lead to a simplistic approach, to punish or not to punish, with little shared accountability or engagement in problem-solving that is seen to be fair or just. All too often the same students repeatedly appear on the detention or exclusion lists, evidencing that no new learning or significant long-term changes in behaviour have been affected by this authoritarian approach. Contrarily, it increases discontent and fosters disconnection between students and teachers, the very people who are there to support their academic and social learning. This strongly echoes the outcomes described when taking the *TO* approach to situations within the Social Discipline Window.

When discussing with teachers the difference between punitive and restorative approaches, many share the misconception that a restorative route is a 'soft touch'. However, RA does not deny consequences for misbehaviour but instead focuses on helping individuals understand the impact of their actions (Zehr, 2002). Rather than punishing for the rule broken, effort is given to identifying the harm that has been caused and encourages accountability and commitment to making reparations for this action. The *WITH* approach is not a 'soft' or excusing approach. We are seeking to hold students accountable for their actions with compassion, recognising the humanity in making mistakes alongside being firm around the consequences for their errors. However, this approach often requires more time. This time investment needs to be weighed against the negative impacts of taking the quicker authoritarian punishment approach that can lead to feelings of shame and shallow, limited learning.

The Social Discipline Window, and its ability to help us reflect explicitly on our 'internal working model' for understanding relationships, helps us to find ways of rebalancing power and knowledge between teachers and children in school. Used skilfully, RA offers us a model to support our attempts to take a values-based approach to our teaching style, to be creating classroom environments which correlate to our desired educational beliefs and reflects the values-based ideology described in the opening quote in our chapter.

Whilst a simplistic understanding of RA can exist within its utility as a process to repair when harm has been caused, securing a whole-school ethos change allows all to 'feel' the full benefits of becoming restorative. For the full impact of a restorative approach to be realised across a whole-school culture, leadership needs to explicitly prioritise the investment in building and maintaining relationships with staff as well as students (Thorsborne (2011) cited in Thorsborne and Blood, 2013, p. 55):

> To change the behaviour of the students in our classrooms and playgrounds, we must change our own behaviours. Adults first … This does not happen by accident. Our relationships must be built and nurtured, and repaired when disconnections occur.

There is a clear need for those in positions of leadership to recognise the power of explicitly focusing on the building and maintaining of relationships and fully understanding the need for all to 'walk the talk' and to explicitly stress the link between RA and wider school pedagogy. However, there are actions that individual teachers can undertake that can foster restorative and relational values within a classroom.

Case study: an RQT reflects on using the Social Discipline Window (Sarah Baggaley)

A recently qualified teacher (RQT) was struggling to manage the behaviour in one of her classes, which was marked by frequent shouting out, students receiving sanctions and certain students being sent out of class. Very little learning was taking place in the classroom. I met to support her and we discussed the issues that she was experiencing. We reflected on the fact that the only behaviour that she

TO	WITH
Who do you have an **AUTHORITARIAN RELATIONSHIP with?**	Who do you have a **COLLABORATIVE RELATIONSHIP with?**
• Me versus you • No effort to connect with the individual • Rigid and rule bound responses • High expectations of behaviour with no understanding or support around needs • Quick to judge & blame • Use of sarcasm • 'I haven't got time...' • 'Just sit down and be quiet.' • 'Do as you're told.'	• We and us • Time spent connecting and showing interest in individual • Authoritative, firm and fair attitude • High standards with guidance around behaviour and effort • Desire to seek to understand & help when errors are made • Seeking to understand others views • 'It sounds as if you are having a difficult time. I think we need some calming down time and then we can get together to solve this problem.'
NOT	**FOR**
Who do you have an **ALOOF RELATIONSHIP with?**	Who do you have a **LENIENT RELATIONSHIP with?**
• No effort to connect • Mindlessly going through the motions • Avoiding challenge and conflict • Lack of involvement often leading to escalation in behaviour • Lack of guidance and instruction • Indifferent responses • 'Whatever'	• Time spent connecting and showing interest in individuals • Desire to help but lack of pressure • Permissive, excusing minimal or poor standards of behaviour or effort • Lack of challenge fostering poor outcomes in learning and behaviour • 'Oh go on then.' • 'Would you like me to do that for you?'

Figure 11.2 Mapping one class onto the Social Discipline Window.

could control was her own and that the best way to improve was to reflect on the ways in which she could change her way of being in the classroom; to move from the authoritarian punitive response towards a more relational connecting approach. We used the Social Discipline Window as a tool to reflect on the relationships in the classroom and the teacher behaviours (Figure 11.2).

The plan

Following this we identified the following action points:

▪ Make sure you know the students' names and connect with them beyond only their academic profile. Seeing the child first, the pupil second.

- Avoid 'nagging' the students in the TO box and make personal connections with them.

- Greet the class at the door with a smile and a named 'hello'. Use this to identify those who seem out of sorts and those that needed a little settling.

- Have a quick 'check-in' at the start of the lesson (e.g. recent TV/box set watched, favourite sport or music, best flavour of crisps). This will help to humanise the relationship between teacher and student.

- Recognise the power of body language, using facial expression, tone of voice and open body language to foster connections. Inject humour into the classroom and attempt to be more relaxed.

- Create a 'needs poster' with the whole class.

How to create a 'needs poster'

A 'needs poster' is a shared agreement developed with the class. Working in small groups, ask students to discuss 'What do we need, from ourselves and each other, to get the best from our lessons together this half term?' Use the feedback to create a list from each group's 'top 3'. From this you can create a 'What we need' poster, which highlights the values of the classroom and reinforces relationships. This is very different from a rules poster, which seeks compliance rather than understanding. Once in place the 'needs poster' provides a shared way of holding each other to account, helping to strengthen accountability and responsibility whilst reminding those in the *FOR* box that they need to show more effort.

Outcomes

After three weeks I returned to chat with the RQT. She reflected on how surprised she had been in the positive responses that the students had shown towards the 'check-ins' at the start of lessons. She reflected how these had provided her with a way of sharing her own interests and that this had led to an increase in pro-social behaviours between herself and the students. She also found that the lesson 'greeting' was working well. Her improved connections meant that she now felt more comfortable having a quiet word with the most challenging individuals, seeking to understand what might be affecting their ability to focus on the learning in her lesson.

She shared that the sessions that she used to create the needs poster had initially caused her some concerns around the lost curriculum time, but this short-term loss had been repaid in the time saved due to improved behaviour in lessons. Each session she refers to the needs poster. This approach has led to the class identity reforming around the affirmations created by identifying their success and has allowed for this teacher to openly increase her challenge around expectations for learning and behaviour without negatively impacting on relationships.

We then returned to the social discipline Window and re-evaluated the class relationships. Students from the *TO* box had moved into, or towards, the *WITH* box, seeing the benefits of her efforts to invite connections with all her students, not just those she naturally connected with. This approach had also seen some students move from the *NOT* box into the *FOR* box. The creation of the needs poster had also helped her to offer more pressure and expectations around academic and behavioural learning challenges, seeing some movement from the *FOR* into the *WITH* box. There was still further work to do to support some individuals, but overall this planning and process had been a useful tool.

Reflections

Want to develop a restorative approach and seek to work WITH your students?
    Why not try some of the following;

- Seek to connect & create relationships through use of check-ins.

- Share the development of a needs poster for your class groups.

- Seek to understand before being understood in your response to unwanted behaviours.

- Use the Social Discipline Window to reflect on your teaching relationships.

- Use circles in your teaching practice.

Compassionate Communication (Mark Sackville-Ford)

Non-violent Communication (NVC) or Compassionate Communication, the latter term I prefer, is a concept developed by Marshall Rosenberg in the 1960s (see Rosenberg and Chopra, 2015). Rosenberg's ideas were influenced by Carl Rogers, with whom he worked, and he acknowledged himself that this was not a new approach. Instead NVC offers a framework to develop language and communication skills, which enhances our humanity. Within a chapter that conceptualises behaviour as a form of communication, this seems an interesting and pertinent idea to explore. As Rosenberg states:

> NVC guides us in reframing how we express ourselves and hear others. Instead of habitual, automatic responses, our words become conscious responses based firmly on awareness of what we are perceiving, feeling and wanting. We are led to express ourselves with honesty and clarity, whilst simultaneously paying others a respectful and emphatic attention.
> Rosenberg and Chopra (2015, p. 3)

The concept is based around four main processes:

1. **Observations** – the concrete actions we observe that affect our well being
2. **Feelings** – how we feel in relation to what we observed
3. **Needs** – the needs, values, desires, etc. that create our feelings
4. **Requests** – the concrete actions we request in order to enrich our lives

Ibid. (2015, p. 7)

Each of these processes is complex and there is insufficient space within this chapter to go into detail; however, I encourage you to read more widely around these. Rosenberg identifies moralistic judgements as the first barrier to achieving compassionate communication. 'Blame, insults, put-downs, labels, criticism, comparisons, and diagnoses are all forms of judgement' (ibid., p. 15). If we fold in the current discourses of education and discipline, it is easy to see how schools and individual staff can fall into these judgemental traps. Some of the system is indeed designed to label and diagnose differences (e.g. SEND discourses) whilst comparisons are rife within the education system (e.g. school league tables, ability streaming, certain reward systems). Indeed, when we work with young people whose behaviour we find challenging, it is quite natural to become emotionally embroiled within this, leading to blame and negative judgements towards the child. NVC offers one way to support us to reframe our responses to children and their behaviours. In Rosenberg's words, when labelling others '… we think and communicate in terms of what's wrong with others for behaving in certain ways or, occasionally, what's wrong with ourselves for not understanding or responding as we would like' (ibid., p. 16). The risk of using moralistic judgements leads to further conflict and erodes relationships and goodwill, factors which are particularly relevant in the classroom. This can lead to a negative cycle for teachers where young people associate you with negative feelings, which further reduces their ability to respond compassionately.

'Most of us grew up speaking a language that encourages us to label, compare, demand and pronounce judgments rather than be aware of what we are feeling and needing' (ibid., p. 23). As I have grown to understand behaviour in more complex ways, I have seen how challenging it is to change, since we are deeply and emotionally involved. NVC in its simplest form offers a way to focus on feelings and needs. This links to other texts that I have written where I have asked teachers to look beneath the surface of the iceberg (e.g. Sackville-Ford, 2018). When working with teachers and explaining the iceberg model, I say that we must look beneath the behaviours to understand what the unmet needs might be. There is a direct link with NVC approaches. Rosenberg's examples is: 'if someone says, 'You never understand me', they are really telling us that their need to be understood is not being fulfilled' (Rosenberg and Chopra, 2015, p. 52). He continues. 'when we express our needs indirectly through the use of evaluations, interpretations, and images, others are likely to hear criticism. And when people hear anything that sounds like criticism, they tend to invest their energy in self-defence or counterattack' (ibid., p. 53).

I believe that NVC needs significant practice and one needs support to develop this. Whilst the individual teacher can implement this in their own classroom, a whole-school culture towards compassionate communication is likely to lead to much more significant change. However, importantly 'the use of NVC does not require that the person with whom we are communicating be literate in NVC or even motivated to relate to use compassionately' (Rosenberg and Chopra, 2015: 5). Maybe this is one way that this differs from RA, where there is often a need for all parties to understand the complexities of restoration.

In summary, NVC in schools seems to offer a framework, leading to:

- Enhanced communication skills.

- A humanistic approach towards behaviour, which it does not seek to manage.

- Development of active listening skills.

- Links behaviour to thoughts and feelings.

- Explicitly allows behaviour to be redirected.

- Enhanced relationships.

Behaviour policy

A challenge to moving schools towards compassionate approaches lies within their behaviour policies. Current behaviour policies tend to construct disruptive behaviour as 'within' the student and fail to recognise that behaviour may be rooted in inadequacies of the curriculum, inappropriate pedagogy or the marginalization of some young people (Maguire et al., 2010). They are dominated by behaviourist approaches that warrant a praise/rewards and sanctions driven policy.

This is compounded by statutory policies such as Behaviour and Discipline in Schools (DfE, 2016, p. 5), which states that 'In developing the behaviour policy, the headteacher should reflect on the following …' with a list that includes 'rewards and sanctions' and 'disciplinary action'. Even when schools have developed an ethos and culture in line with compassionate approaches to behaviour, they struggle to break away from the entrenched language and structure of school behaviour policies. Often it is too difficult (or brave) to stop using praise and sanctions and shift the whole focus. This is particularly challenging in the secondary school sector, where it can be more difficult to establish relationships and cultures. For this reason, my case study is taken from a primary school. However, I believe this is relevant and from my work cross-phase I believe that primary and secondary teachers should collaborate and learn from each other more.

Case study: relationship policy – Barrowford School

Barrowford School is a large primary school in Lancashire that thinks differently about behaviour. In many ways the statistical information about the school indicates that it is a typical primary school, with pupil premium pupils slightly above the average and pupils with special education needs and disabilities just below the national average. The school successfully welcomes a large number of children through managed moves or those who have experienced exclusion in their previous setting. The school also employs a social worker and play therapist and has its own nurture class.

However, this information does not bring to life the unique ethos of the school. Through inspirational leadership, one finds a positive environment where every aspect of school is considered, and where the staff are unafraid to do what they think is right for their school community. Behaviour is thought about restoratively and the policy has been replaced by a 'relationship policy'. This is embedded in their whole-school approach as one aspect of their 'Rounded and Grounded' philosophy. This includes the keywords: respect, compassion, self-regulation, accommodation, communication, co-operation. These words explicitly identify the values that inform their school practices and guide their behaviour choices. The relationship policy states that:

> At Barrowford, we recognise that most children self-regulate their behaviour and behave very well every day and never need reminding about how to behave appropriately … Our relationship policy is not primarily concerned with rule enforcement. It is a tool used to promote good relationships, so that people can work together with the common purpose of helping everyone learn.
>
> Barrowford School (2017)

What is interesting is that the policy does not contain praise or sanctions; they are just not needed. Encouragement and support is given in different ways. Young people and all members of the school community recognise that mistakes happen, but use these as learning opportunities. During the last Ofsted inspection the school was graded as 'good'. Although I place little faith in Ofsted's judgements, which are too often politically motivated, it is interesting to see that schools that resist the dominant discourses of behaviour can still achieve within the statutory inspection framework. Most important for this school is that the children and staff seem to be flourishing. The leadership have been brave enough to distribute their power around behaviour, and restorative approaches appear to have become well-embedded. It seems like a small step to change the behaviour policy to a relationship policy, but it is a giant leap to abolish the traditional rewards and sanctions. With compassionate approaches to education it is an ongoing journey and the staff recognise that there is further work to do. Creating a school built on humanistic theories of education takes energy and continual effort. It is always more than a policy; it has to be the everyday lived experiences of the school.

Reflections

What is your response to the above case study?

What is your position in relation to rewards and sanctions?

How could this apply to your classroom within a secondary setting?

A 'good education' is a 'compassionate education'

What makes 'good education' is unlikely to be precisely defined, due to its intimate connection to the varying needs of the society in which it practices (Noddings, 2005; Biesta 2013). However, Biesta (2015) asserts this lack of an absolute, rather than deterring debates, should confirm its prominence, not only within the spheres of education policymaking but especially within the everyday practice of schooling. 'If we fail to engage with the question of good education head-on there is a real risk that data, statistics and league tables will do the decision-making for us' (Biesta, 2015, p. 27).

Let's return to Noddings (2005) quote at the start of the chapter, presenting the notion that good education should include the aim of happiness. We reflect that it is not the concept that needs to be taught, but the importance of affirming the role that values and ideals enact in guiding our judgements when considering the qualities of good education and the type of teacher we wish to be.

It remains paramount to our belief systems that we advance the human quality within teaching and education. However, it is this bipartisan requirement, 'to serve both individuals and the larger society' (Noddings, 2005, p. 6), that naturally creates friction. This requires us to approach such a debate with progressiveness, acknowledging the complexity, that it is not a 'one size fits all' (Biesta, 2015) domain but a composite field. Such discussions require reflective practitioners, teachers who are able and prepared to work within the '*WITH*' box, to remain open to others' perspectives, to reflect on our own practise and to seek to understand rather than to judge, with ambition to behave thoughtfully and with respect.

To teach is to experience the glorious diversity of human life, with each year bringing a new host of individuals for you to learn more about what it means to be human. Our observation is that this subjectivity, the importance of unique perspectives, is the central influence to the need to view relationships as pivotal to a compassionate educational ontology. As society experiences greater diversity; in gender recognition, sexual identity, religious practices and gender equality etc. ..., the range of possibilities of ways to live one's life is burgeoning. Alongside this, the sonorous use of social media ensures that these unique perspectives are more widely shared now than ever before. If anything connects us as humanity, it is our vulnerabilities, an understanding and accepting of difference. An investment in skills to support unity and understanding into adulthood is key if we are to educate for the future where we are learning to peacefully live together.

It is not what you do but the way that you do it, the intentions and values behind our actions are inherent in our behaviour. So why is it that you are becoming a teacher? How well do you 'know yourself' at the start of your journey as a teacher? A starting point may be in stopping thinking in terms of 'behaviour management' and rather moving towards compassionate classrooms and compassionate education.

Task 3 My philosophy of education.

Return to your reflections from Tasks 1 and 2. Having read about RA and NVC reflect again on the type of teacher you wish to be and recall your influential person and the values that were inherent in that relationship. Now write your own philosophy for what makes a 'good teacher', what is required for an education to be a 'good education'. Where does compassion and the humanistic aspects of teaching feature?

Further reading

Porter, L. (2014) *Behaviour in Schools* (3rd edn). London: McGraw-Hill Education. This book is an excellent exploration of all aspects of 'behaviour' in schools. It theorises comprehensively around different models of thinking with behaviour.

Rosenberg, M., & Chopra, D. (2015). *Nonviolent Communication: A Language of Life* (3rd edn). Encinitas, CA: PuddleDancer Press. This book acts as an introductory guide to NVC and is highly recommended.

Thorsborne, M., & Blood, P. (2013) *Implementing Restorative Practice in Schools: A Practical Guide to Transforming School Communities.* London: Jessica Kingsley Publishers. This book offers a good introductory guide to restorative approaches, which is one of few texts in the context of schools.

References

Baggaley, S.J. (2018) Values can be expensive? Teacher, Know thyself. An autoethnographic study, navigating the tensions to understand what my beliefs and values are in relation what is 'good education'. MA Education. Manchester Metropolitan University.

Barrowford Primary School (2017) Relationship Policy. [Online] Last accessed 5 May 2019. http://barrowford.lancs.sch.uk/page-24.

Bennett, T. (2017). *Creating a Culture: How School Leaders Can Optimise Behaviour.* UK: Department for Education.

Beijaard, D., Meijer, P.C. & Verloop, N. (2004) Reconsidering research on teachers' professional identity. *Teaching and Teacher Education*, 20(2), 107–128.

Biesta, G. (2013) Interrupting the politics of learning. *Power and Education*, 5(1), 4–15.

Biesta, G.J. (2015) *Good Education in an Age of Measurement: Ethics, Politics, Democracy.* London: Routledge.

Coldron, J., & Smith, R. (1999) Active location in teachers' construction of their professional identities. *Journal of Curriculum Studies*, *31*(6), 711–726.

Covey, S.R. (2004) *The 7 Habits of Highly Effective People: Powerful Lessons in Personal Change*. London: Simon and Schuster.

DfE; Department for Education (2016) *Behaviour and Discipline in Schools: A Guide to Head Teachers and School Staff*. London: Department for Education. Ref: DFE-00023-2014.

Hattie, J., & Yates, G.C. (2014) *Visible Learning and the Science of How We Learn*. London: Routledge.

Hopkins, B. (2015) From Restorative Justice to Restorative Culture. *Social Work Review [Revista de Asistenta Sociala]*, *14*(4), 19–34.

Hsieh, B. (2015) The importance of orientation: implications of professional identity on classroom practice and for professional learning. *Teachers and Teaching*, *21*(2), 178–190.

Maguire, M., Ball, S. and Braun, A. (2010) Behaviour, classroom management and student 'control': enacting policy in the English secondary school. *International Studies in Sociology of Education*, *20*(2), 153–170.

Maslow, A.H., & Murphy, G. (1954) *Motivation and Personality (under the Editorship of Gardner Murphy)*. New York: Harper & Bros.

Myatt, M. (2016) *High Challenge, Low Threat: Finding the Balance*. Melton, Woodbridge: John Catt Educational Limited.

Noddings, N. (2003) *Happiness and Education*. Cambridge: Cambridge University Press.

Noddings, N. (2005) What does it mean to educate the whole child?. *Educational Leadership*, *63*(1), 8.

Noguera, P. (1995). Preventing and producing violence: A critical analysis of responses to school violence. *Harvard Educational Review*, *65*(2), 189–213.

Pierson, R. (2013) Every kid needs a champion. TED Talks Education.

Pople, L., Rees, G., Main, G. & Bradshaw, J.R. (2015) *The Good Childhood Report 2015*. London: The Children's Society

Porter, L. (2014) *Behaviour in Schools* (3rd edn). London: McGraw-Hill Education.

Rogers, C. R. (1951) *Client-Centered Counseling*. London: Constable.

Rogers, C. R. (1978) *On Personal Power*. London: Constable.

Rosenberg, M., & Chopra, D. (2015) *Nonviolent Communication: A Language of Life* (3rd edn). Encinitas, CA: PuddleDancer Press.

Sackville-Ford, M. (2018) How might we frame 'behaviour' in primary schools. In C. Carden (Ed.) *Primary Teaching: Learning and Teaching in Primary Schools Today*. London: Learning Matters, pp. 243–260.

Stutzman Amstutz, L., & Mullet, J.H. (2005) *The Little Book of Restorative Discipline for Schools*. USA: Intercourse.

Thorsborne, M. and Blood, P. (2013) *Implementing Restorative Practice in Schools: A Practical Guide to Transforming School Communities*. London: Jessica Kingsley Publishers.

Vennen, M.V. (2015) In B. Hopkins, (ed.), *Restorative Theory in Practice: Insights into What Works and Why*. London: Jessica Kingsley Publishers.

Wachtel, T. (2013) Defining restorative. International Institute for Restorative Practices, 12. https://centre.upeace.org/wp-content/uploads/2019/02/6-defining-restorative.pdf (last accessed January 5, 2020).

Zehr, H. (2002) *Little Book of Restorative Justice*. USA: Intercourse.

Mental health and behaviour management

Anne Guilford

Chapter aims

- To understand how mental health issues may contribute to challenges in behaviour management in classrooms.
- To develop awareness as to how teachers can support pupils both inside and outside the classroom.
- To consider strategies to look after your own mental health.

Keywords: Mental health; emotional disorders; anxiety; disclosure; exam stress; cyberbullying

Introduction

We all have mental health. Put simply, it is our psychological, emotional and social well-being. The majority of the population have good mental health, but a number of factors can contribute towards causing mental health issues. There is a growing concern regarding mental health issues in education, especially for pupils. There is some debate as to whether mental health issues are more prevalent in recent years or being reported more, but there is consensus that modern life brings about a number of challenges for young people and their teachers. This chapter explores some of these and how raising our awareness can help support student teachers and Newly Qualified Teachers (NQTs) as they potentially come across such issues.

Mental health issues have recently risen up the agenda both in the media and politically. The UK prime minister recently stated that mental health is one of the 'greatest social challenges of our time' (May, 2017). The concern is that some children experience a range of emotional and behavioural problems that are outside the normal range for their age or gender. These children and young people could be described as experiencing mental health problems or disorders.

In 2016, almost a quarter of a million children and young people in England were in contact with mental health care services (NHS digital, 2016). 10 per cent of children and young people aged 5 to 16 have a clinically diagnosed mental disorder, the equivalent of three children in every classroom across the country. Within this group, 5.8 per cent of all children have a conduct disorder (this is about twice as common among boys as girls), 3.7 per cent have emotional disorders, 1.5 per cent hyperkinetic disorders and a further 1.3 per cent have other less common disorders, including autistic spectrum disorder, tic disorders, eating disorders and mutism. 1.9 per cent of all children (approximately one-fifth of those with a clinically diagnosed mental disorder) are diagnosed with more than one of the main categories of mental disorder (Green et al., 2004). Beyond this 10 per cent, approximately a further 15 per cent have less severe problems that put them at an increased risk of developing mental health problems in the future (Brown et al., 2012).

It is important that a supportive whole-school framework be in place to support these individuals who are in our classrooms with their mental health issues, and this should be supported by appropriate classroom management, anti-bullying and support strategies. We are coming across an increasing number of pupils who are displaying inappropriate behaviours that are associated with their mental health. Overt behaviour problems often pose the greatest concern for teachers, because of the level of disruption that can be created. These problems may manifest themselves as verbal or physical aggression, defiance or anti-social behaviour.

A further concern is when pupils may become anxious, more introvert and potentially isolated. This can sometimes make attendance to lessons a challenge and can be difficult if you are trying to direct pupils to work collaboratively. Having an awareness of who these pupils are, potential triggers and the most appropriate classroom activities can help you plan to accommodate the pupils, make them feel included and prevent further anxieties or classroom incidents.

Mental health professionals have defined the problems that pupils experience to include:

- emotional disorders, e.g. phobias, anxiety states and depression;

- conduct disorders, e.g. stealing, defiance, fire-setting, aggression and anti-social behaviour;

- hyperkinetic disorders, e.g. disturbance of activity and attention;

- developmental disorders, e.g. delay in acquiring certain skills such as speech, social ability or bladder control, primarily affecting children with autism and those with pervasive developmental disorders;

- attachment disorders, e.g. children who are markedly distressed or socially impaired as a result of an extremely abnormal pattern of attachment to parents or major care givers;

▪ other mental health problems include eating disorders, habit disorders, post-traumatic stress syndromes; somatic disorders; and psychotic disorders e.g. schizophrenia and manic depressive disorder. (Department of Education, 2001)

This information may seem overwhelming but it is very unlikely you will come into contact with such a range of mental health issues during your teaching. What is key is to know who the pupils are who have mental health issues and what strategies, if any, have been identified to support them in the classroom.

Task 1

Look at the student data for your classes. How do you find information about diagnosed mental health issues? Is there a source of information for guidance and classroom strategies to support the pupils in your classes?

Risk and protective factors for child & adolescent mental health

There are many risk factors for children and adolescents that may contribute to their mental health, these are included in Table 12.1 below.

Identifying pupils with possible mental health issues

Pupils that display behavioural difficulties do not necessarily have possible mental health problems. Other issues may be the factor that causes their behavioural difficulties; this could be a special educational need (SEN) or a temporary social issue. Pupils may have experienced negative and distressing life events that have brought about a temporary change in their behaviour and has affected their mental health. It must be remembered that, as with most health issues, mental health issues are not permanent; they can fluctuate in severity and can be bought on by particular triggers. If you have concerns about a pupil then it is important you raise it with the class teacher, pastoral support team, safeguarding officer of other appropriate member of the school staff.

Teachers in schools observe children on a daily basis and could identify those whose behaviour suggests that they may be suffering from a mental health problem or be at risk of developing one. This may include withdrawn pupils whose needs may otherwise go unrecognised. To identify pupils at risk teachers need to have an awareness of changes in patterns of behaviour, attendance and attainment. Medical professionals should make any formal diagnosis, but it is important any concerns are raised so appropriate support and assessment can be put into place (Table 12.2).

Table 12.1 Risk and protective factors for child & adolescent mental health (based on Department for Education, 2018).

	Risk factors	Protective factors
In the child	• Genetic influences • Low IQ and learning disabilities • Specific development delay or neuro-diversity • Communication difficulties • Difficult temperament • Physical illness • Academic failure • Low self-esteem	• Being female (in younger children) • Secure attachment experience • Outgoing temperament as an infant • Good communication skills, sociability • Being a planner and having a belief in control • Humour • Problem solving skills and a positive attitude • Experiences of success and achievement • Faith or spirituality • Capacity to reflect
In the family	• Overt parental conflict including domestic violence • Family breakdown (including where children are taken into care or adopted) • Inconsistent or unclear discipline • Hostile and rejecting relationships • Failure to adapt to a child's changing needs • Physical, sexual, neglect or emotional abuse • Parental psychiatric illness • Parental criminality, alcoholism or personality disorder • Death and loss – including loss of friendship	• At least one good parent-child relationship (or one supportive adult) • Affection • Clear, consistent discipline • Support for education • Supportive long term relationship or the absence of severe discord

https://youngminds.org.uk/resources/tools-and-toolkits/.

It is not your responsibility to diagnose or provide the sole support for a pupil with mental health issues. It is useful, however, to be aware of them and how you could put some additional support into place as part of your lesson, if appropriate.

Task 2

Table 12.2 shows general signs to look for in pupils with mental health difficulties. Consider the classes you have observed or are teaching. Are there any pupils who display any of the signs listed? How might you be able to adapt your teaching to best support the pupils during your lessons?

Table 12.2 Signs to look for and potential support for pupils with mental health issues.

Condition	Signs to look for in Pupils	How to support Pupils
Anxiety Anxiety problems can significantly affect a child's ability to develop, to learn or to maintain and sustain friendships.	The Pupils may • Seem to be worried • Agitated • Feeling fearful or panicky, breathless, tense, fidgety, sick, irritable, tearful • Often hang about trying to start a conversation	When pupils are showing signs of anxiety try and get them to work with other pupils in small groups to support their classroom inclusion and develop problem-solving skills
Depression Feeling low or sad is a common feeling for children and adults, and a normal reaction to experiences that are stressful or upsetting. When these feelings dominate and interfere with a person's life, it can become an illness	• Be unusually quiet • Explode if you say the wrong word to them • Look like they could burst into tears • Look for excuses not to work • Have an unkempt appearance • Show different behaviour to what they usually do.	Getting Pupils to talk and feel included, working in groups, changing thinking patterns and developing problem-solving skills – to relieve and prevent depressive symptoms.
Hyperkinetic disorders (e.g. disturbance of activity and attention) This group includes Attention Deficit Hyperactivity Disorder (ADHD).	It involves three characteristic types of behaviour – • inattention, • hyperactivity • impulsivity Whereas some children show signs of all three types of behaviour (this is called 'combined type' ADHD), other children diagnosed show signs only of inattention or hyperactivity/impulsiveness	Many Pupils will be on prescribed medication, where ADHD is diagnosed and other reasons for the behaviour have been excluded, ensure a s a teacher of this pupils that their medication has been taken. The child may still present behavioural problems, discuss the behaviour with the school SENCO to devise strategies that will work with these pupils this may include **(Continued)**

Table 12.2 (Continued) Signs to look for and potential support for pupils with mental health issues.

Condition	Signs to look for in Pupils	How to support Pupils
Eating disorders The most common eating disorders are anorexia nervosa and bulimia nervosa. Eating disorders can emerge when worries about weight begin to dominate a person's life. Someone with anorexia nervosa worries persistently about being fat and eats very little. They lose a lot of weight and if female, their periods may stop. Someone with bulimia nervosa also worries persistently about weight. They alternate between eating very little, and then binging. They vomit or take laxatives to control their weight. Both of these eating disorders affect girls and boys but are more common in girls.	• Change in weight (either way) • Looks unhealthy (paler) • Often wears the wrong size clothes to hide weight change	Discussion of healthy eating and body images will help pupils identify their issues. School-based peer support groups as a preventative measure (i.e. before any disordered eating patterns become evident) may help improve body esteem and self-esteem; and the family will need to be involved so whole family counselling may take place.
Substance misuse Substance misuse (drugs, alcohol, solvent abuse) can result in physical or emotional harm. It can lead to problems in relationships, at home and at school.	• changes in behavior and mannerism. • frequent change of friends • might get angry unnecessarily when confronted. • withdrawal from usual routines, and activities.	Try to introduction lessons that focus on developing skills that enhance resilience, as a preventative measure as substance abuse is connected to other problems that can be addressed within these settings.
Deliberate self-harm Common examples of deliberate self-harm include 'overdosing' (self-poisoning), hitting, cutting or burning oneself, pulling hair or picking skin, or self-strangulation.	• Wearing long sleeve tops or inappropriate clothing for the weather – don't try to look for marks you probably won't see any. • Jumpy • Moves if you get to close • Unkempt appearance (lack of personal hygiene)	Be available to discuss issues with the pupils, try to get them to discuss with yourself or a supportive peer if they will not speak to you. Refer them for help to a year head or form tutor who will most likely refer them to the educational psychologist or other support services.

(Continued)

Table 12.2 (Continued) Signs to look for and potential support for pupils with mental health issues.

Condition	Signs to look for in Pupils	How to support Pupils
Post-traumatic stress If a child experiences or witnesses something deeply shocking or disturbing they may have a traumatic stress reaction. This is a normal way of dealing with shocking events and it may affect the way the child thinks, feels and behaves. If these symptoms and behaviours persist, and the child is unable to come to terms with what has happened, then clinicians may make a diagnosis of post-traumatic stress disorder (PTSD).		Professional help

Intervention for secondary school pupils

It is important for pupils struggling with their mental health to be identified as early as possible and given appropriate support. Where you feel there may be a problem with particular pupils you may need to enter discussions with others, these could be with teachers, heads of year, class teachers or SENCOs. The pupil may have disclosed an issue to you; do not promise them that you will be able to keep this secret. We are not experts and most pupils with mental health issues will need additional support and professional help. A lot of the work with young people with mental health issues involves working with the family.

In school, all staff have a responsibility for supporting mental health. As a member of staff, it is useful to be empathetic and understanding about mental health issues. Training may be given as part of your school induction or you should know who to go to so that the best support can be given to pupils with these issues; knowledge of when and where to signpost pupils to or to recommend specific interventions or other support to pupils. Schools should have a support team with clear and defined roles for supporting mental health. This should have a visible structure to ensure that pupils know who they can talk to if they have any problems or concerns.

A whole-organisation approach to supporting mental health is most effective. Often teachers can identify potential mental health needs through being alert and noticing changes in the behaviour of pupils. Staff also have a responsibility to be good role models in terms of their own well-being and emotional literacy. If staff are responsive to their own mental health needs, this can help pupils to understand their own needs. Supporting young people to build emotional resilience can help them to cope with, and bounce back from, adversity, and can ultimately help to prevent the development of mental health problems in later life.

Mental Health First Aid England provide some useful resources to use with young people in developing their understanding of mental health and supporting each other. There are also many initiatives around training teachers in mental health issues and identifying a mental health 'first aider' in school who can support pupils in crisis. You may well come across some of these initiatives as your career develops and it is useful for you to be aware of any support or resources for teachers to use to support pupils.

Task 3

Can you identify the structure for the support of pupils with mental health issues your school? Who can they go to? How is information passed on? What agencies or groups do the school work with?

What can school staff do to support a young person experiencing exam stress?

There are certain times of the year and situations that require particular attention; one of these is examination time and the pressure pupils appear to be under. The prominence given to exams and academic attainment within the education system is having a negative impact on pupils, with 80 per cent of pupils asked stating that exam pressure has significantly impacted on their mental health (Health Committee, 2017).

We need to discuss with pupils strategies that will reduce the stresses and promote emotional well-being during these times. It is important that the pupils take care of themselves by eating the right kind of foods, drinking water, exercising and getting enough sleep. At least eight hours of sleep is essential as tiredness can impair concentration and increase anxiety. You will need to reassure pupils and remind them of past successes. It is also important to give pupils the opportunity to say how they are feeling. Revision classes and helping pupils to create a study schedule will help to ease anxiety about forthcoming examinations. Discuss with them at regular intervals how their revisions is going, encourage them to form study groups or partnerships as peer support can help to alleviate the pressure at this stressful time. It is also useful to be aware of your own language and portrayal of examinations. Whilst exams are important, the more this is emphasised the greater the level of stress that can be caused.

Task 4

For one class you are teaching produce an 'Exam Health Check List'. Discuss this with pupils. What do they think will help, what do they need in way of support?

School policies

Schools should have a policy to support the health and well-being of their pupils, with priorities identified and a clear process of 'planning, doing and reviewing' to achieve the desired outcomes.

The school should have a policy that the staff have been involved in the writing of, outlining the risk of mental health problems in their pupils and showing ways that they can support them to become more resilient and preventing problems before they arise. In addition, schools have responsibility for safeguarding and this includes pupils' mental and emotional health. It is important that early interventions are identified and guidance given should include information for schools on ways to improve the emotional literacy of all children, not simply those where a mental health concern has already been identified.

Task 5

Read the school policies on supporting pupils. Reflect on whether you think all aspects of mental health are covered and what, if any, developments the school could make to improve awareness and provision for pupils with mental health issues.

Online and social media risks

Numerous studies have been undertaken to understand the relationship between young people's internet use and their well-being. These explored a range of risks associated with social media, such as:

- the impact of excessive time spent online;
- sharing to much information
- being cyberbullied;
- the influence of social media on boys' self-image;
- sourcing of harmful content or advice, such as websites or social networks enabling the promotion of self-harm.

There is a concern about the excessive time spent online by adolescents. Teenagers do not think they are spending too much time online; however, 72 per cent said they had had missed out on sleep because of their internet habits and 60 per cent agreed they had neglected their school work or studies (OFCOM, Communications Market Report 2016). There is some cause for concern here.

The internet, and social networks in particular, have changed the way we think about privacy and sharing personal information outside our personal friendship networks. Researchers have described an 'online disinhibition effect' where people are more likely to share personal information or display more intense behaviour than they would offline, including anti-social behaviour such as rude language and harsh criticism (Suler, 2004).

The growth of smartphones has increased the opportunities for young people to access social media at times when they are vulnerable, for example, when they have been drinking or are in a very emotional state. This has increased the opportunities for young people to share personal information, photos and video content on social networks, or to livestream their activities. This has increased the risks of young people 'sharing too much'. Although only a small percentage have shared nude photographs online, having had a personal image of this sort shared further without their consent can have damaging consequences for a young person's well-being.

One of the main issues which affects mental health is cyberbullying. This can be defined in different ways, but is most often used to describe any kind of bullying behaviour that occurs online, for example through social networks or instant messaging.

There are many types of bullying online behaviour, including:

- Sending or posting abusive or threating messages.

- Creating and sharing embarrassing photo or videos.

- Sharing secrets about someone online without their consent.

- Intentionally leaving someone out of an online activity or friendship group.

- Voting on someone in an abusive poll.

- Creating a website with mocking or critical content about someone.

- Hijacking online identities or creating a fake profile to damage another's reputation.

- Sending explicit messages or encouraging a young person to send text, then sharing that more widely.

- Cyberstalking: continuously harassing and denigration, including threats of physical harm. (NSPCC, 2019)

Cyberbullying is different from offline bullying as young people can get respite from bullying at school during the evenings and weekends. Online bullying, by contrast, is not limited by school timetables or physical presence within the school building; a single incident can be shared and forwarded multiple times; the use of technology provides anonymity and allows for more frequent sexual or violent content and greater cruelty compared with face-to-face bullying (Frith 2017). Research has suggested that cyberbullying, like offline bullying, has a negative impact on young people's well-being, such as reduced confidence or self-esteem (Spears et al. 2015).

With the advent of smartphone cameras, and the development of online filters and image-manipulation techniques, there has been a rise in the popularity of 'selfies'. This has led to concerns about the abundance of idealised images of beauty on social networks and the impact this has on young people's view of their own appearance and their self-esteem. While the prevalence of photoshopped images of models and celebrities in magazines is not a novel issue, the rise of social media has led to this kind of manipulated image being posted by a teenager's own personal contacts.

Another potential risk is that young people can access harmful information on the internet or make online connections with people who encourage self-harm. For example, some websites imply that unhealthy behaviours, such as anorexia and self-harm, can be normal lifestyle choices (Andrist 2003). Studies have shown that it is very easy to find pro-suicide information, such as detailed information on methods, on the internet (Biddle et al. 2008). Another concern is the risk of 'contagion' where young people are encouraged to take their own lives after witnessing others describing suicidal thoughts or leaving suicide notes on social media. More recently, there have been several reported incidents of young people livestreaming suicides on social media (Frith, 2017).

A systematic review of research on the internet and self-harm amongst young people found that while young people most often use the internet to find help, there is the risk that the internet can normalise self-harm and discourage young people from talking about their problems and seeking professional help (Frith 2017).

Young people use a range of coping mechanisms to deal with online risk. Research by the NSPCC (2014) found that only 22 per cent of children who were upset by something they had seen online talked with someone else face to face about the experience. Adolescents are likely to turn to friends. The fact that only one in five children would tell someone about an upsetting experience indicates the challenges faced by teachers in ensuring that children are supported to cope with such experiences.

As pupils are not always likely to ask for support, it is important that they learn digital skills to protect themselves from online risks. It is important that we teach pupils the skills to keep themselves safe online. This is often completed in computing lessons or PSHE sessions. We need to have a talk about the impact of seeking approval from an online world that does not really know them or comparing their lives to the edited versions of the lives they see online. We need to talk about how it has the potential to effect sleep and therefore their health and through that help them make more informed choices about when to 'switch off' at night. Ultimately, we need to remind them that social media is not the only way of being social and encourage more face-to-face interaction and connection reminding them to be wary of letting online engagement get in the way of good mental health and well-being.

Chapter 8 explores the use of technology and the impact on behaviour within the classroom. It also explores whether online use should be the responsibility of the school or home. A partnership is felt to work best with similar messages and expectations. A number of resources are available to support both parents and teachers with online risks. Among the best-known of these are ThinkUKnow and Childnet.

Task 6

Explore the online resources for parents and teachers
   https://www.thinkuknow.co.uk/
   https://www.childnet.com/
   https://www.Youngminds.org.uk
   Consider what aspects of online safety should be the responsibility of the school, the parents or the pupils themselves. Reflect on how much time do you think pupils should spend online consider if social media can replace face-to-face discussion with others. If you have opportunity, it may be worth discussing some of these thoughts with pupils to see if their views are similar.

Teachers' own mental health

The *Independent* newspaper reported (January 2018) that more than half of Britain's teachers have a diagnosed mental health problem, This was based on a study by Leeds Beckett University, who found that three-quarters of those surveyed believe their poor psychological and emotional conditions could have a detrimental effect on pupils' progress. They cited 'excessive workloads' and growing financial pressures on education staff as among the reasons for the problems. The findings show that of 775 surveyed, 54 per cent reported poor mental health, with 52 per cent of this number saying their illness had been identified by a GP.

Approximately 8 in 10 respondents (81 per cent) said poor mental health had a negative impact on the quality of their relationships with their pupils. The same percentage said it affected their behaviour management skills. The teachers said they had 'lower levels of tolerance' and were 'quick to anger'.

The government are focusing on children's mental health, but it is important to look at the mental health of teachers as well. However, the research showed that teachers feel that their own mental health can have a detrimental impact on the quality of their teaching, the progress of their learners and the quality of the relationships they establish with students and colleagues.

> Teachers feel that they are less effective in the classroom if their mental health is not good. Our on-going research in this area demonstrates that teacher workload contributes to poor teacher mental health.
>
> (Glazzard, 2018)

We cannot ignore the fact that a number of teachers leave the profession before retirement age and that it can also be difficult to recruit to the profession. It is important that student teachers and NQTs feel safe and supported in order to develop their practice and enjoy the process of joining the profession. To help yourself achieve in your teaching you need to take care of yourself. It is important you have a work–life balance.

- Plan time out; do not spend your entire out of school hours working for school.
- Get plenty of sleep – a good eight hours a night.
- Drink plenty of water during the day.
- Watch alcohol consumption.
- Talk to others.

There is support out there for you, during your training and first years in teaching. Your mentors, tutors and peers will be invaluable in supporting you during these initial stages; talk to them often and ensure you discuss any times when you feel overwhelmed or unable to cope. Schools often have councillors who you can go to and teachers' unions have support officers. Do not think it is a sign of weakness to ask for help – at some point we all need support.

Task 7

Reflect on a recent time where you have found something a challenge. This does not need to be teaching-related. What coping mechanisms did you use? Did you talk to anyone about the situation? Look back, would you do anything differently?

Consider how this might help you manage a difficult time during your student teacher or NQT years.

References

Andrist, L. (2003) Media images, body dissatisfaction, and disordered eating in adolescent women. *The American Journal of Maternal/Child Nursing, 28*(2), 119–123.

Biddle, L., Donovan, J., Hawton, K., Kapur, N. and Gunnel, D. (2008) Suicide and the Internet. *BMJ 336*, 800.

Brown, E.R., Khan, L. and Parsonage, M. (2012) *A Chance to Change: Delivering Effective Parenting Programmes to Transform Lives*. London: Centre for Mental Health. https://www.centreformentalhealth.org.uk/sites/default/files/2018-09/chance_to_change.pdf.

Department for Education (2001, June) Promoting children's mental health with early years and school settings. https://www.gov.uk/govenment/publications/DFES-0629-2001.

Department for Education (2018) Mental health and behaviour in schools. November 2018. Online https://www.gov.uk/government/publications/mental-health-and-behaviour-in-schools--2.

Frith, E. (2017) *Social Media and Children's Mental Health: A Review of the Evidence*. Education Policy Institute. https://epi.org.uk/wp-content/uploads/2018/01/Social-Media_Mental-Health_EPI-Report.pdf (accessed 28/6/19).

Glazzard, J. (2018) Pupil progress held back by teachers' poor mental health. Leeds Beckett University. Online https://www.leedsbeckett.ac.uk/news/0118-mental-health-survey/ (accessed 28/6/19).

Green, H., McGinnity, A., Meltzer, H., Ford, T. and Goodman, R. (2004) Mental health of children and young people in Great Britain, 2004. National Statistics. Online https://sp.ukdataservice.ac.uk/doc/5269/mrdoc/pdf/5269technicalreport.pdf (accessed 28/6/19).

Health Committee (2017) *The Government's Green Paper on Mental Health: Failing a Generation*. London: Parliament Publications. Online https://publications.parliament.uk/pa/cm201719/cmselect/cmhealth/642/642.pdf (accessed 28/6/19).

May, T. (2017) The shared society: Prime Minister's speech at the Charity Commission annual meeting. Online https://www.gov.uk/government/speeches/the-shared-society-prime-ministers-speech-at-the-charity-commission-annual-meeting (accessed 28/6/19).

Mental Health First Aid England (2019). Online https://mhfaengland.org/mhfa-centre/resources/?resource_type_id=cf35a863-3ca5-e811-8147-e0071b668081 (accessed 27/6/19).

NHS Digital (2016) Mental Health Bulletin: 2015–16 Annual Report. Online https://digital.nhs.uk/data-and-information/publications/statistical/mental-health-bulletin/mental-health-bulletin-2015-16-annual-report (accessed 28/6/19).

NSPCC (2014) Bullying and cyberbullying - advice to parents and carers. https://www.nspcc.org.uk/what-is-child-abuse/types-of-abuse/bullying-and-cyberbullying/ (accessed June 27, 2019).

NSPCC (2019) Protecting Children from Bullying and Cyberbullying. Online https://learning.nspcc.org.uk/child-abuse-and-neglect/bullying/ (accessed 28/6/19).

OFCOM (2016) Communications Market Report 2016. Online https://www.ofcom.org.uk/research-and-data/multi-sector-research/cmr/cmr16 (accessed 28/6/19).

Spears, B., Keeley, M., Bates, S. and Katz, I. (2015) Research on youth exposure to, and management of, cyberbullying incidents in Australia. Social Policy Research Centre, Australia. Online https://www.sprc.unsw.edu.au/media/SPRCFile/Youth_exposure_to_and_management_of_cyberbullying_in_Australia_Part_A.pdf (accessed 28/6/19).

Suler, J. (2004). The online disinhibition effect. *Cyber Psychology & Behaviour*, 7(3), 321-326.

Young Minds (2019) Online https://youngminds.org.uk/resources/tools-and-toolkits/ (accessed 28/6/19).

Looking at 'behaviour' through the lens of SEND

Mark Sackville-Ford

Chapter aims

- To examine behaviour within the content of Special Educational Needs and Disabilities (SEND).

- To explore the history of differences within the education system, particularly in England.

- To consider how the current legislation and discourses that surround SEND position behaviour in schools.

- To understand how policy, language, models of behaviour and developing understandings of mental health are shifting practices and thinking around behaviour.

Keywords: Special needs; history of behaviour; iceberg models; theories of behaviour; behaviours that challenge; SEND; mental health

A short history of 'behaviour' within SEND discourses

Behaviour within an educational context in the UK has been constructed within official policy for over 100 years, often reflecting the values, beliefs and political ideologies of that time (Wearmouth, 2009). Chapter 2 explores the history of behaviour management, but from a 'classroom management' perspective, whereas here I am interested in the ways that 'behaviour' itself is conceptualised within special needs discourses. Around the end of the nineteenth century, at a time when formal education was emerging, child labour started to reduce and institutions/schools were established, usually by charities or wealthy individuals. Education at this point was mainly for the wealthy with poorer children attending Sunday schools or informal provisions, or indeed nothing at all. Where special educational needs were present in these contexts, they focussed on medical issues, with specific institutions for young people with learning, sensory and physical needs.

For the first part of the twentieth century education remained fairly flat, but changes emerged as the discipline of psychology grew, which recognised differences in children and young people. Indeed the 1913 Mental Deficiency Act sought to identify (and certify) those children aged 7 to 16 years who were identified as 'defective' (Wearmouth, 2017). The language and labels of special needs at this time are offensive to us now but show the way that our understandings of need and difference have evolved over the years. The Education Act of 1944 aimed to provide a national framework for educating a diverse student population, and much of the current education system in England can be traced back to this. During this post-war era the tripartite system of schooling was established with grammar schools for the most able, secondary modern schools for the majority and technical schools for those with particular aptitudes in science. Entry to schools was established via examination at the age of 11 years.

The deficit model of special needs still dominated during this period, although behaviour was not recognised as a distinct category. Eleven categories of need were established: blind, partially sighted, deaf, partially deaf, delicate, diabetic, educationally subnormal, epileptic, maladjusted, physically handicapped and speech defects. Those children identified as 'ineducable' were reported to the local authority under the Mental Deficiency Act mentioned above. The term 'maladjusted' became associated with 'undesirable personal and social characteristics' (Galloway et al. 1994) and acquired a degree of stigma. Local Education Authorities (LEAs) were unsure how to meet the needs of the 'maladjusted' and the later Underwood Report (1955) added more detail to the label. Maladjustment could be associated with six symptoms:

1. *Nervous disorders* – recognised as fear, anxiety, apathy and excitability.
2. *Habit disorders* – recognised through multiple bodily needs, including speech defects, sleep-walking, twitching, thumb-sucking and incontinence.
3. *Behaviour disorders* – recognised through temper tantrums, jealousy, cruelty to others, stealing and sexual troubles.
4. *Organic disorders* – recognised through brain injury, cerebral tumours and epilepsy.
5. *Psychotic behaviours* – recognised as the child being aloof, having repetitive behaviours, delayed speech and other 'bizarre behaviours'.

6. *Educational and vocational difficulties* – recognised through failure at school, being argumentative, disorganised, lack of concentration and not being able to keep employment.

Underwood (1955; Chapter IV, paras 96–115)

Furlong (1985) notes how between 1945 and 1960 the numbers of children labelled as 'maladjusted' rose from 0 to 1742, and by 1975 there were 13,000. Clearly, many of these descriptions now feel inappropriate and our understanding of additional needs has developed so that no children are now labelled as 'maladjusted'. Some of the behaviours listed above can still be exhibited by children but we are now able to understand them differently.

It wasn't until the Warnock Report (1978) that central government began to take responsibility for all children, as the belief was established that all children, regardless of need, were entitled to an education. Behaviour as a concept was increasingly drawn into discourses of psychology and medical models of difference, with behaviour being associated with deviance (Ford et al., 1982). Warnock's report was highly influential, leading to the new concept of 'special educational needs' which formally emerged in the 1981 Education Act replacing the previous categories of need. Under this legislation LEAs were given responsibility to educate all children in conjunction with parents. Behaviour became subsumed into the term 'emotional or behavioural disorders' (EBD) and later the word 'social' was added to the code and the word 'disorders' evolved to become 'difficulties'; Social, emotional and behavioural difficulties (SEBD). These terms have pervaded until the recent iteration of the SEND code of practice in England (DfE, 2015a), which I will discuss next. Special Schools and Pupil Referral Units were established for children with SEBD, designed to educate those who had been permanently excluded from school.

Reflections

Think back to when you were at school.
  Can you recognise the ways that behaviour and special needs was framed at this time?
  How do you think that this has influenced your thinking about behaviour today?
  How do you react to the definitions of 'maladjusted'?

Current thinking around behaviour in relation to SEND

In 2015 the latest SEND code of practice was published in England. Within this code the categories of need, termed 'broad areas of need', were changed and are currently termed:

- Communication and interaction.

- Cognition and learning.

■ Social, emotional and mental health difficulties.

■ Sensory and/or physical needs.

What should be noted is that the word 'behaviour' no longer fits within the broad areas of need; this is a subtle, but significant development. However, there is a strong association between the old term 'social, emotional and behaviour difficulties' and the new term 'social, emotional and mental health' (SEMH). This has led to many individuals and settings concluding that SEBD has become SEMH. This is an unfortunate viewpoint, as it limits the development of schools' understanding of behaviour, and it also negates the importance of mental health. The revised code actually offered an opportunity to recognise 'behaviour' as an outward manifestation of a wide variety of need. We all have needs and we all have behaviours, seeking to communicate how we can ensure our needs are met. This may sound like a controversial point, but the code of practice itself is quite clear about this. It states:

> Persistent disruptive or withdrawn behaviours do not necessarily mean that a child or young person has SEN ... there should be an assessment to determine whether there are any causal factors such as undiagnosed learning difficulties, difficulties with communication or mental health issues.
> DfE (2015: para. 6.21, p. 96)

In other words, all forms of the broad areas of need may contribute to behaviours that challenge. The code also notes that behaviours that challenge may be a result of short-term needs:

> Professionals should also be alert to other events that can lead to learning difficulties or wider mental health difficulties, such as bullying or bereavement. Such events will not always lead to children having SEN but it can have an impact on wellbeing and sometimes this can be severe.
> DfE (2015: para. 6.22, p. 96)

I therefore argue strongly that whilst behaviour will be influenced by SMEH needs it is incorrect to think that this replaced SEBD. All broad areas of needs, and factors outside the children, result in behaviour. Behaviour is just a communication of need. Elsewhere I have represented this using iceberg models (Figure 13.1):

The models shows that the SEND code's 'four broad areas of need' can be hidden under the surface of the water, but in fact it is one or more of these unmet needs that might be producing the behaviour. It begins to capture some of the complexities associated with behaviour. For the teacher or support staff in schools, it is easy to get drawn into the experienced or visible behaviour without acknowledging that this is merely a symptom of something else.

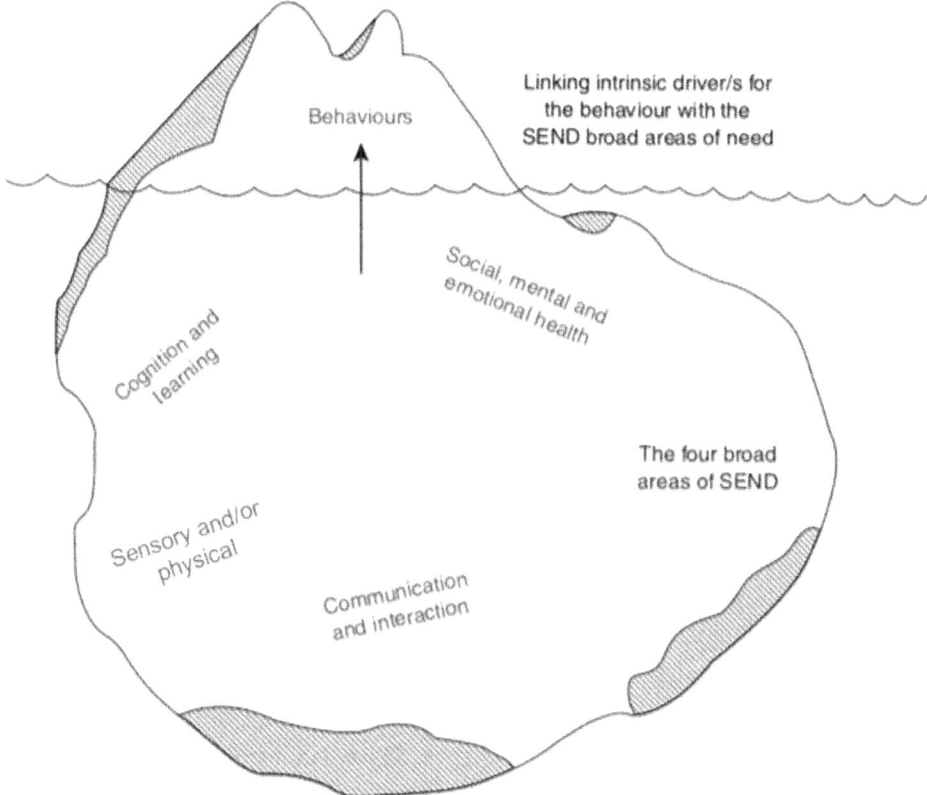

Figure 13.1 SEND iceberg model of behaviour (Sackville-Ford, 2018).

Task 1

Think of a young person that you have worked with whose behaviour could be described as challenging. Based on the SEND iceberg model can you begin to theorise about what the potential drivers for the behaviour were? What areas of need might be linked to the behaviour?

Case study: disrupting the English lesson

I was supporting a Year 8 pupil in a school, whom I will call Joshua. Joshua was struggling to be successful in school and I noted from the online monitoring system that he was most frequently removed from English lessons. I decided that in order to understand what was happening, I would do a lesson observation in English. Prior to the observation I privately questioned the relationship between him and his English teacher, the classroom management skills of that teacher and whether any learning or cognition issues were linked to the issue.

The morning of the observation arrived and in typical style I sat at the back of the classroom, pen and paper at the ready. I immediately noted how skilled the classroom teacher was. The lesson started well, and all children were really engaged. Joshua knew me and kept turning around to talk to me. After some time, I could see that the observation was not going to be productive; Joshua was distracted by my presence. Instead I moved to sit next to Joshua as he completed the independent part of the lesson. Together we completed all the learning and there appeared to be no barriers to the learning. I was left confused as to what the difficulties were and why the lesson observation was so different to what I expected.

When I next worked 1:1 with Joshua I asked him the question 'What was going on in that English lesson?' His reply was that when I sat alongside him, I continually provided verbal prompts. He explained that this helped him to concentrate and he didn't forget what he had to do. I hadn't even noticed that I was giving extra prompts as it happened naturally, but it dawned on me that Joshua was struggling with working memory and executive brain functions. He was later referred to an educational psychologist who identified specific difficulties around working memory. Joshua had established his own classroom coping strategies, including work avoidance, and these had masked his difficulties. The diagnosis enabled Joshua to access further support for him in the classroom and his school behaviours continues to improve. Whilst his presentation in English appeared to be a 'behavioural' issue, in fact this was only an indication of unmet need. The need here related to cognition and learning, one of the four SEND broad areas of need.

Reflections

How do you respond to the case study above?

   Can you critically think about the reasons why Joshua's need might not have been identified earlier in his school years?

   What are your experiences of the ways that different needs impact upon behaviour?

One critique of the iceberg model above is that it falls into the trap of seeing behaviour as something that is within the child. This echoes the historical development of the field of SEND discussed above, built upon medical and psychological models of difference. This discourse still dominates schools as indicated in the case study by the fact that the educational psychologist is seen as the ultimate gatekeeper to further support and advice.

Within this chapter this is, of course, the focus; framing behaviour within discourses of SEND. However, overall it is important to locate the discourses within more holistic terms. Many times that I have supported young people whose behaviour is challenging I have found that the main need is related to contextual factors rather than something within child. To conclude this section, I present two alternative versions of the iceberg models (Sackville-Ford, 2018).

One is a cognitive model (Figure 13.2) and shows how experiences in life, impact upon thoughts and feelings which result in behaviours. In this model there is still a sense that behaviour is within child, whilst acknowledging that this is something that has been produced, and therefore it is not the child's fault or deliberate. It also means that the factors below the surface can be disrupted and ultimately the behaviours changed. This is unlike the SEND model which is often driven by lifelong pervasive needs. When I observe a child, I always start with this model to begin to theorise around what might be producing the observed behaviours.

The teaching and learning iceberg (Figure 13.3) shows how multiple factors around the classroom also impact significantly upon behaviour. This isn't an exhaustive list and you could probably add to these. What it isn't able to show is that the political and social aspects of society also heavily influence education. In the model this should probably be represented by the water that surrounds the iceberg. It is for this reason that I wouldn't use this model to criticise teachers; it is a demanding and complex job. Instead it is to support teachers to ask themselves how their approach might contribute towards observed behaviours. The model encourages us to look at our own practices to see how we might positively impact upon behaviours that challenge, without there being a need to blame teachers.

The three iceberg models should be seen as different faces of the same iceberg. This helps to explain that the observed behaviours may be influenced by multiple factors and this is why understanding behaviour is so complex. As teachers we theorise and experiment until we understand more about what is happening and how we can support young people to develop their behaviours.

Task 2

Think back to the child that you identified in Task 1. In light of the other icebergs, what other drivers do you think were active in this scenario? By incorporating the three models as three faces of the same iceberg, the model begins to approach the complexity of behaviour that is faced daily in the classroom. How would you try to minimise the impact of these behaviours through addressing the drivers rather than the behaviour itself? Try to come up with a short action plan.

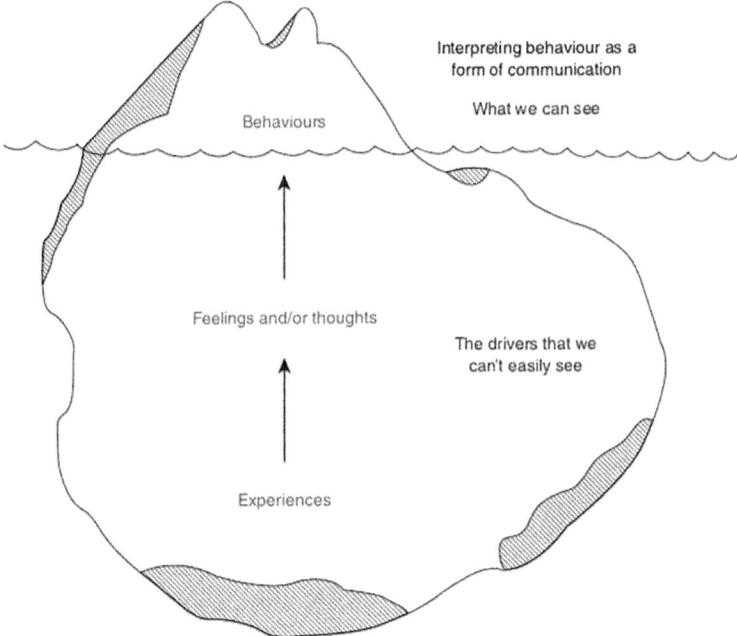

Figure 13.2 Cognitive iceberg model of behaviour (Sackville-Ford, 2018).

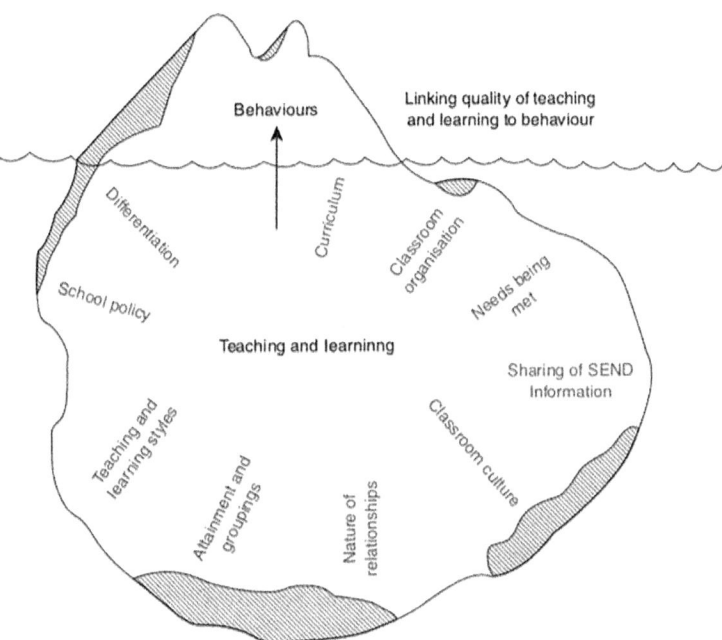

Figure 13.3 Teaching and learning iceberg model of behaviour (Sackville-Ford, 2018).

Aligning SEND and pastoral systems in schools

School ecology is a term that can be used to describe the ways that schools have been organised (see Waters et al., 2010). It is clear that structural characteristics of schools have evolved considerably over the last couple of decades within the UK education system. In the 1980s and 1990s there was a shift in attitudes towards the pastoral care of young people in secondary schools. This emerged in a range of publications from the 1970s and 1980s which recognise the need for a holistic approach for caring for young people that goes beyond instructions and teaching (Marland, 1974; Best et al., 1977; Lang, 1984). This crept into policy when a 1989 HMI report defined pastoral care as:

> concerned with promoting pupils' personal and social development and fostering positive attitudes: through the quality of teaching and learning; through the nature of relationships amongst pupils, teachers and adults other than teachers; through arrangements for monitoring pupils' overall progress, academic, personal and social; through specific pastoral structures and support systems; and through extracurricular activities and the school ethos.
>
> Department of Education and Science (1989, p. 3)

There were many positives of introducing an emphasis on care for individual students, but even decades ago there was a recognition that there were risks in splitting the academic and pastoral aspects of school. Buckley (1980: 182) describes the split well, in defining the students as 'creatures to be 'taught' and creatures to be 'cared for'' and similarly, teachers as 'teaching teachers and caring teachers'. The caring aspect found in the 'form tutor' role slowly evaporated and specific 'pastoral managers' began to be appointed in secondary schools. More recently, Best (2002) notes the continuing dilemma as the system in schools became well-embedded:

> the potentially divisive effect of institutionalizing pastoral care systems as separate from the structure of academic or curricular responsibilities (the pastoral–academic split) has been a concern to those writing about pastoral care for many years, though not often from a research-based perspective
>
> (Best, 2002: 31)

It is surprising that this ecology continues to pervade the school system, whilst this split has been recognised for such a long time. In many schools today there is a non-teacher pastoral manager and/or head of year. This is significant within the debate here because the split has had a massive influence on behaviour in schools, and our attitudes towards it. This is because the pastoral system often creates a divide between systems of SEND. That is, the SEND department in some schools has nothing to do with behaviour and sees behaviour as something that is the responsibility of the pastoral department. Table 13.1 attempts to summarise the thinking and reactions within these differing ecologies.

Table 13.1 Contrasting support between learning and behaviour in schools

Ecology	Cognition and Learning	Behaviour
Situation	A child makes a mistake with their learning (eg. doesn't understand a new concept)	A child makes a mistake with their behaviour (eg. steals some school property)
Teacher responses	Explain in a different way Increase differentiation and support	Blames the child and seeks and explanation Use praise/sanctions to redirect behaviours Punish negative behaviours
Teacher emotions	Feel sympathetic towards the child Question their own teaching	Feels apathetic or frustrated with the child Questions what is wrong with the child
Child emotions	Teacher avoids making the child feel bad about their mistake	Teacher actions might result in the child feeling guilty, shamed or scared about their mistake
If mistake becomes longer-term	Refer to SEND teams Seek further support from outside agencies Teachers take ownership of learning mistakes	Refer to Pastoral team Seek further support from outside agencies Children are expected to change their behaviours (they must take ownership of behaviours)
Outcomes	Children are supported to make progress with their learning	Children may slip into exclusions, managed moves or alternative placements.

Table 13.1 shows the differing ways that schools can respond to behaviour contrasted with learning. I hope what this communicates is a very different ethos between a proactive positive approach by schools (cognition and learning) and a reactive and often negative approach by schools (behaviour). Of course, this is a generalisation, but is based on my professional experiences over the last ten years working in the sector. I have had this discussion with many secondary school SENCOs who see their role as confined to learning needs. I have some sympathy because behaviour is such a complex thing that does not have a quick fix, and there is considerable pressure within the dominant attainment discourses. It is also supported by a recent research project that I was involved in, where interviewees highlighted the two-tier structure of SEND and pastoral systems (Ivinson & Hick, 2018).

As Figure 13.1 highlighted, school staff need further support and guidance to understand behaviour as a form of communication and an indication of unmet need. Where a student continues to experience difficulties with behaviour, I recommend that schools take a systemic approach to resolving the problem. By this I mean that children should be supported through both the SEND and pastoral systems. Further assessments that look beyond the behaviour should focus on attempting to understand the function of the behaviour and if there are unmet needs hidden below the surface. We should not assume that children are challenging on purpose and instead show a sympathetic and supportive attitude. This is, of course, easier said than done and behaviour can become habitual, but it is only through such an approach that we can make changes with behaviour, as I discuss later in the chapter.

Perhaps what is needed is a revised ecology in schools. I would like to see schools where SEND and pastoral departments are merged into one, located in the same offices, and able to work much more holistically together. Children who are experiencing difficulties should be discussed by these larger teams and holistic strategic plans put in place. This will also allow children who are usually drawn into pastoral and disciplinary routes to be able to access further assessments, including time from the educational psychologist. Where SENCOs retain their learning focus there should be a Senior Leadership role like 'Inclusion Manager' that should lead and manage this larger department. More information should be shared with teaching staff about the children and form tutors should be given increasing responsibilities to care for the pupils in their form.

Task 3

Reflect on your pastoral role as a teacher. How can you access further information that would help you to analyse behaviour? Can you ask pastoral and SEND teams to provide you with Individual Education Plans (IEPs) or One Page Profiles? How can you increase your visibility with pastoral teams?

Thinking about Figure 10.1, how might you be able to reframe your approach to behaviour. Is it useful to consider that your young people need more practice at 'behaviour' and will inevitably make mistakes?

Evolving understanding of behaviour

At the start of this chapter the historical perspective on SEND in schools highlighted how rapidly understanding and terminology has changed. Within the context of behaviour, it feels like we are also experiencing rapid changes in understanding. In particular, mental health agendas are promoting a renewed understanding of behaviour. In November 2018, the non-statutory guidance document 'Mental Health and Behaviour in Schools' was published by the Department of Education (DfE, 2018) and this has started to promote fresh thinking about mental health in schools. Of interest here is a paragraph that explains the need to respond to behaviour in schools in more personalised ways:

> Published behaviour policies need to be consistent with the legal requirement that treating all pupils the same may be unlawful where a disability affects behaviour. It may be unlawful to apply a behaviour policy that treats all pupils the same if a pupil's disability makes it harder for them to comply with the policy than other pupils who are not disabled.
>
> DfE (2018: Para 1.3 p.7)

Within this seemingly progressive move towards behaviour the document still explicitly states that behaviour policy should have a 'clear system of rewards and sanctions' which seems designed to support other documentation around discipline in schools. This creates a tension which I will pick up later in the chapter when I explore theories of behaviour. The document must be viewed as a positive step towards understanding mental health and well-being but it struggles to break free of previous policy positions. For example, when the document talks about permanent exclusion it falls into a trap of focussing on the impact of behaviours on the rest of the school community rather than having a human-need driven ethos:

> Permanent exclusion, for example, needs to be very much a last resort. However, in all cases, schools must balance the interests of the pupil against the mental and physical health of the whole school community
>
> DfE (2018: para. 3.16, p. 17)

New guidance coming into schools for September 2020 places greater important on Relationship and Sex Education, and Health Education (see DfE, 2019). This feels much more progressive than the policy above as it demonstrates shifting responses to society and the demands of children growing up in a digital world. This is related at times to mental health in specific ways, but again the whole shifting understanding of mental health and well-being in schools will contribute to a more positive environment for children and young people. In general, our understanding of well-being is developing rapidly and teachers are better equipped to recognise risk and protective factors associated with mental health. Continued work to ensure education, health and social care work in a joined-up fashion will support this, although I feel there is some way to go with this.

As the opening of the chapter suggested, there is a rapidly shifting arena of education and language around behaviour and SEND. Many schools now understand attachment theory and the ways that this might impact upon the well-being and behaviour of children and young people. Key texts such as Bomber (see 2011) have helped to make schools more aware of conditions that we only recently recognise. One limitation around attachment difficulties and/or disorders is the implied blame associated with it. For a child to have issues with attachment there is a need to blame the primary caregiver, which is usually the mother. This adds a layer of complication and acts as a barrier for supporting some children. Whilst recent governmental documentation mentions attachment difficulties, there are currently moves towards a better understanding of 'trauma' in schools. Unlike attachment theories, theories of trauma do not generally become associated with blame. Instead this term encourages school staff to recognise that some children and young people have faced adverse circumstances and will benefit from understanding and support with their education. Organisations such as the Anna Freud National Centre for Children and Families (https://www.annafreud.org/) offer great sources of materials to support schools with mental health, including the Schools in Mind project.

Challenging behaviour vs behaviours that challenge

I believe that the language around behaviour is very important. Here I argue that we should adopt the phrase 'behaviours that challenge' rather than challenging behaviours. Labelling a child with 'challenging behaviour' is a negative term and tends to see the behaviour before the child. It can be spoken in a way that implies that they 'own' these behaviours and therefore there is something intrinsically difficult about that child. It can lead to school staff generalising about these behaviours and ultimately assume that these behaviours cannot be changed. There is a sense of blame associated with the label, with the child, not just their behaviours being seen as challenging.

Instead the phrase 'behaviours that challenge' is emerging in official documentation. For example, it is seen in NICE guidance (2015) around behaviours for people with learning disabilities. 'Behaviour that challenges' is not a diagnosis and is used ... to indicate that although such behaviour is a challenge to services, family members or carers, it may serve a purpose for the person' (NICE, 2015: 6). Such a framing sees that the behaviour can be functional and seeking to communicate need. Rather than seeing the child as challenging, the focus is much more on the behaviours. The focus is away from the child and more towards our responses and reactions to the behaviours. In fact, it supports school staff in asking themselves how they can think and respond to these behaviours.

If we select a behaviour that you might find challenging we can think about this in a reframed way. Take the behaviour 'getting out of your seat and wandering around the classroom'. To address the behaviour we can attempt to use the iceberg models to understand it better. We can consider whether this is a functional behaviour; maybe the young person finds it difficult to sit still and needs regular breaks. Maybe this has become a habitual behaviour and the cycle can be broken through clearer rules and reminders. As a teacher you might put systems in place to support the young person, such as giving them regular jobs in the classroom like handing out equipment, in order to legitimately meet the need. By considering this as a 'behaviour that challenges' we can think about our own responses and the different ways we may be able to address and support the issues.

Task 4

Try to adopt the language of 'behaviours that challenge' whilst in schools. Combining this with the other tasks, how does this reframing of behaviour support your attitudes towards behaviour? Try this out when you are next in school. Does this have any impact on the behaviour in your classroom.

Case Study: 'Kicking off'

When a child or young person displays behaviours that are extremely challenging, we can sometimes describe them as 'kicking off'. This phrase is loaded with power and can act as a way for the young person to develop a pride about their behaviours. One can imagine them saying that they were 'kicking off at school today' with their friends.

Whilst training school staff we suggest replacing the phrase 'kicking off' with 'in need of support' or 'in crisis'. These phrases are much less emotive and judgemental of the behaviours. I argue that this might actually be what is being communicated whilst they are in crisis: 'Help me!' The language here again changes our attitude towards the young person into a more supportive and understanding tone. Young people are unlikely to tell their friends that they were 'in need of support' at school. So try to ban the phrase 'kicking off' from your vocabulary and consider challenging colleagues who use the phrase.

Why behaviour must be theorised about

In the final section of the chapter I want to encourage the reader to theorise with behaviour in order to develop their thinking and understanding. I have written about this in the past (Sackville-Ford, 2018; Sackville-Ford, 2019) but make no apology in raising the issue again. I believe that behaviour in schools is too often reduced to a 'what works' or 'tool kit' approach. This implies that if teachers just implemented the correct strategies then there would be no difficulties with behaviours in schools. CPD training in schools often uses inspirational speakers or behaviour 'gurus' who again can fall into the trap of just sharing their top tips of behaviours. This leads to an approach and understanding of behaviour that is only ever looking at the tip of the iceberg. Instead our focus should be trying to understand the drivers to the behaviour rather than looking directly at the behaviour. For you, at an early stage of your career, it is easy to get sucked into the latest fads or ideas about how to get the young people to behaviour. I encourage you to be cautious and fit new approaches towards behaviour into the theories associated with them.

I believe that one positive development would be for schools to theorise around behaviour aligning it more closely with the values and ethos of their schools. Some would argue that behaviour is a practical application and therefore theory is redundant. However, behaviour in schools is already theorised. It is evident in DfE documentation such as 'Behaviour and Discipline in Schools' (DfE, 2016) and Bennett's (2017) 'Creating a Culture' whilst not being explicitly theorised. Most of the policy position around behaviour in schools draws upon theories of 'behaviourism'. Porter (2014) writes brilliantly around the importance of theory for teachers and she uses the broad umbrella term 'controlling discipline' to describe the approaches of behaviourism. There is not space here to adequately describe behaviourism, but one factor in schools are 'rewards and sanctions' and the ways that this conditioning will teacher children and young people how to behave appropriately.

In the chapter we have already seen that our understanding of behaviour is not static and policy and language rapidly changes. Like Porter (2014), I believe that controlling discipline is no longer suitable for schools today. It evidently clashes against more humanist approaches to behaviour, which Porter (2014) labels as 'guidance approaches'. These position children and young people in ethical ways, who need compassionate support to ensure their needs are met. At a time when SEND discourses are shifting and our understanding of mental health and well-being is developing, one must ask how control and discipline negatively impacts. Guidance approaches need to emerge more strongly in the policy documentation for schools to be able to embrace the approaches. Some schools are already responding in caring and compassionate ways, with schools replacing behaviour policies with relationship policies. As teachers begin to theorise more about behaviour I believe we can change the discourses of behaviour that dominate schools.

Conclusions

In this chapter we explored the ways that behaviour has been framed both historically and recently within SEN discourses. We have understood the dynamic and shifting nature of our understanding of behaviour, which continues to evolve to this day. Here I have used my iceberg models of behaviour to show how behaviour can now be conceptualised as an outward manifestation of need, either originating intrinsically within the child or as a result of contextual factors in schools and the education system. Behaviour in its simplistic terms is a form of communication and it is the role of teachers to understand and interpret what is observed. The complexities of behaviour means that this is a challenging thing to do, but policy and attitudes towards SEND will continue to evolve. Moves towards a better understanding of mental health in policy indicates a commitment to delve deeper to understand behaviour. By doing this we can evolve a school system which views behaviour in compassionate ways; rather than attempting to control behaviour, we can support and challenge children and young people to ensure that their needs are met and communicated in other ways. Such guidance will lead to an ethical, caring approach of behaviour which seems fitting in the current education system. There is some way to go to achieve this vision, but many schools have started their journey to understanding behaviour in more sophisticated ways.

Further reading

Porter, L. (2014) *Behaviour in Schools: Theory and Practice for Teachers* (3rd edn.). Maidenhead: McGraw-Hill. I continue to recommend this book about behaviour as the very best that is currently available. The main reason for this is the excellent way it is built on theory, which is unusual, and the increasingly confident tone that advocates guidance approaches in school. A must-read for all teachers.

Wearmouth, J. (2017) *Special Educational Needs and Disabilities in Schools: A Critical Introduction*. London: Bloomsbury. This book is an excellent starting point to think more criticality about SEND and this includes specific sections around behaviour.

References

Bennett, T. (2017). *Creating a Culture: How School Leaders Can Optimise Behaviour*. London: Department for Education.

Best, R. (2002). *Pastoral Care and Personal-Social Education (A Review of the UK Research Undertaken for the British Educational Research Association)*. Southwell (Notts): BERA.

Best, R., Jarvis, C.B. and Ribbins, P.M. (1977). Pastoral care: Concept and process. *British Journal of Educational Studies, 25*(2), 124–135.

Bombèr, L.M. (2011). *What About Me?: Inclusive Strategies to Support Pupils With Attachment Difficulties Make It Through the School Day*. Brighton: Worth Publishing.

Buckley, J. (1980). The care of learning: Some implications for school organization. In Best, R., Jarvis, C.B. and Ribbins, P.M. (eds.), *Perspectives on Pastoral Care* (pp. 182–195). London: Heinemann Educational.

Department of Education and Science (1989) *Pastoral Care in Secondary Schools: An Inspection of Some Aspects of Pastoral Care in 1987–1988*. London: DES.

DfE (2015) *SEND Code of Practice 0–25 Years*. London: Department for Education, Department of Health.

DfE (2016) *Behaviour and Discipline in Schools: Advice for Headteachers and School Staff*. London: Department for Education

DfE (2018) *Mental Health and Behaviour in Schools*. London: Department for Education.

DfE (2019) *Relationships Education, Relationships and Sex Education, and Health Education in England (Consultation Document)* London: Department for Education.

Ford, J., Mongon, D. and Whelan, M. (1982). *Special Education and Social Control*. London: Routledge.

Furlong, V.J. (1985). *The Deviant Pupil: Sociological Perspectives*. Milton Keynes: Open University.

Galloway, D., Armstrong, D. and Tomlinson, S. (1994) *The Assessment of Special Educational Needs: Whose Problem?* London: Longman.

Ivinson, G. and Hick, P. (2018) Published Written Evidence from Manchester Metropolitan University. Evidence Number ALT0087. http://data.parliament.uk/writtenevidence/committeeevidence.svc/evidencedocument/education-committee/alternative-provision/written/72479.html.

Lang, P. (1984). Pastoral care: Some reflections on possible influences. *Pastoral Care in Education, 2*(2), 136–146.

Marland, M. (1974). *Pastoral Care*. London: Heinemann.

NICE: National Institute for Health and Care Excellence (2015) *Challenging Behaviour and Learning Disabilities: Prevention and Interventions for People With Learning Disabilities Whose Behaviour Challenges*. London: National Institute for Clinical Excellence.

Porter, L. (2014) *Behaviour in Schools: Theory and Practice for Teachers* (3rd edn.). Maidenhead: McGraw-Hill.

Sackville-Ford, M. (2018) How might we frame 'behaviour' in primary schools? In Carden, C. (ed.) *Primary Teaching: Learning and Teaching in Primary Schools Today* (pp. 243–260). London: Learning Matters.

Sackville-Ford, M. (2019) Behaviours that challenge at Forest School. In Sackville-Ford, M. and Davenport, H. (eds.) *Critical Issues in Forest School*. London: SAGE.

Underwood, J.E.A. (1955) *Report of the Committee on Maladjusted Children*. London: HMSO.

Warnock Report (1978) The (1978) Special Educational Needs, Report of the Committee of Enquiry into the education of handicapped children and young people. Cmnd. 7212. Department of Education and Science. London: HMSO

Waters, S., Cross, D. and Shaw, T. (2010). Does the nature of schools matter? An exploration of selected school ecology factors on adolescent perceptions of school connectedness. *British Journal of Educational Psychology, 80*(3), 381–402.

Wearmouth, J. (2009) *A Beginning Teacher's Guide to Special Educational Needs*. Berkshire: Open University Press.

Wearmouth, J. (2017) *Special Educational Needs and Disabilities in Schools: A Critical Introduction*. London: Bloomsbury.

Reflections on behaviour

Mark Sackville-Ford

Chapter aims

- To understand that student and newly qualified teachers will still be developing their thinking and approaches towards behaviour in their classroom.

- To consider 'behaviour' as a concept that requires a career-long engagement with, rather than something that you need to 'get right'.

- To understand how reflection and reflexivity will support your developing expertise in behaviour.

Keywords: Behaviour mistakes; reflection; reflexivity; saying sorry; language of behaviour

Introduction

This is the final chapter of the book. What appears to unite the chapters is a willingness to think differently about behaviour and approach this complex term from a range of angles. Each author successfully brings a wealth of experience that they use to support you in thinking about behaviour as you begin your teaching career. You will see that each author also has their own set of values and beliefs that underpin their arguments. To conclude the book, I want to make a case that this is only the beginning of your engagement with behaviour. I argue that if you can develop a repertoire of reflective practices this will support you on your journey around behaviour management.

If I had a pound for every time I heard or read that newly qualified teachers (NQTs) feel that they should have had more input around 'behaviour management' on their teacher education courses, I would be a rich man. This frustrates me because this viewpoint is built upon a notion that not only is that there is something we can call 'behaviour management', but also that this can be easily known.

I believe that if we used every taught session on an Initial Teacher Education (ITE) course to learn about 'behaviour management', NQTs would still demand more. What I hope comes across from all the chapters in this book is that there is no 'quick fix' for behaviour management. It is a highly nuanced and complex field of education.

Learning to be a teacher is rightly a university-level qualification and, as such, I believe we should resist calling it teacher training. We cannot 'train' to do something so complex. Instead what we aim to achieve is to develop a critical and broad understanding of behaviour. Rather than refer to your PGCE or QTS course as 'training' you should call it 'teacher education course' (ITE not Initial Teacher Training (ITT)). Such a shift is important for behaviour because it helps to see how much this is influenced by so much more than the teacher. Instead of learning all the correct 'strategies' for behaviour, I believe it is better to try to think about the teacher you want to be, and what motivates you to be a teacher. Extend this to locate your own ideology/philosophy of education and the values that you think are important. By establishing such a strong foundation, you will only then begin to think about your teaching style, the type of classroom you want to have and the way that relationships exist in your classroom. There is no 'right way' to *do* behaviour; it is a constant experimentation and behaviour is an adapting beast which envelops and changes shape around the shifting educational and political landscape.

The following subheadings aim to give you some practical advice or provoke thinking that is aiming to support you during the early phase of your teaching career.

Have realistic expectations of yourself

In Chapter 11, along with Sarah Baggaley I argue that young people should be expected to make 'mistakes' with their behaviour, because this is an important part of the learning process. I think this advice is equally true for student and early career teachers. I believe that you should have realistic expectations of yourself. Expect that you will make mistakes and use these as learning opportunities. Remember that you will need different approaches according to the age of the students you are working with as well as other contextual factors, such as the time of day or the spread of ability. There is no 'one size fits all' model to be used. When you are new to a school it also takes time to build your reputation. Once this is established, you will find it easier to work with new classes because they will already have some understanding of the type of teacher you are.

Our student teachers often have very high expectations of themselves. For example, they want to achieve outstanding grades by the end of their placement. However, I caution that whilst having high expectations of yourself is important, you are in a marathon not a sprint. It is easy to become obsessed with demonstrating proficiency against the Teachers Standards, but rather, see these early years as a teacher as a learning opportunity. Use every opportunity you have to work with young people to learn. Use your school colleagues, other students and university tutors to think and debate aspects of behaviour and classroom management. Being a 'good' teacher is fantastic; 'being an 'outstanding' teacher is also great but be mindful that this is not linear. Instead consider that as a human we will have good lessons, outstanding lessons and also weaker lessons. All of these are acceptable.

Case Study: The power of the word 'sorry'

One of the worst moments during my teaching career occurred when I ripped up a young person's work and threw it in the bin. This young person had been challenging for most of the academic year and I felt like I had tried everything I could to support her. The lesson came towards the end of a difficult week and I was already feeling stressed. This context is relevant as my behaviours weren't just about the young person's behaviours. She walked up to me (again!) whilst I was interacting with another student and presented a piece of work which I judged to be unacceptable. I remember thinking that she was so bright, and capable of doing so much more ... and in that moment I snapped. As she ran out of the room, I understood what a major mistake that I had made.

Very rarely do we admit to our mistakes. I knew I had work to do with this student to repair the harm done to our relationship and to rebuild her as a positive learner in my classroom. The word 'sorry', when used meaningfully by a teacher, can be very powerful. Students do appreciate it when we own our mistakes. For the student in this case study we were able to move beyond this moment. I never again responded negatively to students whose work was disappointing and this experience helped me to be more conscious of my emotional state and stresses.

Task 1

What strategies do you have to help you to de-stress? What clues are you aware of that you are becoming overwhelmed with your workload?

Schools have a natural rhythm and during the year there will be variations in your workload. In your first year at a school it is difficult to know these rhythms, which can lead to quite a reactive experience. Talk to your colleagues and ask them about the 'pinch periods', then put a plan in place to you can respond to these proactively.

Understand that this is a career-long learning process

Your understanding and approach to behaviour in schools will always be in a state of flux. By this I mean that you will go through different periods where you will think and act differently in response to behaviour. This is for many reasons, which I will explore in this section of the chapter.

Early phase

During the earliest phases of your career you will be experimenting and building experiences in the classroom that will feed into your own values and philosophy of education. This, in turn, will lead to your own repertoire of beliefs and responses to behaviour. As a student teacher you may have very little autonomy in the ways that you will approach behaviour in schools. Some schools will have very strict behaviour policies that you are required to follow, regardless of your own beliefs. Some school mentors will advise you to follow their strategies and techniques in the classroom. This frustrates some of our students, but I believe that you should be understanding and expect this. Remember that you are at the school for a relatively short period and some staff will not want there to be a loss of the culture and routines that they have created. Schools with strict policies will need everybody to follow them, otherwise they are immediately undermined and become ineffective. Accept that there may be an imbalance of power, but continue to reflect upon what you are learning. Having said this, there will be schools and teachers who are happy for you to experiment. This can also be challenging because you will not have a full repertoire of strategies and approaches to draw on, and I would still continue to seek support from more experienced colleagues. Schools also have a responsibility in educating you on what it means to be a teacher and we should not separate university from the school placement; they holistically contribute a range of theoretical and practical skills and knowledge.

In the early phase of your career as a teacher it is important that you begin to consciously shape the type of teacher that you would like to be. I was fortunate that when I was an NQT I had an inspirational mentor. I would watch her teach and observe her interactions with young people, and within a term I knew I wanted to be a teacher like her. I noted that she had found a balance between having high expectations of behaviour and strong relationships with young people. I never saw or heard her raise her voice, but the students understood what was expected of them. I distinctly remember thinking, 'I want to be like you'. It took me several years to achieve this ambition, but I am fortunate that I had such positive early mentorship. Even if you are not this fortunate, look for other staff in your school that inspire you. Notice what they do in all settings, both informally (out of the classroom) and formally (in the classroom). Where possible, ask if you can observe them teach as this can be a powerful way to build up your own ideas of how to interact with students and manage a classroom. I learnt from one colleagues in my school that it was okay to share a little bit of your personal life with students, such as talking about what you did at the weekend. This helped to build the relationship and encourage students to recognise you as a human being with perhaps some shared interests. Sharing football teams (or rivalries) or music or family helps you to make connections which can be crucial to the relationships when behaviour is seen as challenging.

When I was faced with a challenging class, at this stage of my career, I struggled to understand how to respond. I was most worried about the noise levels and the general disruption in the classroom and the strategies that I was trying weren't working. At this point I returned to a key practical textbook from my PGCE course by Bill Rogers (see Rogers, 2015). I had been struck particularly by the use of language and how this could be used to influence behaviour. I read the book ferociously, writing down key points and trying out things such as a noise wheel. I'm not sure that everything that I tried worked, but the recognition that there was an issue and my willingness to try to work on my classroom management did help.

In the early phase of your career the following things may assist you:

- Attempt to locate your own philosophy of education and type of teacher you want to be.

- Watch other colleagues and particularly those you aspire to be like.

- Try out different things you see – note which work for you and which don't.

- Try these with different year groups and different classes.

- Continue to read about ways to think about and manage behaviour.

- Try to be yourself; this is important.

Establishing phase

After three or four years of being a teacher, I believe I achieved my aspirations about the kind of teacher I wanted to be, albeit with the occasional bump in the road. By then I had experimented with different approaches towards behaviour, and had therefore built my own repertoire of strategies and approaches that worked for me. What had also become significant, since I had stayed in the same school, was that my reputation had been built. Students that I didn't teach had met me in the corridor, or been in assemblies that I led, or I had taught their siblings. Parents had met me at parents' evenings and at other events. In a way that I am not fully aware of, students had learnt and understood my own philosophy of education even though I hadn't articulated it. I believe this is quite significant as I found that I no longer had to work as hard with a new class at establishing the ground rules and my expectations. Therefore behaviour management started to become less of an issue that I had to work at.

Whilst my management of the classroom had become quite automatic, there were occasions when this would be challenged. A particularly difficult class or a child whose behaviour was extremely challenging would stop me in my tracks. Here I would have to revert to the *early phase* described above and work harder to resolve the issues. However, having a certain level of confidence meant that you could talk to colleagues and use them to help you think through the problems. Often you are too close to the issue and there is value in getting the perspectives of others. Seek advice from respected colleagues such as support staff who may know the class/child well, or from pastoral staff or SEND staff. Sometimes there is information that has not be shared with all staff, but will help you to understand some of the behaviours that you are experiencing. By being reflective and informed, you are more likely to be able to work at the difficulties in the classroom and support the young person to make positive changes.

At this stage of your career you may also be taking on additional responsibilities in school, either departmental responsibilities or whole-school ones. I found that at times this would mean that you are pulled in multiple directions and sometimes your focus is away from your own classes that you teach. At these times there can also be a deterioration in behaviour in your classes as you have stopped working at it. Continue to be reflective and be prepared to have to return back to the basics with classes to get routines back on track.

In the establishing phase of your career the following things may help:

■ Know the range of strategies that work in your classroom and continue to use them.

■ Be prepared to experience difficulties despite the fact that you are feeling more confident and competent.

■ Seek support from a range of colleagues to help you resolve issues.

■ Be conscious that additional responsibilities may distract from your core teaching role which can impact upon the behaviour in your classes.

Experienced phase

You may not be that interested in this phase as you read this chapter. However, I think it is important to mention this so that behaviour is put into this wider context. There will come a point in your career where your behaviour management, values and relationships are well established. You will have probably worked in several schools and maybe in different contexts. You no longer have to really think about behaviour as you have so much experience and such a range of ideas and strategies to draw upon. This doesn't necessarily mean that this is easy or simple, but it recognises the importance of your experiences. You will probably mentor and support less experienced colleagues and this gives you an opportunity to watch others and reflect upon your own practices.

However, as I alluded to at the start of the chapter, behaviour management is a lifelong learning process. Most teachers feel that they are always evaluating and adapting their approaches to meet changing contexts as well as class dynamics. One of the main reasons for this is the changing policy. Behaviour is a popular topic for new governments or Ofsted to address, as it tends to communicate how 'serious' they are about the 'problem' of behaviour – regardless of whether a problem actually exists or not. As a result, policy will continue to change and evolve around behaviour. Similarly, society will also change and our attitudes and understandings of childhood and behaviour will always grow and shift. We need to understand that such changes are natural and to be expected; as an experienced teacher you will need to keep abreast of these changes. By now you should be able to think critically about new policy or understandings. Some you will readily incorporate into your practice and others you will be able to reject. The work you will have done early in your career to establish your teacher identity and values should underpin the decisions that you make about what you accept and reject.

In the experienced phase of your career the following things may help:

- Be confident in your ability, knowledge and experience around behaviour management.

- Mentor student teachers and less experienced colleagues.

- Continue to engage in training around behaviour to keep your knowledge up to date.

- Expect new policy and languages of behaviour and use your experience to decide which you should accept and which you should reject.

Case Study: Changing languages of behaviour

Language and its meaning is constantly changing and this is true of behaviour too! As teachers, it is also easy for us to slip with language and begin to use that which is being used around us. A good example of this is 'behaviour for learning' which emerged towards the end of the national strategies around ten years ago. I was attending a conference where I was delivering some training. As I walked around the room, I kept hearing the phrase 'behaviour for learning' being used. It had slipped into the teacher vernacular with little critical thought or questioning. What does behaviour for learning really mean? As we experience constantly changing policy we should be able to question the meaning of language. You will also note that the phrase is rarely used by teachers now.

Another example of language is 'low-level disruption', which emerged from an Ofsted briefing document in 2014. This describes typical low-level behaviours such as: talking unnecessarily or chatting; calling out without permission; being slow to start work or follow instructions; showing a lack of respect for each other and staff; not bringing the right equipment; and using mobile devices inappropriately. 'Low-level disruption' is a phrase that is now frequently used by teachers but I think is problematic. The document is a political one, built upon a certain ideological position, and is not supported by robust educational research. It fails to understand behaviour and places it completely within the child or simplifies something that is usually highly complex (for example being 'slow to start work'). More worryingly, it can be used as a tool to criticise teachers, which is something I would always resist.

Reification is the process of turning something abstract into something real. Through using the phrase 'low-level disruption', we actually reify this and it becomes a real 'problem' in education. I suggest we never use the phrase and thus stall the process of reification. That is not to say that these behaviours might not exist and indeed there may be a child shouting out in your classroom, for example. However, I believe that labelling this 'shouting out' as 'low-level disruption', a meaningless and useless umbrella term, is redundant. Describe the behaviours that you see and then work to reduce and teach alternative behaviours. As student and newly qualified teachers be cautious about the language of new policy and be critical about what these might produce.

Task 2 Policy reading

Based on the case study above, it would be useful for you to critically read some educational policy around behaviour. Select an official document, such as *Behaviour and Discipline in Schools* (DfE, 2016). Read through and attempt to identify 'sticky areas', something that you might not have noticed before or accepted without thought.

The importance of being reflective

The term 'reflective practitioner' is often used when talking about teachers, often with the assumption that this is universally understood. Here I would like to explore the processes and importance of reflection and the way that this might contribute to your engagement with 'behaviour'.

Those of you who are currently student teachers will inevitably have been asked to write reflectively about your experiences in schools. This may be used as part of assessment. I want to argue here that the practices that you begin as a student teacher may have value as your move on with your career. Schön (1987) classically wrote around reflection, identify two distinct forms:

- *Reflection-in-action* – reflecting upon what you do as you are going about your practices, thinking on your feet.

- *Reflection-on-action* – deeper reflection 'in the head' after the event.

Many of you will take part in 'reflection-in-action' without consciously giving this much thought. With regards to behaviour this will involve constantly assessing what is happening in the classroom, and working out how to respond. You are in the moment, reflecting in order to make informed decisions. Conversely, 'reflection-on-action' happens when you are driving home or discussing the class with a colleague, friend or family member. You are thinking or discussing a difficult moment or a specific child, often with the intention of trying to make better sense of what happened or gain the experience and viewpoint of others. Moore and Ash (2002) argue that 'reflection-on-action' becomes deeper and more meaningful when you are able to write this down. Bolton (2010) is another key author who recognises the power of reflection and states that this writing can be 'transgressive of stable and controlling orders: they lead cogs to decide to change shape, change place, even configure whole new systems' (Bolton, 2010: 7). As this is my own position, I feel that reflective writing can be a powerful driver for change, particularly in the context of behaviour.

It should also be recognised that behaviour in schools evokes emotions in all parties, including the staff. We feel hurt and frustrated at times, as well as the converse feelings of joy and elation. As Davenport (2012: 152) reminds us, reflective writing can facilitate the 'unloading of powerful emotions' and 'allows the author ... to make sense of vulnerable thoughts'. Such emotive writing can help one to process thinking and get us out of moments where we get stuck. As this book has hopefully communicated, behaviour is inherently complex and we should expect to get stuck at times.

Case Study: 'Alecia walked in swearing her little head off'

Many secondary schools use electronic systems to monitor aspects of behaviour in school. In one school that I worked in the staff would record details of behaviour incidents on the computer with a description of what happened included. Several of these would stand out for me and make me feel uncomfortable. One of these included the phrase:

'Alecia walked into my classroom swearing her little head off'

This student was immediately ejected from this classroom. My discomfort related to the fact that the use of language within the piece told the reader more about the emotional state of the person writing it than about the facts of actually what happened. This teacher was upset or frustrated or exhausted with Alecia. This is legitimate, but I question whether such 'angry' writing (Davenport, 2012: 152) has a place in official documents. Remember that parents have the right to request anything that is recorded about their child. When completing reports about behaviour consider how this could be interpreted by parents. Such angry writing may be productive in your personal reflections, but here it is better to state the facts. The above phrase could perhaps be written in a more factual and neutral tone. For example:

'Alecia walked into the room swearing loudly'

This reminds us that behaviours do indeed evoke emotions. This is to be expected as we are humans too. However, when writing up reports it is better to do this later in the day when you are calmer and able to think more rationally and objectively about what happened.

Supervision and reflexivity

Many professions who work with vulnerable children and families receive a form of professional supervision, including those working in social care and health.

When I worked as a behaviour specialist teacher I was also fortunate enough to receive supervision, which alternated between the headteacher and deputy head-teacher. Supervision can take on many different forms and have varying degrees of formality. For me, this was a structured conversation where I reviewed 'out loud' the cases that I was involved in. I raise this here because it acted as a verbal 'reflection-on-action' without the need for writing. Through the careful support of a more experienced colleague there was a process that allowed reflective thinking to occur. For me, it included some of the following features:

- Active listening from the supervisor.

- Shared problem-solving.

- Shared ownership of difficulties.

- Times where my thinking was challenged.

- Forms of accountability (e.g. planning).

- Forward action planning.

Sometimes the supervision would be on a 1:1 basis and at other times there would be group supervision whereby one would work with a group of peers. I found supervision to be an extremely useful process which allowed me to offload 'difficult' moments and avoid worrying about vulnerable children. From this experience I explored how supervision might be used more in schools. Very few schools use professional supervision as a process; this is unfortunate and something that I think could change. In schools, it is more likely that mentoring takes place, but this has a very different purpose and power dynamic. Of course, many of us talk to our colleagues, which acts as an informal type of supervision, but there is something special about having a protective type on a regular (weekly or fortnightly) basis.

In this section there is a difference between reflection and supervision; something that can be referred to as reflexivity. Above I have called this 'forward action planning'. Reflexivity allows the reflection to fold in on itself and orientates this towards action. It is much more than just thinking about what has happened to you in the classroom. As Bolton (2010: 10) notes, 'reflexivity is making aspects of the self strange: focusing close attention upon one's own actions, thoughts, feelings, values, identity, and their effect on others, situations, and professional and social structures'. This then leads the reflexive practitioner to think about how this can be negotiated in the future. This moves from a mode of 'what happened in my classroom?' towards 'now that I have thought about what happened, I will do this next time …'. It goes beyond questioning practice to thinking actively about practice. Such reflexivity can be present in personal journal writing, but often occurs later in the analysis phase, and is also found in professional supervision. It therefore avoids a notion of 'navel gazing' and allows reflection to move beyond that, which is pertinent at a period when teachers' time is extremely precious.

Action points for reflection

- Reflecting and thinking about behaviour is a good starting point.

- To take this further you may want to do some reflective writing; maybe once a week.

- Begin to extend your thinking to move to reflexivity, thinking about what you might change or do differently.

- Use your colleagues to seek advice through informal supervision.

- Use your line manager and/or head of department to have more formal supervision, even on an ad hoc basis. Seeking support should be seen as a sign of strength as you develop your strategies and approaches towards behaviour.

- Remember that each person has a different standpoint on behaviour based on their values and identity. What works for a colleague might not work for you.

Conclusions

In this chapter I have aimed to explore how behaviour is highly complex and show how early career teachers are at the beginning of an exciting engagement with behaviour. One should not begin their career expecting to be fully formed as it will take time to form your own values, philosophy and set of strategies that will work for you. As the chapter echoes, this should still be a time for you to experiment with behaviour and seek further support and guidance from colleagues and wider reading. Reflection through writing or discussion with others will always be a positive tool to help you, particularly where this leads to action and helps you to identify new ways to work with classes and individuals.

Further reading

Bolton, G. and Delderfield, R. (2018) *Reflective Practice: Writing and Professional Development* (5th edn). London: Sage. This latest update version of Bolton's book is the main starting point for beginning to understand the importance of reflective practices.

References

Bolton, G. (2010) *Reflective Practice: Writing and Professional Development* (3rd edn). London: Sage.

Davenport, H. (2012) Reflective journals and portfolios. In Hansen, A., Copping, A., Clough, N., Pezet, M., Dudley, P., Murtagh, L. and McVittie, E. (eds.) *Reflective Learning and Teaching in Primary Schools*. London: Sage.

Department for Education (DfE) (2016) Behaviour and Discipline in Schools: Advice for Headteachers and School Staff. DFE-00023-2014. London: Department of Education.

Moore, A. and Ash, A. (2002) Reflective practice in beginning teachers: Helps, hindrances and the role of the critical other. Paper presented at the Annual Conference of the British Educational Research Association, Exeter University, 12–14 September.

Ofsted (2014) Below the Radar: Low-level disruption in the country's classroom. Available at: https://assets.publishing.service.gov.uk.

Rogers, B. (2015) *Classroom Behaviour: A Practical Guide to Effective Teaching, Behaviour Management and Colleague Support* (4th edn). London: SAGE.

Schön, D.A. (1987) *Educating the Reflective Practitioner.* San Francisco, CA: Jossey-Bass

Index